A History of the AbaThembu People from Earliest Times to 1920

Jongikhaya Mvenene

SUN PRESS

A History of the AbaThembu People from Earliest Times to 1920

Published by African Sun Media under the SUN PReSS imprint

All rights reserved

Copyright © 2020 African Sun Media and the author

This publication was subjected to an independent double-blind peer evaluation by the publisher.

The author and the publisher have made every effort to obtain permission for and acknowledge the use of copyrighted material. Refer all enquiries to the publisher.

No part of this book may be reproduced or transmitted in any form or by any electronic, photographic or mechanical means, including photocopying and recording on record, tape or laser disk, on microfilm, via the Internet, by e-mail, or by any other information storage and retrieval system, without prior written permission by the publisher.

Views reflected in this publication are not necessarily those of the publisher.

First edition 2020

ISBN 978-1-928480-66-2
ISBN 978-1-928480-67-9 (e-book)
https://doi.org/10.18820/9781928480679

Set in Myriad Pro 9.5/13.5

Cover design, typesetting and production by African Sun Media

SUN PReSS is an imprint of African Sun Media. Scholarly, professional and reference works are published under this imprint in print and electronic formats.

This publication can be ordered from:
orders@africansunmedia.co.za
Takealot: bit.ly/2monsfl
Google Books: bit.ly/2k1Uilm
africansunmedia.store.it.si (*e-books*)
Amazon Kindle: amzn.to/2ktL.pkL

Visit africansunmedia.co.za for more information.

Contents

	List of Maps	vi
	Iminombo (Genealogical) Tables	vii
	List of Abbreviations	viii
	Acknowledgements	ix
	Note on Terminology	xi
1	Introduction	1
2	Precolonial and Early History of AbaThembuland, 1650-1828	9
3	Internal and External Pressures on the AbaThembu Polity, 1828-1848	25
4	The Origins of Emigrant AbaThembuland, 1848-1865	53
5	The Division of AbaThembuland into Magisterial Districts, 1865-1881	83
6	Tile and the Formation of the African Separatist Church Movement in AbaThembuland, 1881-1894	103
7	Colonial Assault on the House of Ngubengcuka, 1894-1920	119
8	Conclusion	143
	Appendices	147
	References	155

LIST OF MAPS

1. Former Transkei region depicting abaThembu settlement during the 20th and 21st centuries (areas numbered 1-7) 2

2. The Eastern frontier, 1795-1858 6

3. Cape Colony, 1806-1865 19

4. AbaThembu areas of settlement by the 1800s (areas numbered 1-7) 21

5. The Eastern Cape frontier and amaXhosa land losses, 1779-1850 22

6. The Eastern Cape frontier area, 1847-1850 55

7. The Eastern Cape frontier area, 1858-1866 75

8. British annexations on the Eastern frontier, 1848-1894 113

9. The South African War, 1899-1902 131

10. South Africa in 1910, showing the four provinces of South Africa (Transvaal, Orange Free State, Cape Province and Natal). Swaziland and Basutoland were separate British Crown territories 135

Iminombo (Genealogical) Tables

1	AbaThembu Primary Lineage	15
2	The House of Nxeko	16
3	The House of Dlomo	17
4	The House of Ndaba	18
5	The House of Ngubengcuka	19
6	The House of Joyi	58
7	The House of Ngangelizwe	87
8	The House of Dalindyebo	111

List of Abbreviations

AME	African Methodist Episcopal Church
ANC	African National Congress
CMT	Chief Magistrate, Thembuland
CPSA	Communist Party of South Africa
FAMP	Frontier Armed and Mounted Police
SANAC	South African Native Affairs Commission
SANNC	South African Native National Congress (ANC since 1923)
SNA	Secretary for Natives Affairs
TTA	Transkei Territorial Authority
TTGC	Transkei Territorial General Council (Bhunga)
USNA	Under Secretary for Natives Affairs
UTTGC	United Transkei Territorial General Council

Acknowledgements

I owe debts of gratitude to many people without whom this book would not have been completed. In particular, I am indebted to those who in various ways have also helped me to write this book. I have had informal discussions with uNkosi (Chief) Sindile Zwelodumo Mthikrakra, Mr Mda Mda, the late Messrs Phondolwendlovu Mncedi Nyoka, F.M. Njozela, James Kati and Auto Mnyande, and from these discussions I have benefitted immensely.

During the research for this book, I conducted interviews with various people who keenly gave me invaluable information. They were uKumkani (King) Buyelekhaya Dalindyebo, heir to the late abaThembu uKumkani Sabata Jonguhlanga Dalindyebo, the late uKumkanikazi (Queen) NoMoscow Dalindyebo, the Great Wife of the late abaThembu uKumkani Sabata Jonguhlanga Dalindyebo, abaThembu iiNkosi (chiefs) and amaKhosikazi aKomkhulu (chieftainesses), Professors J.B. Peires and Wandile Kuse, as well as men and women whose knowledge of the abaThembu history has enriched this book.

I sincerely thank the staff of the Mthatha Arhives, Africana Library at Walter Sisulu University (WSU), Cory Library at Rhodes University, Western Cape Archives and South African Library in Cape Town, for their readiness and willingness to help me. I also express my gratitude to the Directorate of Research and Innovation at WSU under Senior Director Professor Wilson Akpan and Manager Mrs Penny Dawson for their financial support towards the publication of this book.

My affectionate thanks to my wife, Nongcwalisa (nee Jadezweni), for her constant support and interest in my work, and our children, Mveni, Mbasa and Lindisipho for unfailing support when I could have fallen by the wayside. Most of all, I must thank my late mother, Nophumele (nee Nontloko), my late father, Nyembezi, and the Lord God for the successful completion of this book. I dedicate this book to my children.

Note on Terminology

In this book, 'Africans' refers to *abeNguni*[1] communities, namely amaZulu, amaXhosa, abaThembu, amaNdebele and amaSwati, who speak Nguni languages. 'Blacks' refer to *abeNguni* communities and all other South Africans, namely Indians and coloureds, previously referred to as 'non-whites'.

Such terms as *amabuto, Baca, Mbashe, Mbolompo, Tembu, Tukela, Tyalara* and *Tyhopo* are spelt in accordance with new orthography, thus *amabutho, Bhaca, Mbhashe, Mbholompo, Thembu, Thukela, Tyhalarha* and *Tyhopho*, respectively. However, for purposes of directly quoted extracts or statements, no changes or modifications are effected in the spelling of words, e.g. Gangelizwe, Tambookie Location, Kreli and Sandili.

African place names, such as Umtata, Idutywa and Engcobo, are written as Mthatha, Dutywa and Ngcobo, as were – and are – better known and understood by the *abeNguni* communities.

In instances where an isiXhosa word is used for the sake of clarifying a certain concept as is understood by *abaThembu* or *amaXhosa*, its English equivalent is placed in brackets, e.g. Gatyana (Willowvale), iNdlu eNkulu (Great Place), Nciba (Kei), *amagqobhoka* (converts) and *amaphakathi* (councillors). In certain cases, however, some isiXhosa terms are explained in a footnote, e.g. *inkosi inkulu* (a corrupted form of *inkosi enkulu*), *amabutho, amagogotya, amathamba, umtsheko* and *umngqingo*.

Izikhahlelo (praise names) are used to refer to traditional leaders as were – and still are – used as a gesture of honour by the southern *abeNguni* communities. "A!" is prefixed to the traditional leader's *isikhahlelo*.

---

1 AbeNguni are divided into Northern abeNguni, namely amaZulu, amaSwati and amaNdebele, as well as Southern abeNguni referring to isiXhosa speaking communities.

1

Introduction

This book is an account of the history of abaThembu, from the reign of uKumkani Nxeko in c.1650 to the death of uKumkani Dalindyebo in 1920. The importance of this cut-off date lies in the fact that uKumkani Dalindyebo's reign was characterised by relative stability compared to those of his predecessors. His prestige, however, was demeaned by the Department of Native Affairs' Secretary whose instruction was that uKumkani Dalindyebo should not be addressed as a 'paramount chief' as that title applied exclusively to the government, thereby strengthening the government's position and elevating it to be above customary law.[2]

AbaThembuland was – and still is – central to the history of the former Transkei region and South Africa. Not only does it form part of the former Transkei region, but it also constitutes South Africa, and so divisions, conflicts, developments and/or underdevelopments in abaThembuland inevitably affected not only the former Transkei region, but also the greater part of South Africa in no small measure. Thus, the history of abaThembuland and the divisions thereof overlap with the history of the former Transkei region and South Africa.

The former Transkei region (see Map 1) stretches from the Nciba (Kei) River to the Mzimkhulu River, and lies between the Drakensberg Mountains and the Indian Ocean. AbaThembuland, being part of the former Transkei region, stretches from the Mthatha River to Komani (Queenstown[3]), and lies in the region west of amaXhosaland. The abaThembu inhabit the former Transkeian districts of Xhorha (Elliotdale), Mqanduli, Mthatha, Ngcobo, Cofimvaba, Lady Frere and Xhalanga.

---

2 D.S. Yekela, "Unity and Division: Aspects of the History of AbaThembu Chieftainship c.1920 to c.1980", (PhD. Thesis, University of Cape Town, 2011), 42.
3 Mager posits that the district of Queenstown (Komani) was named after Cape Governor Sir George Cathcart's (1794-1854) home town. See A.K. Mager, "Gungubele and the Tambookie Location, 1853-1877: End of a Colonial Experiment", *Journal of Southern*

Although abaThembuland today is divided into two independent kingdoms, viz. Eastern and Western abaThembuland (sometimes referred to as abaThembuland Proper and Emigrant abaThembuland, respectively), before the arrival of whites in South Africa, abaThembu were one big, united nation. They inhabited the area covering Glen Grey, Komani, Aliwal North, Sterkstroom, Dordrecht, Elliot and Indwe.[4] AbaThembu had one iKumkani (king) under whom were iiNkosi (chiefs) of varying status. AbaThembu iiKumkani (kings) and iiNkosi are of common origin, are members of the same royal lineage and are descendants in the direct line of their common founding father, uMthembu, who had ruled probably in the fifteenth century.

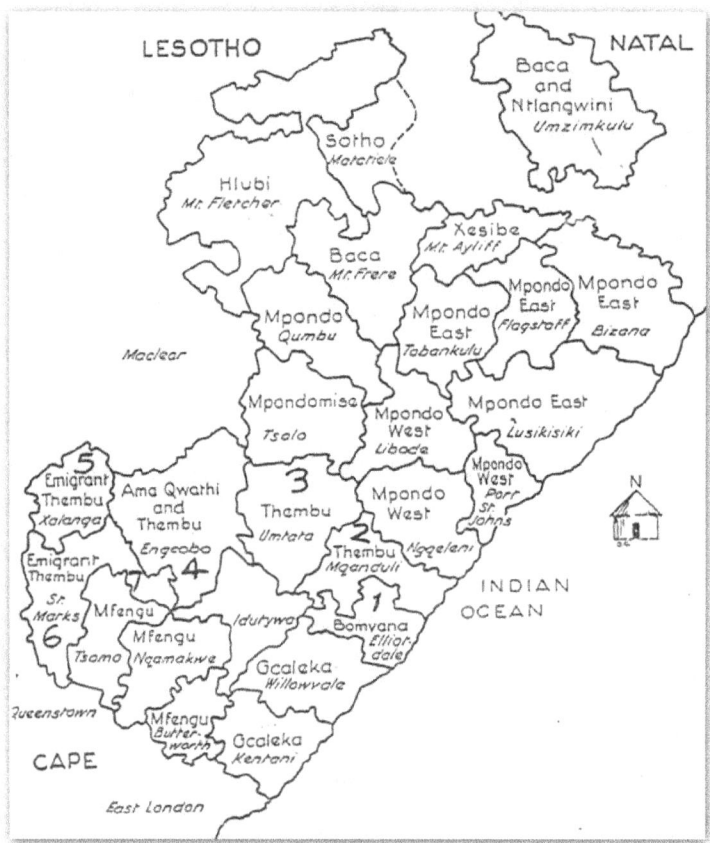

MAP 1: Former Transkei region depicting abaThembu settlement during the 20th and 21st centuries (areas numbered 1-7)[5]

African Studies, 40, 6 (2014), 1159. However, uNkosi Mbuzo Ngangomhlaba Mathanzima asserts that the name referred to uKumkanikazi Nonesi, that is 'the town of Queen Nonesi'. UNkosi Mbuzo Ngangomhlaba Mathanzima, Interview, Myezo, Mthatha, 25 July 2018.

4   W.D. Cingo, *Ibali laba Thembu* (Palmerton: Mission Printing Press, 1927), 25; A.O. Jackson, *The Ethnic Composition of the Ciskei and Transkei: Ethnological Publications No. 53* (Pretoria: Government Printer, 1975), 11; W.D. Hammond-Tooke, *The Tribes of Umtata District* (Pretoria: Government Printer, 1956), 41.

5   H. Campion, *The New Transkei* (Sandton: Valiant Publishers, 1976), x.

iiNkosi played a significant role in ensuring that "everyone had an equal share of the available resources".[6] Not only did they regulate access to, and use of, communal land, but iiNkosi also allocated land for pasture and for fields, supervising hunting privileges.[7] IiNkosi were the custodians of their culture and environment, and exercised the role of guardianship amongst their people. They also, on account of their wealth, acted as patrons for the people who needed food, shelter or cattle to pay *lobola*.[8]

AbaThembu, along with amaBomvana, amaXhosa, amaMpondo, amaMpondomise and amaMfengu, constitute one of the Southern abeNguni communities. AbaThembu, amaXhosa, amaMpondo, amaMpondomise and amaBomvana are also amongst the earliest inhabitants and oldest nations in the former Transkei.[9] AbaThembu, amaXhosa, amaMpondo and amaMpondomise are the indigenous kingdoms in the former Transkei. AmaBomvana, amaBhaca, amaXesibe and amaQwathi arrived later. AmaHlubi, amaBhele and amaZizi set foot in the former Transkei much later. AmaMfengu and other refugees of the Mfecane/Difaqane wars migrated to the former Transkei in the 1820s, having been "displaced directly or indirectly by the military activities of Shaka's Zulu impis, ... [producing] waves to affect not only the former Transkeian and Ciskeian peoples, but the [Cape] colony too".[10] Being dispersed amongst the amaMpondomise and abaThembu, the amaBhaca communities of uNkosi Madzikane did not only disturb the settlement pattern of abaThembu, especially the amaTshatshu and amaGcina, but their pressure led to the abaThembu fission and secession, resulting in the migration of abaThembu northwards and westwards.[11] Though distinct from amaXhosa, abaThembu, like amaMpondo, amaMpondomise, amaBhele, amaHlubi and amaBhaca, are Xhosa speakers. AbaThembu have a long and proud history of their own.[12] This book explores this history.

This book brings the account of the abaThembu history from c.1650-1920. It puts the spotlight on abaThembu relations with whites, missionaries and other abeNguni communities, and how and why their conflict with amaXhosa and collaboration with whites gradually weakened the abaThembu kingdom to such an extent that they lost power to whites. Nevertheless, the abaThembu kingdom and chiefdoms had instances of cultivating good and diplomatic relations with other southern abeNguni communities, as will be seen in the ensuing chapters.

---

6   L. Switzer, *Power and Resistance in an African Society: The Ciskei Xhosa and the Making of South Africa* (Pietermaritzburg: University of Natal Press, 1993), 35.
7   Ibid.
8   Ibid.
9   J.A. Broster, *The Thembu: Their Beadwork, Songs and Dances* (Cape Town: Purnell and Sons, 1976), 1; P. Maylam, *A History of the African People of South Africa: From the Early Iron Age to the 1970s* (Cape Town: David Philip, 1986), 35; R. Derricourt, "Settlement in the Transkei and Ciskei before the Mfecane", in C. Saunders and R. Derricourt (eds), *Beyond the Cape Frontier: Studies in the History of the Transkei and Ciskei* (London: Longman, 1974), 39.
10 Derricourt, "Settlement in the Transkei and Ciskei", 39.
11 *Cape of Good Hope, Report and Proceedings of the Government Commission on Native Laws and Customs* (Cape Town, 1883), 403-409.
12 J.B. Peires, *The House of Phalo: A History of the Xhosa People in the Days of their Independence* (Johannesburg: Ravan Press, 1981), ix; S.M. Molema, *The Bantu: Past and Present* (Cape Town: Longmans, 1920), 387.

While examining the collaborative relations of the abaThembu iiKumkani and iiNkosi with the colonial governing authorities and the consequences thereof, which brought about a further split within the abaThembu kingdom, this book also analyses the relations within the abaThembu traditional but unequal leaders. Such an analysis is intended to put the reader in a position to comprehend how and why both internal and external factors and influences were in varying degrees responsible for the rise and development of a split in the House of uKumkani Ngubengcuka.

It is worth mentioning that internal forces were a basis for a split, while external factors impinged on the abaThembu internal socio-political constitution to create the division. For example, the division of the king's houses into the iNdlu eNkulu (Great House), the iNdlu yase Kunene (Right-Hand House) and amaQadi (Supporting Houses) encouraged secession, envy, conflict and division.[13] Though the colonial authorities used the division of these houses to their own benefit by using the policy of divide-and-rule, these were intended for expansion of the abaThembu nation. For a clear understanding of the origins of the division within the abaThembu, one needs to critically examine the colonial attack on kingship and chieftainship, and the incompatibility of the Christian missionary outlook on life with the abaThembu beliefs and practices. Throughout the history of abaThembuland whites had taken it upon themselves to initiate, promote and accelerate conflict and divisions within the abaThembu kingdom.

The heavy concentration is on how the colonial and missionary influences adversely affected abaThembu unity during the period of conquest. abaThembu conflict with the amaGcaleka–Xhosa, amaNgwane, amaMpondo of Ndamase and Faku, amaMpondomise of Mditshwa and abaThembu inter-tribal tensions, is explored in relation to how it paved the way for the subjugation of this kingdom. The amaMpondo of Faku had settled between the Mthatha and the Mzimvubu Rivers, while amaMpondomise of Mditshwa lived north of the Mthatha and Ncambele Rivers.

AbaThembu acceptance of non-abaThembu clans, e.g. amaQwathi, amaVundle, amaGcina, amaTshezi, amaTshomane and the amaNqanda is assessed in terms of how and why these alien clans made the abaThembu kingdom a heterogenous and loosely structured polity. These clans of non-abaThembu origins are only a portion of the abaThembu by adoption who continued to show allegiance to their own original chiefs. This resulted in uKumkani Ngubengcuka ruling a conglomeration of clans whose sympathies were divided between the abaThembu king and their own chiefs. This, in turn, made the abaThembu kingdom vulnerable to outside attacks. Thus, the abaThembu kingdom could not face its enemies in

---

13 Traditionally, a traditional leader has four houses of importance, viz. iNdlu eNkulu (the Great House), iNdlu yase Kunene (the Right-Hand House), iQadi leNdlu eNkulu (the support of the Great House) and iQadi lase Kunene (the support of the Right-Hand House). While the Great House son comes first in the line of succession, the support of the Great House comes around.

unison. Wagenaar concludes that uKumkani "Ngubengcuka's greatest defect as ruler was his inability, at such a critical time, to reconcile dissident groups under his rule".[14]

The main factor responsible for the acceleration of this division was the Mfecane wars, which resulted in the infiltration of the amaNgwane into abaThembuland and the drifting of the abaThembu section closer to the colonial territory and amaXhosaland. It is demonstrated how, as a result of the Mfecane wars, some abaThembu clans, e.g. the amaTshatshu under uNkosi Bawana, amaGcina under uNkosi Tyhopho, the amaHala under uNkosi Mathanzima, amaNdungwana under uNkosi Ndarhala and two non-abaThembu clans (the amaGcina and amaQwathi), moved towards Komani. These clans chose as their own iNkosi, Mathanzima, son of uKumkani Mthikrakra in the Right-Hand House. With the passage of time, Mathanzima became the senior Emigrant abaThembu chief. This heralded and marked the origin of Emigrant abaThembuland of 1865. However, ooNkosi Mfanta, Duli and Mathanzima, all members of the House of Mthikrakra, were subordinate to the abaThembu uKumkani, Ngangelizwe.

A number of general works discuss abaThembu, but these are not done in great detail.[15] However, a number of recent works have appeared on the history of the abaThembu[16] but these do not address and analyse the theme of abaThembu relations with other abeNguni kingdoms and chiefdoms during pre- and postcolonial times, abaThembu interaction with the colonial government, colonial control in abaThembuland and the division of abaThembuland in great detail. Moreover, many of these works are based mainly on written sources. Oral sources in all their forms have been sadly neglected. This book attempts to close this gap.

This book is based upon documents, journals, newspapers, unpublished manuscripts and what the people themselves know and remember, that is oral tradition, oral evidence (oral history) and oral testimony. My interviewees were uKumkani Buyelekhaya Dalindyebo, the late uKumkanikazi NoMoscow Dalindyebo, abaThembu chiefs and chieftainesses, Professors J.B. Peires and Wandile Kuse, as well as men and women who possess valuable knowledge about the abaThembu history.

---

14   E.J.C. Wagenaar, "A History of the Thembu and their Relationship with the Cape, 1850-1900" (PhD. Thesis, Rhodes University, 1988), 7.
15   For example, Peires, *House of Phalo*; Maylam, *History of African People*; D. Williams, "The Missionaries on the Eastern Frontier of the Cape Colony, 1799-1853" (PhD. Thesis, University of the Witwatersrand, 1959).
16   For example, Cingo, *LabaThembu*; V.M. Master, "Colonial Control in Thembuland and Resistance to it, 1872-1885" (M.A. Dissertation, University of Cape Town, 1966); Wagenaar, "History of the Thembu"; W. Kuse, "The Thembu Right-Hand House: An Institutional Problem", Bureau for African Research and Documentation, University of Transkei, 1991.

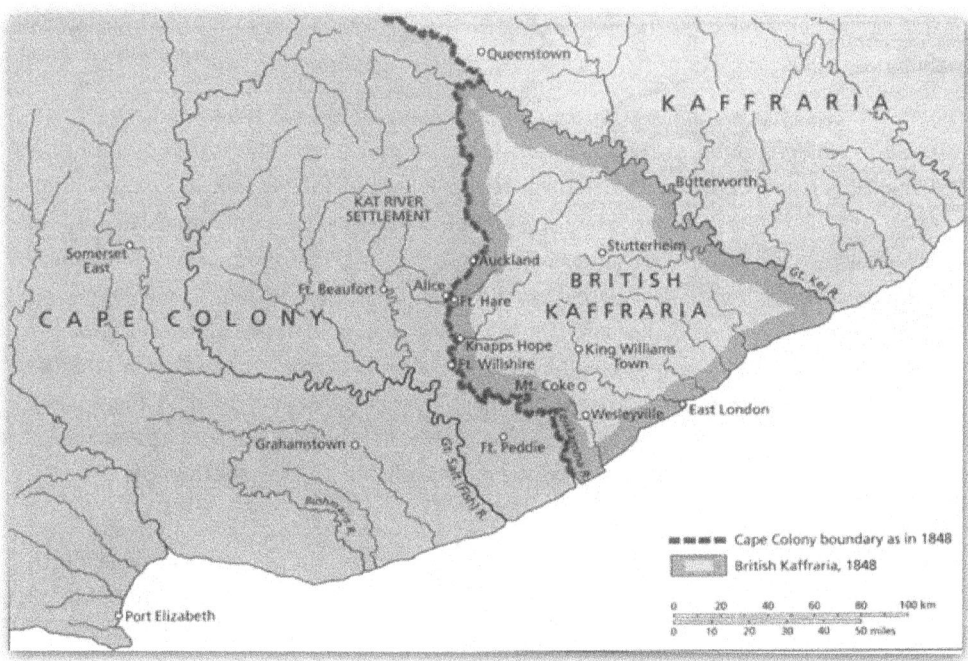

MAP 2: The Eastern frontier, 1795-1858[17]

While oral history encompasses all that the informants have experienced, oral tradition is what has been handed down from generation to generation by word of mouth, and is widely or universally known in a society. Those recollections of the past, which are not widely understood are referred to as oral testimony.[18] Oral tradition is one of the main available sources for reconstructing the past, particularly amongst the non-literate society.[19] However, oral tradition may be contaminated with flaws and distortions due to political beliefs and social pressures on the part of the informant. Tisani puts it neatly that "the contamination of oral sources by extraneous material is a problem researchers have to contend with".[20] Stapleton observes that amaXhosa informants whom he interviewed in his research on uNkosi Maqoma (1798-1873), though some had never been to school, were influenced in their narratives by those who had formal education.[21] Tisani argues that, while Stapleton regards oral tradition as sources of evidence that are not found in written sources, Peires observes that oral tradition does not yield much objective information, which is not already recorded in written sources. The latter uses oral tradition to corroborate written sources.[22]

---

17   R. Price, *Making Empire: Colonial Encounters and the Creation of Imperial Rule in Nineteenth-Century Africa* (Cambridge: Cambridge University Press, 2008), xxvi.
18   D. Henige, *Oral Historiography* (London: Longman, 1982), 2.
19   J. Vansina, *Oral Tradition: A Study in Methodology* (London: Routledge and Kegan Paul, 1965), 1.
20   N.C. Tisani, "Continuity and Change in Xhosa Historiography during the Nineteenth Century: An Exploration through Textual Analysis", (PhD. Thesis, Rhodes University, 2000), i.
21   T.J. Stapleton, "The Memory of Maqoma: An Assessment of Jingqi Oral Tradition in Ciskei and Transkei", *History in Africa*, 20, 1993, 329.
22   Tisani, "Continuity and Change", viii.

The principal purpose of oral historiography is to complement written documentation. Oral sources can fill in gaps that have plagued oral practitioners; they can rectify some errors; they can contradict or confirm documentary evidence. Oral sources may change, in whole or in part, the content and/or context of historical knowledge, and thus result in the detailed reconstruction of the past. In other words, oral records have a historical significance and, if used with great caution, are the other means whereby the historian can learn about the past. Yet, oral traditions are sadly underutilised by researchers.[23]

The historian derives much meaning from these sources when he or she is familiar with the language of the informant(s). The historian's mastery of the informant's language puts the former in a position to appreciate and comprehend the exact meaning of words used in their oral communication. The historian will not take words out of context but will understand the varying signification of words. Oral records, like any source, should not be accepted at face value. They should be subjected to critical analysis. Even though oral accounts can be conflicting, they must be approached critically, and evaluated against non-oral sources.

---

23   Stapleton, "Jingqi Oral Tradition", 333.

2

PRECOLONIAL AND EARLY HISTORY OF ABATHEMBULAND, 1650-1828

For a proper historical perspective on the origins, expansions, migrations and eventual establishment of the abaThembu in the former Transkei region, one needs to pay attention to their encounters from the sixteenth century and later with white explorers, other abeNguni communities and whites. However, this view does not purport that the history of physical contact between abeNguni and whites started in the sixteenth century. In the words of Du Pre, "the history of Black-White relations dates back to 1488 when Bartholomew Diaz first landed on South African soil and met the indigenous peoples living at the tip of the continent of Africa."[24] On arrival in South Africa, Diaz and his successors found the subcontinent inhabited by the San and the Khoi,[25] who had established themselves in the Cape hundreds of years before the arrival of Europeans.[26] Thus, the history of the abaThembu kingdom is interwined with that of other African kingdoms and closely interwoven with that of whites. Therefore, the history of abaThembu cannot be examined and presented as a factor on its own, but only in relation to white and African communities.

The arrival, exploration and settlement of whites in South Africa ushered in an era of colonisation that gave rise to racism, sexism, ecocide, ethnocide and genocide.[27]

---

24 R.H. du Pre, *The Making of Racial Conflict in South Africa* (Johannesburg: Skotaville, 1992), 9.
25 The colonially-inspired concept of the Khoi or Khoikhoi is no longer in use. The concept presently preferred is Khoe or Khoekhoe in terms of the Nama language.
26 Du Pre, *The Making of Racial Conflict*, 9-10.
27 W. Mignolo, "Delinking: The Rhetoric of Modernity, the Logic of Coloniality, and the Grammar of Decoloniality", *Cultural Studies*, vol. 21, No. 2, 2011, 512; J. Mvenene, "Embedding Chiefs' Bulls and Iminombo in Decolonising South African History in the Further Education and Training Phase", *Indilinga: African Journal of Indigenous Knowledge Systems*, vol. 18, No. 1, 2019, 29.

Odora-Hoppers and Richards highlight that the colonised were "captured..., their physical assets were taken away ... and their minds were colonised".[28] The colonisers either replaced or supplemented beliefs, practices and culture of the aborigines, undermining all that was African.[29]

While relatively little is known about the abaThembu polity prior to the reign of uKumkani Nxeko in 1650, it is acknowledged by some historians that the abaThembu are one of "the most prominent kingdoms to emerge after the sixteenth century".[30] Stapleton notes that "despite the fact that the [aba]Thembu were and are one of the largest groups in the eastern Cape, their history has received little attention."[31]

However, the actual abaThembu occupation of the former Transkei probably began far earlier than the sixteenth century. The abaThembu, along with other southern abeNguni communities, viz. amaBomvana, amaMpondo, amaMpondomise and amaXhosa, are the earliest inhabitants of the region of the former Transkei, which is part of the Eastern Cape Province of South Africa.[32] AbaThembu were united by a sense of belonging to a common ancestor, Mthembu, who died in Lesotho probably towards the end of the fifteenth century.[33] Mthembu had two sons, viz. Mvelase from the iNdlu eNkulu and Bhomoyi from the iNdlu yase Kunene. Bhomoyi, though not the heir of uMthembu, became the legitimate father of the former Transkei abaThembu who eventually settled in abaThembuland, a stretch of territory lying within the southwestern portion of the former Transkei, between the Nciba (Kei) and the Mbhashe Rivers. Yekela observes that "Bhomoyi's amaDlomo cluster eventually became assimilated into the Southern abeNguni unit, where they established themselves as a great house in their own right."[34] Both the descendants of Mvelase and Bhomoyi are referred to by the name of their common founding father, uMthembu. They are collectively termed abaThembu.[35]

It is difficult to fix the exact date of abaThembu arrival in the former Transkei. It is, however, generally accepted by most historians that they moved from Natal and migrated towards the Dedesi River near the upper reaches of the Mzimvubu River probably at the end of the

---

28 C. Odora-Hoppers and H. Richards, *Rethinking Thinking: Modernity's 'other' and the Transformation of the University* (Pretoria: Unisa Press, 2011), 73.
29 Mvenene, "Embedding Chiefs' Bulls and Iminombo in Decolonising South African History", 29.
30 W. Beinart and C. Bundy, "State Intervention and Rural Resistance: The Transkei, 1900 to 1965", in M. Klein (ed.), *Peasants in Africa* (California: Hoover Institution Press, 1980), 273; M. Wilson, "The Nguni People", in M. Wilson and L. Thompson (eds), *The Oxford History of South Africa*, vol. 1 (Oxford: Oxford University Press, 1969), 79 and 120; W.A. Bellwood, *Whither the Transkei?* (Cape Town: Howard Timmins, 1964), 16; N. Parsons, *A New History of Southern Africa* (London: Macmillan, 1982), 36.
31 Stapleton, "The Expansion of a Pseudo-Ethnicity in the Eastern Cape: Reconsidering the Fingo 'Exodus' of 1865", *International Journal of African Historical Studies*, 29, 2 (1996), 248.
32 Maylam, *History of African People*, 35; Hammond-Tooke, *Umtata District*, 14.
33 J.H. Soga, *The South-Eastern Bantu* (Johannesburg: Witwatersrand University Press, 1930), 73-74; Kuse, "Thembu Right-Hand House", 78.
34 Yekela, "Unity and Division", 42.
35 "Aba" in 'abaThembu' is an isiXhosa prefix, which denotes the plural form of 'umThembu'.

fifteenth century, and in the mid-seventeenth century were established along the Mbhashe River.³⁶ AbaThembu, being a small nation, settled along with the amaMpondomise and the amaXesibe at Dedesi. After a century or so, having emerged as a large kingdom at the end of the sixteenth century by natural growth and assimilation of conquered nations like aBambo, aMazizi and aMahlubi, the abaThembu gradually expanded.³⁷ In the former Transkei, abaThembu had peaceful contact with white explorers and interacted with other southern abeNguni communities, viz. amaXhosa, amaMpondo, amaBomvana and the amaMpondomise.

During the reign of uKumkani Nxeko in the first half of the seventeenth century, the abaThembu and amaBomvana migrated southwards, and came to be situated south of the amaMpondo and amaMpondomise. Shipwrecked travellers provide accounts of contact with the abeNguni communities, of which the abaThembu are part. The Portuguese survivors of the shipwrecked Santo Alberto reported their encounter with the 'Tizombe' in the western part of the former Transkei.³⁸ Around the year 1600, an abaThembu cluster was spotted at the sources of the Ntsele and the Qhudeni mountains, while in 1635 the survivors of the *Nossa Senhora de Belem*, wrecked at the Xhorha mouth, came into contact with abeNguni communities between the Mbhashe and the Mthatha Rivers.³⁹ Around February 1686, an abaThembu group was spotted along the south coast of Natal by the survivors of the Dutch ship, the *Stavenisse*. The survivors reported to have seen "the Semboes, the Mapontemousse, the Maponte, and the Matimbes".⁴⁰ The shipwrecked survivors travelled through five kingdoms, viz., amaXhosa, Griqua, Khoekhoe, abaThembu and abaMbo. There is further evidence that abaThembu were found by shipwrecked seamen in 1688 occupying the country between the Mbhashe and the Mthatha Rivers, and they were still living there at the commencement of the present century (1880s).⁴¹

Trading was the abaThembu form of contact with explorers. Bartering was practised as a form of trade between abaThembu and explorers. AbaThembu encounters with the explorers suggest that the former practised mixed farming.⁴² They were herdsmen and agriculturalists. Their economy was based on cultivation and herding, while the homestead served as the basic social and economic unit. They had great fertile pastures for their cattle. They subsisted on milk and butter and used hunting and the collection of wild plants to supplement their diet of sorghum and maize, the latter having become their staple food since 1635. The abaThembu reared dogs for purposes of hunting wild animals.

These accounts also inform us that the abaThembu, like other abeNguni communities, esteemed cattle. They prized cattle highly because of the part they played in marriage customs and in sarifices to the *izinyanya* (ancestors). They used cattle as the basis of their economy. In the

---

36 Parsons, *New History*, 36; Kuse, "Thembu Right-Hand House", 78.
37 Molema, *The Bantu*, 387.
38 Soga, *South-Eastern Bantu*, 467.
39 C.C. Saunders, *Historical Dictionary of South Africa* (London: Government Printer, 1983), 173.
40 Wilson, "The Nguni People", 84; Soga, *South-Eastern Bantu*, 467.
41 *Blue Book on Native Affairs*, 1885, 20.
42 Saunders, *Historical Dictionary*, 173.

marriage transaction, the groom paid lobola, that is marriage payment of cattle to the bride's father. It is believed that lobola was a means to solemnise and bring stability to the marriage, amongst other things. It cemented relationships between the two families. Wealthy men and traditional leaders practised polygamy. Owning cattle was a "means of sustaining the practice of polygamy, which underpinned the gender division of labour".[43] Jack Lewis sums it up this way:

> The transfer of cattle from a man's homestead to that of his wife's father on marriage was primarily compensation for the loss of the productive and procreative power of a woman. By lowering or raising the age of marriage or by marrying additional wives themselves, the homestead heads could affect the rate of demographic and hence of social cohesion.[44]

According to Joseph Cox Warner, most abaThembu men had two wives, while the wealthy ones preferred three to four wives.[45] Even though wives

> shared the burdens of growing crops, and preparing food and drink for the homestead..., [by the 1850s] technology was slowly changing the nature of work. Metal hoes, spades and picks, as well as ploughs – bought at one of the white trading stores that sprang up in the [Tambookie] location – meant that women no longer needed to plough on their knees, with wooden spades.[46]

IiKumkani and iiNkosi used polygamy as a mechanism to preserve social order amongst conflicting nations. It signified the mutual bond of the two kingdoms or chiefdoms.[47] In this sense, they used it for diplomatic purposes. As regards abaThembu sacrifices to the *izinyanya* (ancestors), it needs be stated that the abaThembu believed in the survival of the dead and the existence of a spiritual world. In line with this belief, the deceased was buried with certain clothes. The sacrificial ceremonies offered to the *izinyanya* (ancestors) indicated the mutual and reciprocal relationship between the *izinyanya* (ancestors) and the members of the family. Thus, ownership of cattle and wives was not only a standard of wealth, influence and power to owners, but it was also the centre of their existence.[48]

The location and distribution of the abaThembu kings' graves substantiates the fact that the abaThembu had a long history of inhabiting abaThembuland. This also provides evidence relating to the abaThembu expansion and distribution over centuries. For example, uKumkani Nxeko (c.1640) who had died in the 1680s was laid to rest at Msana, a tributary of the Mbhashe

---

43 Mager, "Gungubele and the Tambookie Location", 1162.
44 J. Lewis, "Materialism and Idealism in the Historiography of the Xhosa Cattle-Killing Movement 1856-7", *South African Historical Journal*, 25 (1991), 248.
45 *Cape of Good Hope Proceedings of and Evidence taken by Commission on Native Affairs 1865*, Joseph Cox Warner's Testimony, 11 February 1865, 70.
46 Mager, "Gungubele and the Tambookie Location", 1161.
47 R.L. Cope, "Christian Missions and Independent African Chiefdoms in South Africa in the 19th Century", *Theoria*, vol. L.ii, May 1979, 4; L. Callinicos, *A People's History of South Africa, 1886-1924* (Johannesburg: Ravan Press, 1981), 3.
48 Williams, "Missionaries", 292.

River. His legitimate heir, Hlanga, was buried at Nkanga in the Gatyana (Willowvale) district. UKumkani Thatho (c.1730) was buried at Mkhuthu, east of the Mbhashe River, in 1700. His son, Zondwa (c.1750), was laid to rest at Darhabe in the Mqanduli district in 1725. In 1800, uKumkani Ndaba (c.1780) was laid to rest at Mthentu on the east of the Mbhashe River.[49] UKumkani Vusani, A! Ngubengcuka! was buried at Tyeni in the Ngcobo district on 10 August 1830. His son, Xokiso, A! Mthikrakra! was laid to rest at Gqebenya in Komani in 1850. UKumkani Qheya, A! Ngangelizwe! was buried at Tyhalarha in the Mthatha district in 1884. And so was his son, Aliva, A! Dalindyebo! in 1920, his grandson, Sampu, A! Jongilizwe! in 1928 and his great-grandson, Sabata, A! Jonguhlanga! in 1986.[50]

Though little is known of the early history of the abaThembu nation, oral tradition claims that uKumkani Nxeko succeeded his father, Mnguthi. A look at the lineage of the abaThembu *umnombo* (genealogy) depicts an orderly succession of iiKumkani who reigned before and after uKumkani Nxeko towards the end of the sixteenth century. The abaThembu *iminombo* (genealogies) also show the relationship of the abaThembu kings and chiefs to one another.

The historical significance of *iminombo* is enormous in the history of African societies. They are the means whereby the historical roots of traditional leaders are traced from the womb of history. They shed light on the historical origins of the ruling house and its relation to other houses.[51] Furthemore, *iminombo* throw light on the dating of certain historical events. As Van Jaarsveld observes, *iminombo* function "chiefly as proof of the ruling group's right to rule".[52] They yield a new insight into South African history, and contribute towards preserving traditions that might, without them, have been lost. No wonder that they are used by the traditional leaders to justify and buttress their claims to legitimacy, seniority and authority.[53]

The death of uKumkani Nxeko in the 1680s was to have far-reaching implications and enormous destabilising consequences for the abaThembu. It marked the beginning of a political cleavage within the abaThembu kingdom and reversed the southern abeNguni tradition of succession, which laid down that amongst the sons of an iKumkani or iNkosi, it is only the eldest son of the iNdlu eNkulu who is entitled to succeed his father, or if he is a minor on the death of his father, it is the iQadi of the iNdlu eNkulu who is to act as regent or even to succeed as heir to the patrimony in the event of the iNdlu eNkulu having no issue. According to the abeNguni general rule, "the regent is never ever the Right-Hand House".[54]

---

49 Derricourt, "Settlement in the Transkei and Ciskei", 59.
50 UNkosi Dalagubha Joyi, Interview, Bhaziya Village, Mthatha, 7 May 1994; uNkosi Ngubethafa Mnqanqeni, Interview, Mbhashe Village, Mthatha, 8 September 1994; Mlahleni Xundu, Interview, Manzana Village, Ngcobo, 16 April 1996.
51 Mvenene, "Embedding Chiefs' Bulls and Iminombo in Decolonising South African History", 35.
52 A. van Jaarsveld, "Oral Traditions of the Ndzundza Ndebele", in H.C. Groenewald (ed.), *Oral Studies in Southern Africa* (Pretoria: Human Sciences Research Council, 1990), 16.
53 Mvenene, "Embedding Chiefs' Bulls and Iminombo in Decolonising South African History", 35.
54 Kuse, "Thembu Right-Hand House", 85; Headman Ntsikelelo Sotyatho, Interview, Clarkebury Village, Ngcobo, 28 June 1995; Sizakele Matiwane, Interview, Ntlalukana Village, Ngcobo, 24 June 1995.

UKumkani Nxeko had three sons, viz. Hlanga of the iNdlu eNkulu, Dlomo of the iNdlu yaseKunene and Ndungwana of the iQadi of iNdlu eNkulu (see Umnombo 2). Hlanga was born of an umMpondo princess, Mqiyakazi. As Ndungwana was iMvelatanci, the natural successor to the late king was Prince Hlanga.[55] Prince Hlanga, however, lacked desirable qualities, such as courage, open-mindedness and wisdom to guide, which would commend him to the abaThembu. This counted in favour of Dlomo who gradually had a growing influence on the abaThembu.[56] Notwithstanding, Dlomo fought Hlanga for succession at the Battle of Msana in 1680. Ndungwana put his weight behind Dlomo, and this action turned the outcome of the battle in favour of Dlomo. Having defeated Hlanga, Dlomo assumed the abaThembu kingship, something which was out of place with regard to the abaThembu tradition of succession. Since then, the House of Dlomo became the reigning house. Not traditionally justifiable and having no known precedent in the abaThembu customary law, this friction and its ominous outcome were subversive to the abaThembu social and political equilibrium. While representing one of the inter-tribal conflicts, which was to lead to the disempowering of the abaThembu kingdom, it was the major factor that contributed in no small measure to the rupturing of the social fabric that had cohesively held the abaThembu kingdom intact. While it did not only intensify a split within the abaThembu nation, it also led to the political and military fragility of the abaThembu kingdom.

---

55 Traditionally, the king's or chief's Great Wife (great because she is heir-producing) is chosen from the royal house by his councillors and is lobola-ed by the nation. His first wife is not allocated to the iNdlu eNkulu as she is regarded as 'umosulimdaka', that is, the one who has removed the white clay (or 'ingceke') of his initiation and thus is not heir producing. Her son is the first born and not an heir. Hence he is termed 'imvelatanci'.

56 Soga, *South-Eastern Bantu*, 470.

Umnombo (Genealogy) 1: AbaThembu Primary Lineage[57]

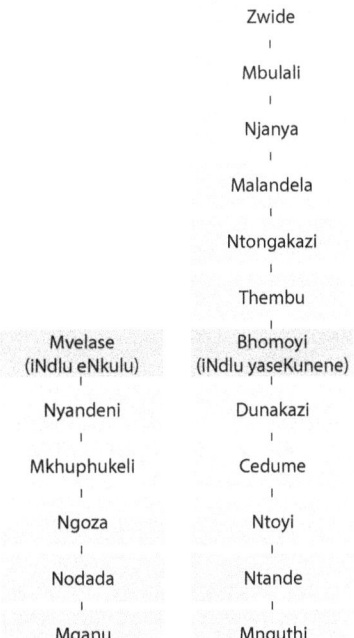

Consequential to Dlomo's assumption of power, his subjects assumed the name Hala and were since then termed amaHala. As the majority of the Mbhashe clans recognised Dlomo's supreme authority, uKumkani Nxeko's legitimate heir, Hlanga, became a chief of a separate but subordinate cluster, which assumed the name Hlanga or Qhiya. Since then, Hlanga's subjects were called amaHlanga or amaQhiya. Hlanga established his political domain on the west of the Mbhashe River. Observing with alarm and anxiety the turning of the tables in the House of Nxeko, Ndungwana established his hegemony, which comprised the descendants of the royal house on the north of the Mbhashe River. He was granted chieftainship and semi-autonomous status by his youngest brother, Dlomo, whom he had given military support during the Battle of Msana. His section, though remaining quasi-independent, was referred to as amaNdungwana.

---

57 Jackson, *Ciskei and Transkei*, 13.

Umnombo (Genealogy) 2: The House of Nxeko[58]

iNdlu yaseKunene	Nxeko	iQadi of kwiNdlu eNkulu
Dlomo	Hlanga	Ndungwana
Hala	Mndlovu	Diya
Madiba	Maleki	Gungu
Thato	Thela	Langa
Zondwa	Ngxoxo	Khono
Ndaba	Ngcutsha	Bhejula
Ngubengcuka	Bhacela	Nene
Mthikrakra	Siphendu	Qhwesha
Ngangelizwe		Ndarhala
Dalindyebo		Tshaka
Jongilizwe		Mvumbi
Jonguhlanga		Siyabalala

The abaThembu kingdom had thus become divided into three notable sections, viz. amaDlomo, amaHlanga and amaNdungwana (see Umnombo 2). There emerged from the descendants of Dlomo's Right-Hand House a section called amaTshatshu (see Umnombo 3). Another section called amaJumba mushroomed from uKumkani Ndaba's Right-Hand House (see Umnombo 4). This was to set in motion a train of fissions, which adversely affected the abaThembu socio-political threads. Furthermore, the abaThembu incorporated clans of alien blood into their kingdom, viz. amaMvulane, amaGubevu, amaGambu, amaHegebe, amaQwathi, amaTshezi, amaTshomane, amaNqanda, amaGcina, amaNtshilibe, amaVundle, amaNgabi, amaXesibe and amaBhayi. These clans had originally migrated over a period of a century or so from the northern parts of Africa before eventually settling in abaThembuland.[59] With the passage of time, however, they ultimately settled in various places. For example, amaGubevu, amaGambu and amaVundle migrated from Lesotho. AmaBhayi moved from the Herschel district. AmaQwathi and amaXesibe came from Mount Ayliff, while AmaGcina were from Lady Frere. AmaTshezi, amaTshomane and amaNqanda were from Mpondoland. They were absorbed and accommodated with the intention of placing them at strategic points so that they could with ease and promptitude help in the defence of abaThembuland, "lest the

---

58   D.L.P. Yali-Manisi, *Izibongo Zeenkosi ZamaXhosa* (Lovedale: Lovedale Press, 1952), 62.
59   UNkosi Dalagubha Joyi, Interview, 7 September 1994; Mlahleni Xundu, Interview, 19 April 1996.

enemies could penetrate and launch an attack on the abaThembu kingdom".[60] Even though the abaThembu and these refugees interacted and influenced one another, abaThembu retained their language and cultural identity.

Some of these refugee clans were, however, powerful, had varying ideologies and as a consequence paid allegiance not to the abaThembu kings but to their own original chiefs. As a result, the abaThembu kingdom had no social and political cohesion, and this rendered this kingdom vulnerable to outside attacks and influences. Lacking within the abaThembu kingdom was the "powerful element of union".[61] This laid the foundation for the inherent weakness of the abaThembu kingdom, which culminated in the division of abaThembuland.

Umnombo (Genealogy) 3: The House of Dlomo[62]

Dlomo	iNdlu yaseKunene
Hala	Manusi
Madiba	Thukwa
Thato	Xhoba
Zondwa	Tshatshu
Ndaba	Bawana
Ngubengcuka	Maphasa
Mthikrakra	Gungubele
Ngangelizwe	Gcuwa
Dalindyebo	Sobantu
Jongilizwe	
Jonguhlanga	

---

60 Professor Wandile Kuse, Interview, University of Transkei, Mthatha, 20 April 1996.
61 F. Brownlee, *Transkei Native Territories: Historical Records* (Lovedale: Lovedale Press, 1923), 21.
62 Soga, *South-Eastern Bantu*, between 466 and 467.

Umnombo (Genealogy) 4: The House of Ndaba[63]

Ndaba	iNdlu yaseKunene
Ngubengcuka	Jumba
Mthikrakra	Mgudlwa
Ngangelizwe	Langa
Dalindyebo	Ligwa
Jongilizwe	Dalikhulu
Jonguhlanga	Mvulankulu
Zwelibanzi	Ngubesizwe
Zanelizwe	

While adapting themselves to their environment, the abaThembu had considerable peaceful and sometimes violent contact with their western neighbours, the amaGcaleka-Xhosa.[64] Since the reign of King Thatho (c.1760), the abaThembu-Xhosa contact was a recognisable feature.[65] This contact, however, was also characterised by physical friction. For example, the physical conflict between uKumkani Ndaba's abaThembu and uNkosi Rharhabe's amaXhosa culminated in the death of Chief Rharhabe[66] and his son, Prince Mlawu, in 1782. The abaThembu–Xhosa rivalry, coupled with their divided attitude towards whites, who sought to play one kingdom against the other, ultimately led to the subjugation of these kingdoms in general. and division of abaThembuland, in particular. As a matter of fact, the abaThembu were, in comparison with the amaXhosa, weaker owing to their socio-political heterogeneity.

---

63   Hammond-Tooke, *Umtata District*, 35-36.
64   AmaXhosa nation comprises amaGcaleka and amaNgqika. AmaGcaleka belonged to the Great House of Phalo, who died in 1775. AmaNgqika descended from Phalo's Right-Hand House. AmaNgqika are also called amaRharhabe.
65   By 'Thembu-Xhosa', I refer to the abaThembu contact with both the amaGcaleka and the ama-Rharhabe, which constitute the whole amaXhosa nation.
66   As each iKumkani and iNkosi had his *ingoma* (traditional song), uNkosi Rharhabe's was: *uMdudo*. Iingoma are other forms of historical sources that paint a picture of a particular period and portray the milieu of the time. Iingoma carry a historical message about the culture, customs and traditions of a nation. They were sung on important occasions, such as those performed during the rituals of passage from boyhood to manhood (uSomagwaza), during war times (iGwatyu) and during ancestral worship rituals (uMdudo). For more on *iingoma*, see S.E.K. Mqhayi, *Ityala Lamawele* (Lovedale: Lovedale Press, 1914), 64; J. Mvenene, "The Implementation of Indigenous Knowledge Systems in the Teaching and Learning of South African History: A Case Study of Four Mthatha High Schools" (DEd. Thesis, Walter Sisulu University, 2018).

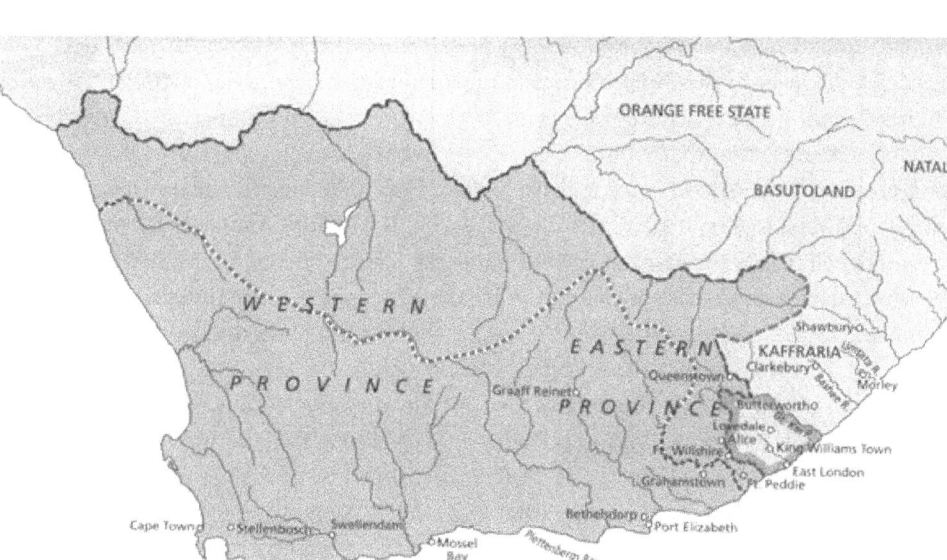

MAP 3: Cape Colony, 1806-1865[67]

Despite these intermittent physical conflicts, these two dynasties could still forge marriages links, which "were [indeed] particularly strong".[68] However, the abaThembu engaged in these marital links with reluctance owing to the fact that the amaXhosa used these kinship ties to intervene in the abaThembu internal affairs, as uNkosi Tshatshu's son-in-law, uNkosi Ngqika (c.1775-1829),[69] sought to influence abaThembu administration through his mother who was also an umThembu. As can be seen, the abaThembu–Xhosa interaction was one of diverse forms, and it did not have the effect of welding the abaThembu together.

Umnombo (Genealogy) 5: The House of Ngubengcuka[70]

Ngubengcuka	Ekunene	iQadi of (iNdlu eNkulu)	iXhiba
Mthikrakra	Mnqanqeni	Joyi, Shweni and Ngxitho	Mandela
Ngangelizwe	Mbambonduna	Gobinamba (GH): Makhawula (RHH)	
Dalindyebo	Phalele	Mgubhuli, Zwelibhangile and Zanengqele	
Jongilizwe	Nqabisile		

---

67 Price, *Making Empire*, xxv.
68 Wilson, "The Nguni", 120.
69 UNkosi Ngqika's *ingoma* was: *iNjinana*. His sons from various houses were Sandile (1820-1878), Maqoma (1798-1873), Tyhali (d. 1842), Anta (1810-1877), Xhoxho (d. 1878), Matwa (1810-1847) and Thente (d. 1842).
70 Author's version, 2019.

In 1810, uKumkani Vusani, Aa! Ngubengcuka! assumed power. UKumkani Ngubengcuka had Princes Mthikrakra in the iNdlu eNkulu, Mnqanqeni in the iNdlu yaseKunene and Mandela in the iQadi of the iNdlu eNkulu (see Umnombo 5). The first king to permit the missionaries to work amongst the abaThembu, uKumkani Ngubengcuka grappled with the herculean task of ruling a conglomeration of clans. While giving allegiance to uNkosi Qhwesha,[71] the amaNdungwana section blatantly frowned upon the abaThembu kingdom. UNkosi Tshatshu, uNkosi Sandile's father-in-law through his daughter, Suthu, challenged the abaThembu king. While dissuading the amaNtshilibe clan from paying allegiance to uKumkani Ngubengcuka, uKumkani Hintsa, A! Zanzolo! abortively sought and exerted authority over the abaThembu kingdom. UNkosi Tshatshu, whose status was increasingly inflated through his kinship ties with uKumkani Hintsa (1789-1835), the king of the whole amaXhosa nation and the most powerful of all the kings, set out to build his little chiefdom, thereby challenging uKumkani Ngubengcuka.[72] UKumkani Hintsa's political domain stretched from the Mbhashe River to the Xelexwa (Gamtoos) River and covered iNtaba zikaNojoli (Somerset East).[73] UNkosi Tshatshu's challenging plans and uKumkani Hintsa's intrusions and ambitions disrupted and further disintegrated the abaThembu kingdom.

AmaGcina, amaVundle (of abeSuthu origin), amaQwathi (of amaXesibe origin), amaNgabi and amaNtshilibe presented the abaThembu people with insurmountable problems. Though acknowledging the supremacy of Ngubengcuka, the amaGcina, amaVundle and amaQwathi "maintained their chiefship and their territorial integrity".[74] More disturbing to uKumkani Ngubengcuka was the tendency of amaQwathi to regard the amaHala as no match for them, while the amaNgabi and the amaNtshilibe constantly paid allegiance to King Hintsa (1789-1835). The amaQwathi, having been incorporated into the abaThembu kingdom shortly after Ngubengcuka became king, "became more contemptuous than ever before, claiming supremacy over the Mbashe area".[75] Under these circumstances and upheavels Wright's remark that the abeNguni kingdoms were composed largely of discrete chiefdoms, which had been subordinated by, or had given their allegiance to, a dominant chiefdom, seems applicable to the abaThembu kingdom.[76] Such an atmosphere justified a strong leader to weld the abaThembu nation together and to deal with the arising problems of the day.

---

71   UNkosi Qhwesha was uNkosi Maqoma's brother-in-law.
72   W.B. Boyce, *Memoir of the Reverend William Shaw: Late General-Superintendent of the Wesleyan Mission in South Africa* (London: Wesleyan Conference Officer, 1874), 96; N. Mostert, *Frontiers: The Epic of South Africa's Creation and the Tragedy of the Xhosa People* (London: Jonathan Cape Ltd, 1992), 606.
73   Mqhayi, *Ityala Lamawele*, 58.
74   Peires, *House of Phalo*, 84.
75   Wagenaar, "History of the Thembu", 5.
76   J. Wright, "Popularizing the Precolonial Past: Politics and Problems", *Perspectives in Education*, vol. x, No. 2, 1988, 48.

Precolonial and early history of AbaThembuland, 1650-1828

MAP 4: AbaThembu areas of settlement by the 1800s (areas numbered 1-7)[77]

---

77 J.W. Macquarrie (ed.), *The Reminiscences of Sir Walter Stanford, vol. i, 1850-1885* (Cape Town: Van Riebeeck Society, 1958), between 198 and 199.

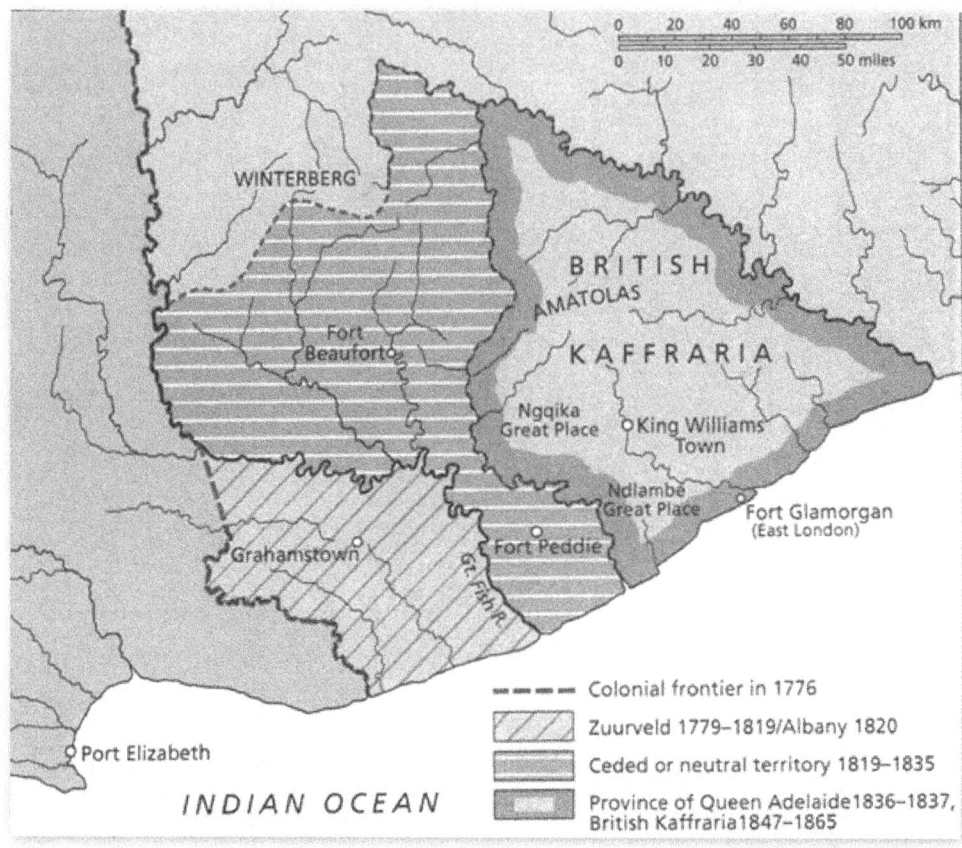

MAP 5: The Eastern Cape frontier and amaXhosa land losses, 1779-1850[78]

The worst was yet to come with the Mfecane wars, which had catastrophic consequences for the abaThembu. Not only did it bring about a truce in the abaThembu–Xhosa rivalry but it also drove the abaThembu closer to the colonial government. With the the advent of the Mfecane wars, some abaThembu clans under Chiefs Mathanzima, Bawana and Ndarhala made their way towards Komani and settled there as a separate abaThembu section. This had the effect of disrupting the abaThembu nation more so that whites interfered in the abaThembu relations. While some authorities define the Mfecane wars as "the prolonged and widespread inter-tribal warfare",[79] characteristic of the nineteenth century, and "the migratory wars which disrupted the lives of Africans in central South Africa",[80] abaThembu used the term 'Mfecane'

---

78 Price, *Making Empire*, xxvii.
79 Cope, "African Chiefdoms", 4.
80 R.L. Watson, "Missionary Influence at Thaba Nchu, 1833-1854: A Reassessment", *International Journal of African Historical Studies*, 10, 3 (1957), 394.

to refer to "enemy bandits or sometimes to local rivals".[81] The Boers used the term "to describe any people whose cattle they happened to be raiding".[82]

The socio-political structure of the abaThembu kingdom was partly responsible for conflict within the House of Nxeko. It also encouraged expansion and secession. It naturally led to the rivalry between members of the iNdlu eNkulu and the iNdlu yaseKunene and it fostered conflict and envy within the abaThembu kingdom. Furthermore, Nattrass's remarks are apt in showing that the Mfecane wars were not the root causes of a rift within abaThembu:

> Many myths and distortions have arisen about those troubled years [the 1820s and 1830s] … the 1820s and 1830s were a time of warfare, migration, consolidation and change,… some powerful black kingdoms emerged – notably the Zulu, Sotho and Ndebele. The Mfecane produced some of our most famous historic leaders: Shaka (Zulu), Manthatisi (Tlokwa), Mzilikazi (Ndebele, Moshoeshoe (Sotho), Moletsane (Taung), Sekwati (Pedi) and Montshiwa (Rolong), all of them leaders who gathered together what was left of their tribes and rebuilt consolidated communities.[83]

---

81 J. Cobbing, "The Mfecane as Alibi: Thoughts on Dithakong and Mbholompo", *Journal of African History*, 2 (1988), 500.
82 Ibid.
83 G. Nattrass, *A Short History of South Africa* (Johannesburg and Cape Town: Jonathan Ball, 2018), 58.

3

INTERNAL AND EXTERNAL PRESSURES ON THE AbaThembu POLITY, 1828-1848

By 1828, the abaThembu people were living as one nation under one uKumkani, Ngubengcuka. They had had contact with whites who sought land, labour and cattle. Clashes between the abaThembu and the amaGcaleka-Xhosa were also taking place. These clashes, and the fragmentary nature of the abaThembu socio-political constitution, had weakened the abaThembu kingdom for years to come. Had there been strong ties between these kingdoms, viz. abaThembu and amaXhosa, their history would have taken a different course. Perhaps, they could have jointly faced their enemies. Had there been no whites' interference in the abaThembu relations, there could not have been rivalries within the abaThembu kings and chiefs. Also, there could not have been acute rivalries between abaThembu and amaGcaleka-Xhosa. The weakness of abaThembu was to lead to their collaborative relations with whites, who had taken it upon themselves to initiate, promote and accelerate divisions with the abaThembu kingdom and between the abaThembu and the amaGcaleka-Xhosa. The Cape Government did not hesitate to use this to its advantage and its interference in the abaThembu relations gave rise to the division of the House of Mthikrakra. Once divided the abaThembu were subjugated by whites who used the policy of divide-and-rule as one of their weapons in their attempts to undermine kingship and chieftainship.

This chapter briefly addresses the current debate and the polemical discussion surrounding the Mfecane wars; the Mfecane wars and its effects on the abaThembu socio-political structure; the disastrous results of the abaThembu participation in the war of 1846-1847; and finally the missionary influences on the abaThembu religion, beliefs and practices.

Because of the divisive and disruptive effects of the Mfecane wars on the abaThembu, it is proper and fitting to explore the nature of these great battles and migrations, which took place in South-East Africa. The main significance of the Mfecane wars is that they escalated a rift within the abaThembu people. A proportion of abaThembu fled towards Komani.[84] Thus, it discolated the abaThembu nation and so rendered them vulnerable to piecemeal attacks.[85] In this way, the Mfecane wars marked a watershed in the history of the abaThembu. Therefore, the notion of the Mfecane wars and the debates surrounding them deserve historical analysis.

Conflicting accounts of the Mfecane wars have been given by historians who battle to make sense of the events that occurred in South-East Africa during the first half of the nineteenth century. Some historians advance the view that the Mfecane was a great series of wars and raids carried on by the abeNguni communities during the 1820s and 1830s.[86] They claim that whites did not participate in these wars, and rather stood as helpless observers. They further state that these wars were precipitated by the rise of uKumkani Shaka's amaZulu empire and overpopulation in South-East Africa. These wars caused the displaced and refugee abeNguni communities to flee over the Drakensberg passes, leaving their lands depopulated and littered with bones of the dead. These wars spread into abaThembuland, threw the area into disorder and destroyed traditional patterns of socio-political life of the abaThembu. They maintain that the Mfecane wars as black-on-black confrontation, a Shakan revolution, a period of revolutionary warfare, were not only accompanied by deprivations, but also resulted in widespread migrations of peoples in different directions and to different destinations, abaThembu themselves included. These migrations sometimes led to conquest, raiding, dislocation of tribal organisation and orderly life, social and political disintegration and regeneration.[87] They maintain that these migrations and displacements led to tribal land settlement around the depopulated regions, and in this way use the Mfecane wars as the basis of land division of 1913, through the Native Land Act. Thus, these historians use the Mfecane wars to justify segregation, which became the basis on which apartheid policies were built. In short, the Mfecane wars wrought havoc, trauma and turmoil on the southern Highveld.

As a matter of fact, the Mfecane wars were not carried on by the abeNguni communities alone, but were a South African affair, involving even abeSuthu and whites. Furthermore, the above-mentioned historians uncritically and incorrectly attribute the Mfecane wars to the aberration and cruelty of uKumkani Shaka whom they depict variously as the ruthless tyrant, the bloodthirsty and warlike king. UKumkani Shaka is not only portrayed as a "cruel monster", who engaged in a mission of "massacre" and "destruction", but also as one of the most ruthless

---

84 Jackson, *Ciskei and Transkei*, 11.
85 Maylam, *History of African People*, 55.
86 J.D. Omer-Cooper, *The Zulu Aftermath: A Nineteenth-Century Revolution in Bantu Africa* (London: Longman, 1966), 6-7; Peires, *House of Phalo*, 84-85; Maylam, *History of African People*, 55; J. Benyon, *Proconsul and Paramountcy in South Africa, 1806-1910* (Pietermaritzburg: University of Natal Press, 1980), 11 and 145; W.D. Hammond-Tooke, "Segmentation and Fission in Cape Nguni Political Units", *Africa*, vol. xxxv, No. 3, 1965, 145 and 161.
87 W.D. Hammond-Tooke, "Segmentation and Fission", 145 and 161; J.A. Templin, *Ideology on a Frontier* (London: Greenwood Press, 1984), 103; Maylam, *History of African People*, 55; J. Guy, *The Heretic: A Study of the Life of John William Colenso, 1814-1883* (Johannnesburg: Ravan Press, 1983), 37; D. Guise, *Freedom for All* (Natal: Natal Publishing Company, 1983), 5.

conquerors amongst the abeNguni traditional leaders.[88] By claiming that Shaka "considered himself above morality, responsible to none and free from ordinary restraints",[89] these historians likened uKumkani Shaka to Napoleon Bonaparte. They, nevertheless, attest to the fact that there is no recorded account given of Shaka's cruelty by his contemporaries.

It was traders, missionaries and settlers who depicted uKumkani Shaka in a poor light. In their own interests, Henry Fynn, Nathaniel Isaacs and Francis Farewell (white traders), Robert Moffat and John Melvil (missionaries) depicted Shaka not only as a villain, but also as insane, despotic and merciless. For example, Isaacs urged Fynn to portray Shaka and the amaZulu in a poor light by making them appear as extremely bloodthirsty.[90] This was meant for outside consumption and to justify the extension of white control into amaZululand. It is evident that these historians adopt an Afrocentric or Zulucentric approach to the Mfecane wars.

However, during the 1980s, other historians re-examined the Mfecane wars and came up with new interpretations.[91] These views gave rise to the current debate surrounding the Mfecane wars. Precipitating the debate was Julian Cobbing who regards the term 'Mfecane' as "a twentieth century invention of European academics",[92] which was meant to cover up white intrusions into African lands by exaggerating black-on-black confrontation while whites were observers. He considers the Mfecane as a historiographical concept, which white historians have anthropomorphised. He claims that "the [ama]Zulu were never the primary stimulus of forced migrations, and most frequently were not involved at all".[93] He points out that wars that were engulfing South-East Africa at the same time were a result of various factors relating to already turbid relations between African societies and whites. At the core of these wars was the shortage of land and labour on which white farmers were dependent for their sustenance. Cobbing maintains that it was the increase of whites in South-East Africa that led to the excessive demand for land, labour and cattle. He also points to the Griqua raids for cattle and labour from the 1760s onwards, which gave rise to conflict in the middle of the Orange and Lower Vaal Rivers by the 1810s. Thus, the Mfecane wars originated in the west and spread down to the east before affecting Africans. Cobbing also attributes the Mfecane wars to the slave trade in Delagoa Bay, which took place from about 1800 to 1825. As the Portuguese

---

88 W. Eveleigh, *The Settlers and Methodism, 18201920* (Cape Town: Methodist Publishing Office, 1920), 76; E.H. Brookes and C. de B. Webb, *A History of Natal* (Pietermaritzburg: University of Natal Press, 1965), 11; B. Guest (ed.), *Natal and Zululand from Earliest Times to 1910: A New History* (Pietermaritzburg: University of Natal Press, 1989), 68; *Cape of Good Hope Government Gazette*, No. 1535, 22 May 1835: Report by W.H. Dutton, Military Secretary, on Hintsa, 3 May 1835.
89 Brookes and Webb, *Natal*, 33.
90 C.A. Hamilton, "An Appetite for the Past: The Re-creation of Shaka and the Crisis in Popular Historical Consciousness", *South African Historical Journal*, 22 (1990), 144; Du Pre, *The Making of Racial Conflict*, 20.
91 Cobbing, "The Case against the Mfecane", Unpublished Seminar Paper, University of the Witwatersrand, 1984, 9; Cobbing, "Mfecane as Alibi", 500; J. Wright, "Political Mythology and the Making of Natal's Mfecane", *Canadian Journal of African Studies*, 23, 2 (1989), 273.
92 Cobbing, "Mfecane as Alibi", 487.
93 Ibid., 517.

slave traders sought labour, land and cattle they raided their neighbours. These raiding activities led to violence and forced migrations.

Cobbing disputes any possibility of depopulation of the interior of South Africa.[94] This view is supported by other revisionist historians who also claim that the notion of the empty land was propagated by Natal's settlers to justify the annexation of Natal in 1843.[95] These historians view the notion of the empty land as one of the perpetrated myths in the history of South Africa, and regard it as intended to justify the extension of white power into the lands previously inhabited by Africans. They also claim that whites' negative portrayal of Shaka was pursued for a variety of related reasons. For example, missionaries wanted to convince the British government of a need to annex Natal so that Western civilisation and Christianity could be used to change the character of the 'savages'. Merchants wanted to influence the British government to allow traders to establish businesses in Natal. White settlers tried to justify the white master-status over Africans. Hence, partly as a result of these white interest groups, the region between the Thukela and the Mzimkhulu Rivers was annexed to the Cape in 1843.

Indeed, myths have characterised the history of South Africa. From the middle of the nineteenth century, British officials used history "as a tool to justify their colonial expansion".[96] On consulting Dutch and British archives, Theal selected evidence to depict that amaXhosa were of recent origin into South-East Africa, and were immigrants.[97] This kind of historical writing by Theal implied that Africans are relative newcomers just like white settlers. Furthermore, Tisani notes that early travellers frequently remarked on unoccupied land through which they passed, and expresses her view on the possible causes of this notion of the empty areas as follows: "firstly, the indigenous people could have temporarily moved away from a place because of seasonal migration. Secondly, during the process of colonisation, Europeans assumed ownership of the lands of the indigenous people."[98]

Similarly, Seton aptly asserts that the amaMpondo "had been known to Europeans since 1686 [but incorrectly and wrongly states] but it was not until Wesleyans began work among them that their history and customs were discovered".[99] While Cobbing disputes the notion of the Mfecane, Peires has contributed to the debate by coming out strongly against what he terms the "Cobbing hypothesis".[100] However, Eldredge neatly concludes that "neither great leaders, nor environment and ecology, nor overpopulation, nor trade (including the slave

---

94 Cobbing, "Jettisoning the Mfecane with Perestroika", Unpublished Seminar Paper, University of Cape Town, April 1989, 10.
95 Wright, "Political Mythology", 274; N. Worden, *The Making of Modern South Africa: Conquest, Segregation and Apartheid* (Oxford: Blackwell Publishers, 1994), 13 and 14; Du Pre, *The Making of Racial Conflict*, 19 and 21.
96 Tisani, "Continuity and Change", i.
97 Ibid.
98 Ibid., iv.
99 B.E. Seton, "Wesleyan Missions and the Sixth Frontier War" (PhD. Thesis, University of Cape Town, 1962), 51.
100 Peires, "Matiwane's Road to Mbholompo: A Reprieve for the Mfecane?" *The Mfecane Aftermath: Towards a New Paradigm*, University of the Witwatersrand (6-9 September 1991), 2-3; V. Nhanha

trade and raiding) alone set off the wars and migrations that plagued the area through these decades."[101] The Mfecane wars, therefore, should be seen in terms of the complex interplay of environment, society, economy and demands or pressures of the time.

Nevertherless, if the Mfecane episode is to be accepted then it appears as if the Mfecane wars started in Natal as a result of both internal and external conflicting forces that were at work in the Phongolo–Mzimkhulu region during the Shakan era (c.1810-1830). Having been attacked by the amaNdwandwe of Zwide in 1818, Shaka set out to assert his authority by removing all opposition forces. Determined to protect and expand his territorial domain against outside attacks, uKumkani Shaka increased his army and centralised its control so as to make it wieldly. His behaviour was shaped by the amaZulu quest for more cattle to provide the amabutho and threats presented by the amaNdwandwe, the amaGasa and the amaNgoni in the north.[102]

It is noteworthy that the history of the early nineteenth-century African societies was characterised by numerous violent conflicts resulting from interacting forces within and outside the amaZulu kingdom. Conflicts between groups of kingdoms, genealogically unrelated, occurred while political alliances between those with the same descent and genealogy took root. Moreover, European traders' and farmers' greed for land and labour from African societies also contributed to the tense atmosphere of the Shakan period. As the product of his times Shaka was no different from Matiwane of the amaNgwane, Zwide of the amaNdwandwe, Ngoza of the abaThembu and Mzilikazi of the amaKhumalo. In adapting to the arising circumstances of the time, he used the system of amabutho to amass personal power and status and also to establish amaZulu supremacy in South-East Africa. The amabutho system served as an instrument of internal social control and a means of external defence.[103] Though Shaka is accused of committing atrocities and crimes previously unknown to mankind, he had to protect the amaZulu from inside opposition generated by internal ethnic differentiation, and from outside attacks during the turbulent period. Even though whites are presented as bearers of civilisation who were innocent, nonetheless "African 'aggresion' and 'savagery' were primarily to resist the white aggressor and invader and to protect or recover their ancestral homes".[104]

The Mfecane wars adversely affected the socio-political structure of the abaThembu. Madzikane was the first leader at the end of 1823 to challenge the might of uKumkani Vusani, A! Ngubengcuka! Chief Madzikane, like whites and other African chiefdoms and kingdoms, had a quest for more land and was attracted by the fertility of abaThembuland. The

---

and Peires, "Introduction", in R.T. Kawa, *Ibali LamaMfengu and Kunganjani Kusiyiwa eKapa?* 2nd Edition (Grahamstown: Cory Library, 2011), i.

101 E.A. Eldredge, "Sources of Conflict in Southern Africa, c.1800-1830: The Mfecane Reconsidered", *Journal of African History*, 33 (1992), 2.

102 'Amabutho' is a Zulu word that refers to a military system, practised by the abeNguni communities, whereby men and women of almost the same age were called up for military service.

103 Wright and Hamilton, "Traditions and Transformations", 69.

104 Du Pre, *The Making of Racial Conflict*, 14-15, 19 and 21.

amaBhaca of Madzikane launched an attack on the amaTshatshu and the amaGcina. A mixed abaThembu, amaXhosa and amaMpondomise force routed the amaBhaca, killing Madzikane at Gqutyini in 1825. Part of Madzikane's followers joined the ranks of the abaThembu and amaGcaleka begging for succour. However, the amaBhaca's "continual inroads greatly sapped the strength of the monarchy [uKumkani Ngubengcuka]".[105]

March 1825 saw the abaThembu under uNkosi Bawana contemplating crossing south into the neutral territory between the Keiskamma and the Nxuba (Fish) Rivers from which they had been evicted by the British after 1820. Between 1826 and 1827 the amaNgwane settled on the upper reaches of the Mbhashe River. The amaNgwane had migrated from Zululand and devastated Lesotho before crossing the Drakensberg to set foot in abaThembuland. The amaNgwane raided the abaThembu, forcing many victims into the Colony.[106] However, the abaThembu successfully resisted amaBhaca and amaNgwane raids.[107]

Owing to the amaNgwane raids, a section of the abaThembu led by the amaTshatshu migrated from the danger zone between the Mbhashe and the Mthatha Rivers and settled in the regions of present-day Komani (Queenstown), Cacadu (Glen Grey), Aliwal North, Burgersdorp, Sterkstroom and Dordrecht.[108] Thus, the Mfecane wars were partly the roots of a rift within the abaThembu. What was more disturbing was that uKumkani Shaka threatened uKumkani Ngubengcuka of the abaThembu and King Hintsa of the whole amaXhosa nation by sending them messages that they should submit. At the time, King Ngubengcuka lived along the Mbhashe River, while uKumkani Hintsa had his great place where the town of Gcuwa (Butterworth) is situated.[109] Du Plessis uncritically describes uKumkani Hintsa (1789-1835) as a "brave but avaricious and cunning chief…, whose duplicity embroiled him in constant troubles with neighbouring tribes and with the Government, and led to his death in 1835".[110]

Both uKumkani Hintsa and uKumkani Ngubengcuka appealed to the colonial authorities for 'protection'. The gathering of refugees on the colonial boundary was cause for alarm to the colonial authorities. This precipitated a frontier crisis as thousands of abaThembu refugees encountered white farmers who sought more land and labour. To counteract the looming frontier crisis, the colonial authorities responded positively to the abaThembu and the amaGcaleka kings' request for colonial military aid. Richard Bourke, the acting Governor, ordered a small force to make an in loco inspection in the areas reportedly traversed by the amaZulu army. The expedition, led by Major Dundas and Colonel Henry Somerset, spotted in July 1828 the amaNgwane, led by their iNkosi Matiwane, and not the amaZulu, against whom

---

105 Wagenaar, "History of the Thembu", 7.
106 W.F. Lye, "The Difaqane: The Mfecane in the Southern Sotho Area, 1822-24", *Journal of African History*, 8, 1 (1967), 122; E.G. Sihele, "Ngobani na AbaThembu, Bevelaphi na?", 18-19; *Blue Book on Native Affairs*, 1885, 21.
107 Peires, Telephone Interview, 30 July 2018.
108 Cingo, *Laba Thembu*, 25; Jackson, *Ciskei and Transkei*, 11; Hammond-Tooke, *Umtata District*, 41.
109 Mqhayi, *Ityala Lama Wele*, iv.
110 J. du Plessis, *A History of Christian Missions in South Africa* (Cape Town: C. Struik, 1965), 174.

Ngubengcuka and Hintsa sought colonial assistance. Acting Governor Bourke instructed Henry Somerset, the eldest son of Lord Charles Somerset, to form a large force comprising regular soldiers and burghers. Under Henry Somerset's command, this colonial force joined up with a large abaThembu, amaGcaleka and amaMpondo army and broke up "the [ama] Ngwane at Mbholompo on the Mthatha river on 27 August 1828".[111] Thus, the amaNgwane "were routed and nearly exterminated by a combined military and burgher commando aided by bodies of Tembu and Gcaleka warriors".[112]

Generally, the consequences of the Mfecane wars upon the abeNguni society were profound. It had far-reaching implications and traumatic effects for the abaThembu. It had thrown the abaThembu into disorder and drawn them closer to the colonial authorities -- a circumstance, which accounted for the ruling house collaborating with whites by allying with them in times of wars of resistance. That the abaThembu–Xhosa truce came to an end in 1830 owing to disagreement over the division of spoils was also an ominous event for the abaThembu. It was not conductive to cordial relations between these kingdoms, and drew the abaThembu closer to the colonial authorities, with catastrophic consequences for both the abaThembu and the amaXhosa, as will be seen in the subsequent chapters.

As a result of the Mfecane upheavals, the majority of the remnants of Madzikane and Matiwane were scattered in all directions. They sought food and refuge and merged with the amaXhosa and the abaThembu whom they served as clients and herdsmen.[113] This merging did not have the effect of consolidating these kingdoms. Others, however, had become "part of the composite group known as the Mfengu".[114] The amaMfengu were largely drawn from the ranks of the amaBhele, amaHlubi, amaZizi and amaNtlangwini chiefdoms.[115]

Like the Mfecane wars, the question of the amaMfengu has become a source of debate. Having been precipitated by Cobbing, the amaMfengu debate has been expanded by Webster and Stapleton.[116] Webster denounces the notion that the amaMfengu were the remnants of Shaka's victims from Natal. He disputes any holding of these refugees as bondsmen by uKumkani Hintsa (1789-1835). He regards the story of the amaMfengu as devoid of truth and full of exaggeration. He asserts that whites invented the story to justify their extraction

---

111 C.C. Crais, *The Making of the Colonial Order: White Supremacy and Black Resistance in the Eastern Cape, 1770-1865* (Johannesburg: Witwatersrand University Press, 1992), 113; J. Milton, *The Edges of War: A History of Frontier Wars, 1702-1878* (Johannesburg: Juta and Company, 1983), 90; Molema, *The Bantu*, 387; Saunders, *Historical Dictionary*, 173; Peires, "Matiwane's Road", 3.
112 *Blue Book on Native Affairs*, 1885, 21.
113 Peires, "The British and the Cape, 1814-1834", in R. Elphick and H. Giliomee (eds), *The Shaping of South African Society, 1652-1840* (Cape Town: Maskew Miller Longman, 1989), 486.
114 *Cape of Good Hope Government Gazzette* No. 1535, 22 May 1835: Report by Dutton, on Hintsa, 3 May 1835; M. Ndima, "A History of the Qwathi People from Earliest Times to 1910" (M.A. Dissertation, Rhodes University, 1988), 42; Eveleigh, *Settlers and Methodism*, 76.
115 M.S.B. 428, Statement of Silayi, May 1884 15; Peires, *House of Phalo*, 88.
116 A.C. Webster, "Land Expropriation and Labour Extraction under Cape Colonial Rule: The War of 1835 and the 'Emancipation' of the Fingo" (M.A. Dissertation, Rhodes University, 1991); Stapleton, "Oral Evidence in a Pseudo-Ethnicity: The Fingo Debate", *History in Africa*, vol. xxii, 1995, 359-360.

of labour and cattle from uKumkani Hintsa's people whom whites had enslaved. He points out that whites disguised their enslavement of the amaXhosa as philanthropic activity. As he puts it:

> Fingo consisted of mission collaborators, mercenaries, refugees and voluntary labourers ... included a large number of Gcaleka and Rharhabe women and children ... It was this heterogenous conglomeration that formed the Fingo, and not a refugee Natal ethnic unit who escaped from Shaka's rapacity. [They had no] natural chiefs [but only] collaborators and opportunists, who were prepared to follow British orders on the management of the Fingo.[117]

The amaMfengu debate aside, it is claimed that uKumkani Hintsa (1789-1835) once called these fugitive remnants of various clans his 'dogs' and expressed surprise that he could not kill them at his pleasure.[118] UKumkani Hintsa's allusion to these refugees as his 'dogs' should not be taken in a literal sense, but should be put in the context of his times. What he could have meant was that the amaMfengu were his subjects who had the duty of providing him with protection in times of wars with whites and other African kingdoms. The literal interpretation of 'dogs' is a gross exaggeration and was used to alienate the refugees from Hintsa. In actual fact, Wesleyan missionaries had been influencing the amaMfengu to regard their being given shelter by Hintsa as implying that they were held in bondage by the amaGcaleka-Xhosa.[119] Yet, when the amaMfengu left amaGcalekaland for Ngqushwa and Oxkraal, they took 20,000 head of amaGcaleka cattle, before settling in the lands belonging to the amaNgqika.[120] Wesleyan missionaries' influence resulted, as was intended, in the deterioration of amaMfengu–Gcaleka relations.

According to Kawa, uKumkani Hintsa (1789-1835) never ill-treated amaMfengu, but were well-received by Hintsa, though they were deceived by whites "into thinking that the only paradise is the government of the English".[121] He cites uNkosi Mbovane Mabandla, who, on justifying why Mabandla and Njokweni and other amaMfengu chiefs left amaGcalekaland in 1835, said:

> The thing which caused [them] to leave the amaGcaleka was not bad treatment by Hintsa's government, but they were promised land, and that their chiefship would return to the way it used to be on the Tukela. To govern with their own chiefship and to dispose of their own lands, and not to be subjects any more. The person who made this speech was Reverend Ayliff [1797-1862], translated by Hermanus Matros (Ngxukumeshe).[122]

---

117 Webster, "Land Expropriation and Labour Extraction under Cape Colonial Rule", 58.
118 *Government Gazzette*, no.1535, 22 May 1835: Report by Dutton on Hintsa.
119 Mostert, *Frontiers*, 606.
120 R.A. Moyer, "The Mfengu Self-Defence and the Cape Frontier Wars", in Saunders and Derricourt (eds), *Beyond the Cape Frontier*, 107.
121 Kawa, *Ibali LamaMfengu*, 46.
122 Ibid., 46-47.

Echoing Kawa, Moyer concludes that the amaMfengu "had been well received by the Xhosa when they arrived in the Transkei and Ciskei".[123] Whatever the merits of the situation may be, the merging of these refugees rendered the abaThembu kingdom more heterogenous than ever before and thus made it vulnerable to whites and abeNguni attacks. In a way, it disrupted the socio-political structure of the abaThembu and amaXhosa. It frequently led to abaThembu cooperation with whites and their eventual impoverishment and subjection. AbaThembu collaboration with whites was the former's strategy to ensure their own survival in the light of their proximity to the strong and compact amaXhosa.

The Mfecane wars were characterised by a period of human agony, disintegration, division and confusion amongst the abeNguni in general and the abaThembu in particular. They created havoc and socio-political upheavals. The destructive effects of the Mfecane wars are evident in the fact that they led to a further rift/split of the abaThembu nation, thereby accelerating what Nattrass regards as "the emergence and decline of chiefdoms [which] had been going on for centuries".[124] Some abaThembu clans "migrated into a country previously occupied only by a few wandering Bushmen".[125] These clans, comprising the amaTshatshu under uNkosi Bawana, amaHala under uNkosi Raxothi (A! Mathanzima!), the amaNdungwana under Ndarhala and two non-abaThembu clans, viz. amaGcina and amaQwathi, fled towards Komani (Queenstown) and settled near uNkosi Maqoma's (1798-1873) land. They also established themselves on the banks of the Black Kei River on the doorsteps of white farmers. Whilst settling in what later came to be known as the Tambookie location (Lady Frere), "the location superintendent, J.C. Warner, divided the Tambookie Location into sub-locations allocated to four Thembu clans – the amaTshatshu, amaNdungwana, amaHala and amaGcina"[126] in the 1850s.

Wagenaar posits that the "north-westward migration ... [and] the settlement of these clans on the banks of the Black Kei River, then the Cape frontier, marked the beginning of an epoch characterised by group formation and by military alignment and re-alignment, as the [aba]Thembu, like the [ama]Xhosa before them, came face to face with white colonists."[127] These clans later became a separate, supposed subsection, which could challenge the abaThembu kings. These clans, having established themselves as a separate abaThembu section, chose as their own reigning iNkosi, Mathanzima, son of uKumkani Mthikrakra in the iNdlu yaseKunene.[128]

In another vein, the Mfecane wars, having set off a train of events, which led to the exacerbation of a rift in the abaThembu kingdom, could also be viewed as an era of social and political adaptation and reconstruction amongst the abaThembu and other abeNguni

---

123 Moyer, "The Mfengu Self-Defence", 107.
124 Nattrass, *A Short History of South Africa*, 58.
125 *Blue Book on Native Affairs*, 1885, 21.
126 A.K. Mager, "Gungubele and the Tambookie Location, 1853-1877: End of a Colonial Experiment", *Journal of Southern African Studies*, 40, 6 (2014), 1161.
127 Wagenaar, "History of the Thembu", 7.
128 Jackson, *Ciskei and Transkei*, 11.

people.[129] Wagenaar asserts that the migration had tremendous territorial gains, as these clans (Emigrant abaThembu since 1865) "had spread themselves thinly over the territory between the Stormberg in the north and the Winterberg in the south, and from the Indwe River in the east to the Black Kei and Klaas Smit Rivers in the West".[130]

All the evidence tends to the conclusion that the emergence of new political structures and strong and able leaders provided fresh challenges both for the abaThembu kings and the colonial authorities. It was to have a major influence on the policies of white governments. It led to the abaThembu adopting a divided attitude towards the colonial government. Even so, the Mbhashe-Thembu and the abaThembu refugees (Emigrant abaThembu since 1865) were – and still are – one nation.[131]

The split and the senior chiefly position held by uNkosi Rhaxothi (A! Mathanzima!) were destructive features within the abaThembu polity, even though the abaThembu ancestral faith and genealogical link united them.[132] The westward movement of the abaThembu section was to bring about disunity and political fragmentation within the abaThembu political units because, since migration, the abaThembu were not united in their struggles against the establishment of white domination and colonial rule. Nevertheless, the abaThembu migrations referred to above should be regarded as an expansion process that was characterised, amongst other things, by the abaThembu refugees' interaction with whites and adaptation to their environment. As Wagenaar has observed, "the most important result of these migrations, was the breaking up of national cohesion."[133]

The impact of the Mfecane wars on the abaThembu and the debates surrounding both the Mfecane wars and the origins of the amaMfengu aside, the drought of 1829 was something to reckon with. It exacerbated amaXhosa–Thembu relations owing to the practice of the colonial authorities of sowing seeds of rivalries between African kingdoms by playing one kingdom against the other with the purpose of weakening these kingdoms. Consequential upon the severity of the drought, uNkosi Bawana, who was not a colonial ally, was raided by uNkosi Maqoma[134] of the amaNgqika, in the iNdlu yaseKunene of uNkosi Ngqika, A! Lwagandal.[135]

---

129 C. de B. Webb, "The Mfecane", in *Perspectives on the Southern African Past*, University of Cape Town, 1979, 135 and 141.
130 Wagenaar, "History of the Thembu", 7-8.
131 Broster, *The Tembu*, 2.
132 G.M. Carter, T. Karis and N.M. Stultz, *South Africa's Transkei: The Politics of Domestic Colonialism* (Evanston: North-Western University, 1967), 83.
133 Wagenaar, "History of the Thembu", 8.
134 UNkosi Maqoma (1798-1873) was older by 22 years than uNkosi Ngqika's heir, Prince Sandile (1820-1878). He was made regent for 10 years on the death of uNkosi Ngqika in 1829. His sons were Namba (1828-1860), Kona (1818-1907), Makrexana (1830-1878), Thini (d. c.1910), Mfazwe (d. 1860) and Ngqabe. He and Princess Nongwane were twins born of uNkosi Ngqika's first wife, uKumkanikazi Nothonto (daughter of Nxiya), who originated from a common Ngqosini clan.
135 The concept of the Right-Hand House emerged during the reign of uKumkani Phalo, when Prince Gcaleka (d. 1778) was allocated to the iNdlu eNkulu, while Prince Rharhabe was *lawulwa'ed* to the iNdlu yase Kunene. See Mqhayi, *Ityala Lamawele*, 60.

UNkosi Bawana's subjects fled into the colonial territory. The Commissioner-General for the Eastern Districts, Andries Stockenström, became increasingly indignant and brooked no delays in working to have what he had vied for since 1828 – to settle the landless Hottentots (referred to as Khoikhoi[136] since the 1960s) in Maqoma's land so that they could form a human buffer against the amaXhosa. Thenceforth, Andries Stockenström pressurised Governor Sir Lowry Cole to sanction the ejection of uNkosi Maqoma (1798-1873). UNkosi Maqoma's huts were burned down and kraals plundered, despite his remonstration. Eventually, he was expelled from the Ngxwengxwe (Kat) River Valley in Bhofolo. In his land, the landless Khoekhoe and bastards were settled.[137] About 4,000 people settled in the Kat River Valley during mid-1829, while by "1833, more than 2,000 Khoikhoi [Khoekhoe] had been settled as smallholders".[138] As Mostert correctly remarks, the "expulsion became the spur to Maqoma's own anti-colonial militancy. It rankled to the end of his life, never forgotten, nor forgiven."[139]

The expulsion of uNkosi Maqoma (1798-1873)[140] had no factual basis, but it contributed to the outbreak of the Sixth Frontier War of 1835. UNkosi Maqoma's expulsion could be seen in the light of the colonial government's tradition of settling strangers on the land of African kings and chiefs. This strategy was intended to disrupt these kingdoms so that they acted disjointedly against white intrusion and encroachment.[141] It was a smokescreen to deal uNkosi Maqoma (1798-1873) a heavy blow. It is no wonder that Maqoma's expulsion was to contribute to the outbreak of the Sixth Frontier War, 1834-1835.

There can be no doubt that Chief Maqoma's successful raiding activities against Chief Bawana's subjects could have been averted if the abaThembu were politically united. The abaThembu division of purpose and reaction to external challenges was cause for their weakness. UKumkani Ngubengcuka was not an ally of the amaXhosa kingdom. He was well-disposed towards the colonial authorities, while uNkosi Bawana was at loggerheads with a chief of the amaGcina, Mtyhalele, who died in 1829. On the death of Mtyhalele, uNkosi Bawana's people were suspected of having poisoned the former, and in revenge, they murdered Chief Bawana.[142]

These unhealthy relations within the abaThembu were exploited by the Cape Government, which sought to have the abaThembu refugees as useful neighbours – much to detriment of the entire abaThembu nation. Indeed, it was a matter of political expediency that Governor Sir Lowry Cole (1828-1833) came to the rescue of Chief Bawana not only because Bawana's people had flocked to the colonial territory but also due to the fact that he saw the conflict

---

136 But today, they are termed 'Khoe' or 'Khoekhoe' in terms of the Nama language in contrast to the colonially-inspired concept of the Khoi or Khoikhoi.
137 'Bastards' referred to people of mixed race that included runaway slaves, whites and Khoekhoe.
138 Peires, "The British and the Cape", 484.
139 Mostert, *Frontiers*, 66.
140 UNkosi Maqoma's ingoma was: uGusawe.
141 *Cape of Good Hope Debates in the House of Assembly*, 10 July 1894: John Hemming, Civil Commissioner, to Secretary for Native Affairs, 30 December 1882, 14-15.
142 Wagenaar, "History of the Thembu", 10 and 40.

as an opportunity to play one chiefdom against the other. Thus, uNkosi Maqoma's expulsion seemed unfounded. It was meant "to create a human buffer west of the [Nxuba] Fish River to enforce the border as a line of separation".[143] It is not surprising that uNkosi Maqoma's expulsion and the consequent loss of territory created turbid relations between the amaXhosa and the colonists. Furthermore, the expulsion in 1833 of uNkosi Maqoma's brother, uNkosi Tyhali,[144] by Acting Governor Wade and the wounding in the head by a British patrol in October 1834 of uNkosi Xhoxho, Maqoma's and Tyhali's brother, did not only add to the tense atmosphere but also resulted in the amaXhosa–colonial conflict in December 1834-1835. It is no wonder that uNkosi Maqoma (1798-1873) ordered "retaliatory stock raids against the colony in late 1834".[145]

The period of the Mfecane wars witnessed the advent of white missionaries in abaThembuland and amaXhosaland. However, abaThembuland had been lagging behind in accepting missionaries. This delay was partly due to the geographic situation of abaThembuland, which stood the abaThembu in good stead to evaluate missionary activities amongst the amaXhosa, and therefore to see its negative effects. Also, it was partly due to the fact that missionaries viewed abaThembuland as thinly populated, and therefore not worth the expenses to be incurred in erecting mission stations. It was the Mfecane pressures that prompted the abaThembu to reluctantly encourage the missionaries to settle in their midst. Less drawn into encounters with white colonists and also viewing the colonial military power as an ally against the Mfecane onslaught, the abaThembu regarded the presence of missionaries as a matter of inflating their prestige. The presence of a mission station in a chief's or a king's territory meant that the traditional leader could use the missionary in communicating with the colonial authorities. In similar fashion, the Cape governors used the missionaries to relay their messages to the traditional leaders, who held the missionaries in high esteem.

No sooner did the missionaries set foot on abaThembuland than their presence caused strife and divisions within the abaThembu. The missionaries influenced the socio-political and religious life of Africans. Their work gave rise to the emergence and rise of a 'civilised' class called *amagqobhoka* (converts).[146] This class emerged from their converts who had taken up residence in the mission stations. Converts believed that being able to read "would endow them with the same knowledge and skill as Europeans".[147] It is worth noting Joseph Cox Warner's observation in the Tambookie location (present-day Lady Frere) in the 1850s. J.C. Warner, a Tambookie agent from 1848 to 1857, reported:

---

143 Maylam, *History of African People*, 97; H.J. van Aswegen, *History of South Africa to 1854* (Pretoria: Academica, 1990), 215.
144 UNkosi Tyhali belonged to the iXhiba House of uNkosi Ngqika, who had died in 1829 at the age of 53. UNkosi Tyhali's sons were Obha and Feni (Feni opposed the cattle-killing movement). See Mqhayi, *Ityala Lamawele*, 49.
145 Stapleton, "Jingqi Oral Tradition", 321.
146 *Amagqobhoka* is an isiXhosa word referring to those converted to Christianity.
147 I. Schapera, "Christianity and the Tswana", *Journal of the Royal Anthropological Institute*, 58, 1 (January–February 1958), 5.

> Some households were beginning to farm comprehensively, with men working alongside women, ploughing 612 acres and planting maize and wheat. Homesteads close to the river used watercourses to irrigate their lands, and a few had small gardens with fruit trees. There was no shortage of skill. Even white settlers recognised that African farming skills were superior to those of European agricultural labourers.[148]

As one observer noted, "indeed, white farmers were dependent on African skills,... their most determined detractor would be puzzled to say what he would do without them [Africans]."[149]

Missionary activities acted as a catalyst in neutralising African opposition to colonialism and the rise of nascent nationalism reflected in the wars of resistance during the nineteenth century.[150] Little wonder then that on the advice of the colonial authorities, Chief Bawana applied to the Cape Governer in 1828 for a missionary to reside amongst his subchiefdom on the north-eastern part of the frontier in the vicinity of Komani (Queenstown). Chief Bawana sought to use the missionary as a diplomatic agent between him and the colonial authorities and to secure protection against his neighbouring rivalries. He wished to have a missionary to introduce his people to trade and agriculture. The Cape Governor, on the other hand, sought to use a missionary as a catalyst in neutralising the amaTshatshu objections to colonialism. In other words, both uNkosi Bawana and the Cape Governor were not so much concerned about the Christianising activities, as much as they were preoccupied with using a missionary for political expediency. While uNkosi Bawana was counteractive to missionary endeavours to penetrate and gain a foothold on other abaThembu chiefdoms and kingdoms, Governor Bourke was eager to gain access to other kingdoms.[151]

UNkosi Bawana's application was supported by Henry Somerset. Hence Governor Bourke had Reverend Hallbeck of the Moravian Missionary Society establish a mission station amongst uNkosi Bawana's amaTshatshu. His son, uNkosi Maphasa, who had established his domain on the colonial border, in the present district of Hewu (Whittlesea),[152] also allowed the Moravian missionaries to set up in 1832 a mission station of Shiloh in his political domain. The Moravian mission stations having been started by Georg Schmidt on arriving in Baviaanskloof (present-day Genadendal) and ministering amongst the Khoekhoe in 1737, played a prominent "and ground-breaking role in the earliest missionary endeavours"[153] in the Western Cape.

---

148 *Cape of Good Hope Proceedings of and Evidence taken by Commission on Native Affairs 1865*, Joseph Cox Warner's Testimony, 11 February 1865, 80.
149 *Cape of Good Hope Proceedings of and Evidence taken by Commission on Native Affairs 1865*, Testimony of A.N. Ella, Field Cornet [local judiciary officer] to Commission on Native Affairs, 38.
150 Maylam, *History of African People*, 70-71.
151 Wagenaar, "History of the Thembu", 29.
152 Whittlesea was established as a military outpost in 1834 during the Sixth Frontier War, 1834 1835. Originally used as a military post, it remained, a very small settlement until 1872, "with a decent inn and a few mud houses surrounding a little mud church". See Megan Voss, "Urbanising the North-Eastern Frontier: The Frontier Intelligentsia and the Making of Colonial Queenstown, c.1859-1877", (M.A. Dissertation, University of Cape Town, 2012), 8.
153 T. de Wet, J.L. Teugels and P. van Deventer, "Historic Bells in Moravian Missions in South Africa's Western Cape", *Historia*, vol. 59, No. 2, November 2014, 94.

Regarded as focused on missionary commitment to evangelise the aborigines, the Moravian missionaries were perceived as the "first Protestant Church in Christendom to undertake the conversion of the heathen".[154]

As a result of the missionary activities of the Moravian missionaries, *Amagqobhoka* emerged amongst the amaTshatshu. The emergence of this class "had serious consequences for the cohesion of [African] life, for it emphasised the cleavage of [these nations] into seemingly irreconcilable parts".[155] Furthermore, non-converts viewed Christianity as proclaimed by missionaries as a disruptive and dangerous religion. The danger of Christianity lay in the fact that there were two class divisions within the abaThembu, viz. *amagqobhoka* and *amaqaba*.[156]

The presence of these class divisions further strained the fabric that had held the abaThembu society intact. The *amagqobhoka* became more antagonistic to their traditional culture and lost their identity as they were estranged from their institutions. The missionary activities militated against African traditionalism, and worked towards destroying the social, political and economic foundations of abaThembu independence. Hence, missionaries found themselves in deep confrontation with non-converts, *amaqaba*. Mission stations were used as a place for "hard work, respect for private property and submission to secular authority".[157] By fostering hard labour amongst the converts, missionaries were knowingly instrumental in providing white farmers with labour. No wonder then that even though the missionaries were in deep confrontation with the *amaqaba*, the former enjoyed the support of white farmers who were in need of a labour force.

Reverend William Shaw of the Wesleyan Methodist Missionary Society (WMMS) masterminded the establishment of a chain of mission stations from Grahamstown to Port Natal (later Durban).[158] His coming to South Africa was consequent to his volunteering "for mission work and was appointed by the WMMS as one of their duly accredited Missionaries, but in the special capacity of Chaplain to the party of [1820] settlers".[159] William Shaw believed that South Africa was inhabited by heathens.

Moreover, William Shaw, like other missionaries of various societies, linked the spread of Christianity with European civilisation, culture and colonial domination.[160] No wonder that Shaw founded the Wesleyville Mission in November 1823, Mount Coke Mission in 1825 and Butterworth east of the Nciba River in 1827.[161] Shaw maintained that, "while Christianity alone can give us influence with the natives, and excite in them a desire of improvement, yet we

---

154 J.E. Hutton, *A History of the Moravian Church* (London: Moravian Publication Office, 1909), 235-236.
155 B. Hutchinson, "Some Social Consequences of Nineteenth-Century Missionary Activity Among the South African Bantu", *Africa*, vol. xxxvii, No. 2, April 1957, 168.
156 *Amaqaba* is an isiXhosa word meaning those not converted to Christianity.
157 Crais, *Making of the Colonial Order*, 101.
158 W.G. Mears, *Mission to Clarkebury* (Cape Town: Longmans, 1973), 15.
159 W. Shaw, *The Story of my Mission in South Eastern Africa* (London, 1860), 5.
160 Peires, "The British and the Cape", 487.
161 Mears, *Clarkebury*, 15.

ought to connect with inculcation of its principles every judicious plan ... to raise them to an improved condition ... [This] plan makes the work of conversion and civilisation proceed concurrently, and therefore more efficiently and rapidly."[162] Charles J. Levey, in his report of 3 January 1894, made the following remark: "the Christian Natives form the brightest feature in the native territories. For the purpose of trade alone one Christianised Kaffir is worth ten reds, so traders tell me, and I believe it is the case, the wants of the former being so much increased. Another advantage is that you rarely find a Christian native in gaol for theft, not one per cent of the stock thieves are school Kaffirs, therefore it must be of advantage to the state to Christianise natives."[163]

By encouraging the establishment of a chain of stations, Shaw sought to spread evangelism throughout the Cape Colony and Natal. As a result of Cape Governor, Lord Charles Somerset's concession, Shaw erected a mission station amongst the amaGcina on the north-eastern frontier. The negative effects of Shaw's missionary activities were evident in the fact that converts from Lesseyton,[164] mostly the amaGcina, took sides with the colonial authorities during the War of the Axe of 1846-1847, while uNkosi Maphasa "a furiously anti-white chief who ruled a substantial part of the [aba]Thembu",[165] participated on the side of the amaRharhabe–Xhosa. UNkosi Maphasa was denounced by Andries Stockenström, the Commissioner-General of the Eastern Districts, as an "apathetic barbarian",[166] while Captain Henry Somerset derogatorily described him as the "ill-disposed, ignorant, grasping savage".[167] Wagenaar, however, described uNkosi Maphasa differently, as a great warrior "who dared situations that were usually avoided by others",[168] an eloquent speaker, and a capable leader, "always unwilling to take up a neutral stance".[169]

Moreover, during the War of the Axe the abaThembu uKumkani Xokiso, A! Mthikrakra! remained neutral. This illustrated the abaThembu kings', chiefs' and converts' division of attitude towards the colonial authorities, owing to the detrimental effects of Christianity, which served the interests of the whites' civilisation. That converts had sided with whites during the War of the Axe was to the detriment of the abaThembu. Comprising many chiefdoms and subchiefdoms, each enjoying political and economic autonomy, the abaThembu kingdom within which there were *amagqobhoka* (converts) was further divided by missionary activitvies, so that their political unity, unity of purpose and action were then no more. This signified the divisive effect of Christianity.

---

162 *Imperial Blue Book 538* of 1836, Evidence of W. Shaw, 56.
163 *Blue Book on Native Affairs*, 1887-1894, Charles J. Levey, Resident Magistrate Xalanga District, Cala, 3 January 1894, 63.
164 Lesseyton, a Wesleyan Mission Station, was roughly 8 miles north of Komani/Queenstown. It was situated in Indlovukazi (she-elephant) below Lukhanji (Hangklip). See Voss, "The Making of Colonial Queenstown", 8.
165 Mostert, *Frontiers*, 1045; Sihele, "Ngobani?", 32-33.
166 Wagenaar, "History of the Thembu", 10.
167 Ibid.
168 Ibid.
169 Ibid.

Wesleyan missionaries, like Glasgow missionaries, were conservative in their evangelical beliefs, and intolerant of abeNguni customs and rites. The Glasgow Missionary Society funded Scottish missions east of the Nciba (Kei) River, such as Cunningham (1856), Thuthurha (1868), Blythswood (1875), Malan (1875), Main (1876), Columba (1878), Duff (1880), Ingcisininde (1900) and Kidston (1905).[170] The Wesleyan missionaries inveighed heavily against the abaThembu culture and traditional religion, regarding these as heathenish and devilish activities. Missionaries urged *amagqobhoka* not to practise polygamy, but rather that each man was to have one wife. They told one Xhosa man

> to put away all his wives but the first, and also told him to read his Bible [to which] the native said he had read his Bible, and found the whole of the respectable people in the Old Testament had from one to a hundred wives. He said he had also found no instruction in the old law that they must remove their wives except one.[171]

It is noteworthy that

> where chiefs have many wives, the first wife is not the principal wife – she is only that one who has removed from him the white paint of his initiation. An important chief's Great Wife is chosen from a Royal House by his counsellors and lobola-ed by the tribe.[172]

Lewis offers a somewhat different interpretation and outcome of this practice as encouraging the characteristic splits between generations of abeNguni kingdoms and chiefdoms, summing it up this way:

> This was encouraged by the practice of appointing the heir to the chieftaincy from the first son of the Great Wife, who was not the first wife and often the last to be married. In this way the legitimate heir was often a minor on inheriting his chieftaincy and a regent was appointed, thus extending the rule of councillors [amaphakathi][173] of his father's generation.[174]

Generally speaking, the missionaries equated the spread of Christianity with the extension of European culture, and wrongly regarded Christianity and Western (European) civilisation as two sides of the same coin. In this connection, Westermann aptly remarks that "Christianity is a factor of its own and has fundamentally nothing to do with European civilization".[175] Thus, these two processes were distinct though closely interwoven.

---

170 J. Mvenene, "Reverend James Macdonald Auld and the Disintegration of Traditional Leadership in Xhosaland", *African Historical Review*, vol. 48, No. 2, 2016, 25.
171 *Cape of Good Hope House of Assembly Debates*, 26 July 1894, 364.
172 S.G. Millin, *The People of South Africa* (London: Constable and Company Ltd, 1953), 264.
173 Amaphakathi were usually drawn from the traditional leader's age-mates and chosen from the richer homestead heads; as senior members of the commoner clans, they were not only the mediators between the chief and his subjects but were also the main decision makers in the Great Place – Komkhulu. Their authority was derived from the people. For more on this aspect, see Switzer, *Power and Resistance in an African Society*, 36.
174 Lewis, "Materialism and Idealism", 251.
175 D. Westermann, *Africa and Christianity* (London: A.M.S. Press, 1935), 28.

UKumkani Ngubengcuka allowed in 1830 the Wesleyan missionary, Reverend Richard J. Haddy, "a man of great energy, who was able to preach fluently in English, Dutch and Kafir"[176] and the lay preacher, Joseph Cox Warner, to establish a fifth link in the chain of stations envisaged by Shaw on the eastern bank of the Mgwali River. The mission was named Clarkebury, after Doctor Adam Clarke, the Methodist author of the famous Clarke's Commentary, and advocate of missions.[177]

The arrival and activities of Methodist missionaries in abaThembuland in the first quarter of the nineteenth century is vital in understanding how the missionaries constituted "part of a broader process of colonial intrusion into the lands and lives of African people beyond the Cape Colony".[178] What was more of an attack on abaThembu traditional leaders as the co-owners of land was the Methodist missionaries' building of mission stations, and enforcing that the residents become black English persons in abaThembuland. Thus, the mission stations introduced their own sphere of influence by insisting that station residents and converts live "according to the rhythms of industrialising England".[179] The chief missionary showed by example that God created African people to labour and work for six days per week, "according to the dictum that if a man will not work neither shall he eat".[180]

What was cause for alarm to uKumkani Ngubengcuka and abaThembu chiefs was the enormous conversion of his abaThembu. As a result, the abaThembu king and chiefs "sought by all manner of means – by persuasion, by persecution, by the enticement of licentious dances – to win them back".[181] However, most Christians continued to embrace their new faith "and endured nobly the reproach of Christ".[182]

Furthermore, the missionaries took it upon themselves to record the history of the African communities. Whether or not this history was accurate, objective, reliable and trustworthy is a matter of conjecture. And more efforts should be executed in order to Africanise, transform and decolonise this history, using archival documents, pictorial figures, and oral sources. Their journals or correspondence focused, as Lambourne posits, not on everyday occurrences, but were narrowed to weekly accounts of Sunday services and prayer meetings.[183]

UKumkani Ngubengcuka was not so much interested in Christian principles as in the missionaries' material and technological benefits, such as irrigation, the plough, firearms and ammunition, and education that would accrue from his interaction with them. Thus, uKumkani Ngubengcuka accepted the missionaries "as a means of acquiring British skills and

---

176 Du Plessis, *Christian Missions*, 174.
177 W.G. Mears, *Clarkebury*, 20.
178 B. Lambourne, "Methods of Mission: The Ordering of Space and Time, Land and Labour on Methodist Mission Stations in Caffraria, 1823-1835", African Studies Seminar Paper, University of the Witwatersrand, African Studies Institute, 24 August 1992, 1.
179 Lambourne, "Methods of Mission", 1.
180 Ibid., 6.
181 Du Plessis, *Christian Missions*, 175.
182 Ibid.
183 Lambourne, "Methods of Mission", 2.

advantages"[184] through Christian missionary education, which was used to Westernise and detribalise Africans so that converts could adopt Western standards, thoughts, behaviour and ideas.

UKumkani Ngubengcuka had accepted the missionaries for diplomatic and secular motives, so that they could give aid in abaThembu negotiations with the militarily superior Cape Colony and strong amaGcaleka–Xhosa. By having a mission station in his midst, he hoped to enhance his tottering prestige. He also wanted to use missionaries to liaise on cattle-raiding and other matters, which exacerbated relations with whites. In another context, the missionaries "discouraged at the frustration of their work"[185] began to advocate British domination by attacking chiefly power and authority. John Cumming of the Glasgow Missionary Society wrote the following about the might of the chiefs: "Their power must be broken; and then there is a brighter prospect of the benign influence of the gospel being more generally diffused over those who may be spared from the judgements which are now abroad in the land."[186] This went hand in hand with the missionaries' attack on African religion, beliefs and practices. In this sense, the missionaries, more so the Wesleyans, became "the vanguards of British colonialism",[187] while mission stations had become "a powerful source of social disruption and change ... a source of new material wants and technical innovations".[188] Etherington asserts, and rightly so, that the WMMS missionaries had come to view residential stations as "asylums for the extremely poor or incorrigibly idle".[189] It is worth noting that Wesleyans had "never made a distinction between their colonial and their mission work".[190]

Not only did the Wesleyans establish mission stations amongst the amaTshatshu, the amaGcina and the abaThembu of uKumkani Ngubengcuka, but they also built the Glebe mission station, at Bholotwa amongst the amaNdungwana through the endeavours of Reverend C.F. Patten. The Bholotwa station's infrastructural appearance was relatively unsightly, as it had "a broken down, impoverished appearance ... where but little appears to be done to improve the condition of the people".[191] This mission station had the same effect, like others before it, of enforcing that converts should dissociate themselves from non-converts and rather stay within the premises of the mission. In this way, it also widened the gulf between the abaThembu converts and non-converts. Consequential upon missionaries'

---

184 Mostert, *Frontiers*, 598.
185 Cope, "Christian Missions", 1.
186 Williams, "The Missionaries", 175.
187 J. Comaroff and J. Comaroff, "Through the Looking Glass: Colonial Encounters of the First Kind", *Journal of Historical Sociology*, 1, 1 (March 1988), 6; N.D. Southey, "Christianity", in C.C. Saunders (ed.), *An Illustrated Dictionary of South African History* (Sandton: Vois Books and Editorial Services, 1994), 71.
188 Hutchinson, "Missionary activity", 162.
189 N. Etherington, "Mission Station Melting Pots as a Factor in the Rise of South African Black Nationalism", *Africa*, 47, 1 (1977), 592.
190 J. du Plessis, *A History of Christian Missions in South Africa* (Cape Town: C. Struik, 1965), 595 and 832.
191 *Cape of Good Hope Blue Book on Native Affairs 1878*, G.17 – '78, John Hemming, Civil Commissioner Queenstown, 18 January 1878, 45.

promotion of manual labour in mission stations, the division of labour according to gender was increasingly becoming old-fashioned and outdated. Hence, by 1838, "[aba]Thembu men were said to be willing to perform manual labour which they had formerly considered the greatest disgrace to engage in".[192]

In order to encourage and promote acquaintance with the traditional leaders, missionaries also engaged in bartering "daily large quantities of European manufactured goods"[193] with abaThembu. They brought "Bibles in their right hands, and beads and buttons in their left".[194] This bartering was accompanied by gift-exchanges, and these processes were regarded by missionaries and colonial authorities as a way of inculcating European values, customs, culture and beliefs. There were also colonial traders who engaged in unfair trade practices with the abaThembu, and in league with the missionaries, usurped control of the abaThembu economy. Many of these alien traders entered abaThembuland without having consulted with the traditional leaders for permission to trade, and threatened the local people with commandos of colonial troops if they did not give way.[195] This meant that these traders undermined chiefs and kings. Worse still, missionaries and colonial traders exchanged cattle for unproductive consumer goods, that is, for beads and buttons, linens, tobacco boxes, knives, scissors, needles, looking glasses, razors, etc. Thus cattle, the abeNguni's productive resource, were exchanged for unproductive consumer goods.[196] These trading activities had a negative effect on the abaThembu socio-economic plane. They destroyed the socio-politico-economic foundations of abaThembu independence, while the missionary activities penetrated the abaThembu traditional institutions and thus were a heavy blow to the chiefs' and kings' authority and power.

Besides such external challenges, there were internal challenges for uKumkani Ngubengcuka. The amaMfengu, some of whom had settled in abaThembuland and amaXhosaland, served as the abaThembu clients and herdsmen but did not hold uKumkani Ngubengcuka in high esteem.[197] UNkosi Bawana and uNkosi Qhwesha of amaTshatshu and amaNdungwana respectively were disdainful to uKumkani Ngubengcuka. AmaQwathi of uNkosi Fubu were contemptuous of uKumkani Ngubengcuka, and this led to a battle "in which the warring parties [amaQwathi and abaThembu] used knives, spears, bows and arrows and other sharp weapons".[198] Aided by his half-brother, uNkosi Jumba, uKumkani Ngubengcuka defeated amaQwathi. Though this battle ended the strife between uKumkani Ngubengcuka and uNkosi Fubu, amaQwathi of uNkosi Dalasile, son of Fubu, were more powerful than abaThembu

---

192 Hutchinson, "Missionary Activity", 173.
193 R.B. Beck, "Bibles and Beads: Missionaries as Traders in Southern Africa in the early Nineteenth Century", *Journal of African History*, 30 (1989), 211.
194 S.E.K Mqhayi, *Inzuzo* (Johannesburg: Witwatersrand University Press, 1943), 73.
195 Peires, "The British and the Cape", 487.
196 P. Kirby (ed.), *Andrew Smith and Natal* (Cape Town: David Philip, 1955), 68.
197 Peires, "The British and the Cape", 486; G.M. Theal, *History of South Africa, 1834-1854* (London: Aberdeen University Press, 1893), 21.
198 Wagenaar, "History of the Thembu", 5.

and treated amaHala, the reigning (but not the ruling house), with contempt.[199] After this battle, writes Sihele, uKumkani Ngubengcuka warned all nations in his domain that they should not in future stand aside when he was engaged in a war.[200] However, all these clans, particularly amaQwathi of Fubu and amaGcina of Mtyhalele, retained their autonomous status. Under these circumstances it became very difficult for uKumkani Ngubengcuka to carry out his titular duties and to preserve abaThembu unity. Hence, he looked towards the Colony for salvation. However, this did not remedy the situation but rather created new divisions and tensions amongst the southern abeNguni in general and within the abaThembu in particular.[201] The colonial authorities readily exploited these cleavages to facilitate the subjugation of African kingdoms and chiefdoms.

On 10 August 1830, uKumkani Ngubengcuka, a shrewd diplomat, a brave and skilled military traditional leader, died.[202] He was stabbed to death by uNkosi Magwa, the iNkosi of amaMaya, a branch of amaDlomo.[203] AmaMaya fled to uKumkani Hintsa, thus increasing tension between abaThembu and amaXhosa. Following the death of uKumkani Ngubengcuka, his brother, uNkosi Fadana, became regent, as the legitimate heir, Prince Xokiso (whose praise name was Mthikrakra), was a minor. However, Prince Xokiso was not the biological son of uKumkanikazi Nonesi, the daughter of uNkosi Faku and the Great Wife of uKumkani Ngubengcuka. He was adopted from a minor house to the iNdlu eNkulu as uKumkanikazi Nonesi was childless.[204] Nonesi raised Prince Mthikrakra, and later, his successor, Prince Qheya (c.1840-1884), A! Ngangelizwe!.[205] His brothers were Joyi, Shweni and Ngxitho, and all were born of the daughter of Vazi, the son from uNkosi Mlawu's iQadi of the iNdlu eNkulu.[206]

As the Mfecane refugees "nominally recognised the [aba]Thembu supremacy",[207] Chief-Regent Fadana cultivated friendly relations with the colonial authorities. And, as whites sought allies against the amaXhosa, they embraced Fadana and his subjects. Chief-Regent Fadana offered protection to whites who were feeling the brunt of the Sixth Frontier War (December 1834 to September 1835). He blatantly refused to aid uKumkani Hintsa. Rather, he gave sanctuary to missionaries, viz. W. Satchell of Buntingville, T. Palmer of Morley, W.J. Davis of Clarkebury and J. Ayliff of Butterworth.

In 1830, abaThembu were attacked by the amaGcaleka-Xhosa and the amaBhaca of Chief Madzikane. They also suffered attacks from the north by the Koranna and the Griqua, and were driven into the colonial border. The increase of the abaThembu on the colonial border

---

199 Sihele, "Ngobani?", 16 and 28; *Blue Book on Native Affairs*, 1883, G.8 – '83: Secretary for Native Affairs to Colonial Secretary, 5 April 1874, 137.
200 Sihele, "Ngobani?", 31.
201 Maylam, *History of African People*, 97.
202 Sihele, "Ngobani?", 28-32; *The Burton Papers*, Glimpses of History, MS 14, 636; Wagenaar, "History of the Thembu", 5.
203 Sihele, "Ngobani?", 36; Wagenaar, "History of the Thembu", 39.
204 *Blue Book on Native Affairs*, 1885, 22.
205 Mager, "Gungubele and the Tambookie Location", 1161.
206 Sihele, "Ngobani?", 28.
207 Theal, *History of South Africa*, 21.

led to mutual cattle-rustling with whites. Furthermore, 1831 saw Chief Maphasa making abortive attempts to avenge his father's death by enlisting the assistance of neighbouring chiefs against the amaGcina. Though assisted by neighbouring chiefs, Chief Maphasa retreated into the Cape Colony where his subjects received a lukewarm and sour welcome. Not long thereafter a Griqua attack on Maphasa's abaThembu in 1833 and Chief Ndlambe's[208] invasion of Maphasa in 1834 led to Maphasa reluctantly seeking colonial assistance. Such attacks on a section of the abaThembu could be attributed to the attackers' realisation of the abaThembu weakness and division. AmaTshatshu increasingly became vulnerable to external challenges, which justified a strong leader of a compact and united nation. The abaThembu were isolated, weak and divided.

The outbreak of the Sixth Frontier War of 1834-1835 was cause for division of purpose and action within the abaThembu. While the Mbhashe-Thembu under Fadana harboured missionaries as a gesture of goodwill towards the Colony, Maphasa at Whittlesea remained neutral. However, Maphasa, who continually acted independently from the abaThembu-regent, Fadana, assured the amaNgqika-Xhosa of his readiness to habour cattle raided from rivalries. Hence, he received stolen cattle in this war.[209] Fadana was always ready to assist the Colony when a need arose.

Sir Benjamin D'Urban, the Cape Governor, placed the blame for the war on uKumkani Hintsa, ooNkosi Tyhali, Maqoma, Nqeno of amaMbalu, Bhotomane of imiDange chiefdom, Ndlambe (1740-1828) and Mdushane. He accused uKumkani Hintsa of having "without provocation, or any previous notice, or declaration of war, suddenly and unexpectedly broke into the colonial frontier along its whole extent",[210] before taking away horses, cattle and sheep. These amaRharhabe chiefs were expelled from their territories along the eastern frontier, and then the boundary was extended to the Nciba River. Governor D'Urban also reprimanded uKumkani Hintsa for holding the amaMfengu as captives.[211] Indeed, Governor D'Urban propagated the myth that the amaMfengu had been shattered as a military force during the Mfecane wars and then cruelly enslaved by the amaXhosa.[212]

To blame uKumkani Hintsa for this war was an exaggeration, which was meant to justify whites' invasion of amaXhosaland and the consequent seizure of land, labour and cattle. After this war, writes Stapleton, many amaXhosa were held in bondage and later became the amaMfengu.[213] These amaMfengu were later placed under government-paid headmen.

---

208 UNkosi Ndlambe's *ingoma* was: u*Wankuntuza* (*ingoma kaMfi*). UNkosi Ndlambe (1740-1828) was the brother of uNkosi Mlawu (d. 1782), and both were sons of uNkosi Rharhabe (d. 1782) and Princess Nojoli. See Mqhayi, *Ityala Lamawele*, 50. On the death of Mlawu in 1782, a regency was created under Ndlambe, who initially refused to surrender his regency to the 17-year-old, Prince Ngqika (1775-1829), in 1795.
209 T.R.H. Davenport, *South Africa: A Modern History* (London: Macmillan, 1991), 123.
210 *Cape of Good Hope Government Gazette*, No. 1536, 29 May 1835: Proclamation, 10 May 1835.
211 *Cape of Good Hope Reports of Select Committee on Native Affairs*, 1873, A.12 – '73: Memorandum by Orpen on Relations with Ngangelizwe and Tambookie Allies, 35.
212 Moyer, "The Mfengu Self-Defence", 108.
213 Stapleton, "The Fingo Debate", 360.

Headmen were introduced during the tenure of Cape Governor Sir George Grey (1812-1898) to weaken the traditional system of justice and render the traditional leaders impotent. Headmen were selected from men who had not participated in the cattle-killing. They were accountable to the resident magistrate and played the role of collecting the hut tax, apprehending people who broke the law, keeping the magistrates informed about those threatening the colonial order in the *iilali*.[214] Majeke observes that

> in the payment of headmen the Government drove a wedge, not only between them and their chief, but between them and their people. They, too, in serving a new master [white magistrate] could be used to betray their people. Grey's immediate purpose, however, was to undermine the power of the chiefs.[215]

In fulfilling this venture, Governor Grey (1812-1898) used white magistrates and headmen as the political pawns. Chiefs, whose authority and power rested on their rights to levy judicial fees and fines, as well as receiving gifts as the arbiters of amaXhosa law and custom, were dealt a heavy blow by Governor Grey (1812-1898).[216] It is fitting to state that during precolonial times, various kinds of levies were collected from commoners, such as death duties, labour levies, judicial fines and occasional gifts to the chiefs. Chiefs were to provide justice, harmony and security to the people. They also had to consult with their counsellors, *izinyanya* (ancestors) and amagqirha (priest-diviners). Africans' religious belief that "the spirits of the dead chiefs hold the destinies of the tribes in their keeping"[217] prompted them to have unquestionable loyalty to their chiefs. Chiefs had to be generous with their subjects and loan them cattle and food as needed.[218] Headmen and subchiefs had the obligation of collecting levies and fines.

As a result of Sir Benjamin D'Urban's postwar settlements of September 1835, uNkosi Maphasa's lands were annexed into the Cape Colony. Colonel Henry Somerset, with an armed force of 200 men, put it to Maphasa that he had to choose between remaining in his lands under 'British protection',[219] and leaving his lands to settle beyond the Nciba River. On account of his precarious position in the face of the compact between the amaXhosa and the Mbhashe-Thembu, he chose to remain in his lands. Differences within the abaThembu were responsible

---

214 Switzer, *Power and Resistance in an African Society*, 95.
215 N. Majeke, *The Role of the Missionaries in Conquest* (Cumberwood: A.P.D.U.S.A., 1952), 67.
216 S. Terreblanche, *A History of Inequality in South Africa, 1652-2002* (Pietermaritzburg: Macmillan, 2003), 199; C.R.D. Halisi, *Black Political Thought in the Making of South African Democracy* (U.S.A.: Maskew Miller, 1999), 23.
217 *Blue Book on Native Affairs*, 1885, 32.
218 S. Redding, "Sorcery and Sovereignty: Taxation, Witchcraft and Political Symbols in the 1880 Transkeian Rebellion", *Journal of Southern African Studies*, 22, 2 (June 1996), 250.
219 K. Shillington contends that African leaders accepted 'British protection' in the hope that they would be protected from their African enemies, but the British government, after defeating African enemies, intepreted 'protection' as signing away the 'protected' kingdom's birthright. See K. Shillington, *History of Africa* (London: Macmillan, 1995), 304.

for D'Urban's annexationist policy, which never materialised and uNkosi Maphasa's concessions, which were prompted by his fear of enraging the Colony: refusal to accept 'British protection' would offend the colonial authorities.

Lord Glenelg, the British Colonial Secretary, rescinded D'Urban's schemes, more particularly the announcement by D'Urban on 10 May 1835 that the territory between the Keiskamma and the Kei Rivers, known as the Queen Adelaide Province, was annexed to the British Crown. AmaXhosa were given a right to occupy parts of the Ceded Territory, the rich lands between the Nxuba and the Keiskamma Rivers where uNkosi Ngqika (1775-1829) had always resided.[220] UNkosi Maphasa's lands were part of the annexed territory – Province of Queen Adelaide.[221] Until 1847 the Nxuba (Fish) River was to remain the official boundary of the Colony. Andries Stockenström, the former Commissioner-General of the Eastern Districts, was appointed Lieutenant-Governor of the Eastern Cape. He was to implement the treaty system, which sought to control relations on the borders between 1836 and 1847, while Henry Fynn was appointed Diplomatic Agent for the abaThembu. He was to act as a link between the colonial authorities and the abaThembu kings and chiefs.

During the 1830s, the combined force of the amaGcina, the amaMpondomise and the ama-Gcaleka-Xhosa overran the amaBhaca of uNkosi Madzikane. Consequently, a section of the amaMpondomise established themselves on the west of the Mthatha River, but subsequent to a clash with the abaThembu, this section returned to the vicinity of Qumbu and Tsolo. The military alliance between uNkosi Faku of the amaMpondo and uNkosi Ncaphayi of the amaBhaca resulted in the defeat in November 1836 of the abaThembu whereupon Faku and Ncaphayi carried off large droves of cattle.[222] It was the alliance between Faku and Ncaphayi, which drove uKumkanikazi Nonesi and Mthikrakra to Rhode in 1837. Fadana's appeal to the Lieutenant-Governor for assistance against external forces was all in vain, even though he had harboured missionaries during the Sixth Frontier War, and had in April 1835 aided Captain Warden in recapturing 4,000 cattle from one of uKumkani Hintsa's kraals. The Lieutenant-Governor's response was to lead to abaThembu losing hope, faith and trust in the Colony. Observing the colonial response to Fadana, uNkosi Faku nurtured a friendship with uNkosi Ncaphayi in 1838 with the objective of capturing cattle from Fadana. The amaBhaca-Mpondo attacks on Fadana's abaThembu and the consequent starvation resulted in some abaThembu migrating towards the upper reaches of the Nciba River in October 1838.

The Moravian mission station at Shiloh was responsible for the conclusion of a treaty of peace and friendship by Andries Stockenström and uNkosi Mphasa in January 1837. In terms of the treaty, Maphasa was burdened with the herculean task of ensuring and maintaining peace amongst other abaThembu clans and with the Colony. However, Maphasa could not discipline the Bushmen (referred to as the San since the 1960s) under Madolo (Mandoor) and other abaThembu clans who paid allegiance to Fadana. Indeed, Maphasa was nominally

---

220 Peires, "The British and the Cape", 482 and 490.
221 Wagenaar, "History of the Thembu", 12.
222 Molema, *The Bantu*, 387.

given power and chiefly authority he could not practically exercise. An attempt to exercise restrictive measures, such as to control other clans, would result in clashes and consequent weakness of uNkosi Maphasa.

Acknowledging the Black Kei and Klaas Smith's Rivers as the colonial boundary, Chief Maphasa's connivance when his subjects crossed the boundary to the colonial territory in 1838 enraged Governor Sir George Napier and Colonel John Hare.[223] Failing to dissuade Maphasa's subjects from intruding into the colonial territory, Colonel Hare and Lieutenant-Governor Andries Stockenström, approached Governor Napier with a view to restoring to the old reprisal system. This system had frequently led to friction and malpractices in instances where whites demanded more cattle than had been stolen by the abaThembu, and as a consequence, the abaThembu refused to surrender all the cattle including the so-called stolen ones.[224] Consequently, the Lieutenant-Governor mobilised and placed one division of his military force under Lieutenant-Governor Colonel Greaves and the other under Major Armstrong in April 1839. These divisions jointly ravaged Maphasa's and Diniso's kraals, and "seize[d] the whole of their cattle, and drove the herds to Shiloh".[225]

The treaty of 1837, which was part of the treaty system by the colonial government with the traditional leaders, was amended in 1841 by Governor Napier and uNkosi Maphasa. In 1844, Prince Xokiso became king of the abaThembu and assumed the name Mthikrakra. In 1845, Governor Sir Peregrine Maitland signed a treaty with uKumkani Mthikrakra on behalf of all the abaThembu, and uNkosi Maphasa as a subchief of the amaTshatshu. In terms of this treaty, uKumkani Mthikrakra and uNkosi Maphasa were to be faithful allies of Her Majesty. They were to be paid one hundred shillings per year or given articles amounting thereto if they cooperated. In turn, the Cape Government promised them 'protection' against enemies.[226]

Through uKumkani Mthikrakra and uNkosi Maphasa were bound by the treaty of 1845, division of purpose and action could still be evident. UNkosi Maphasa, who was related by marriage with the amaRharhabe-Xhosa, disregarded the terms of the treaty by throwing his weight behind the amaRharhabe-Xhosa during the Seventh Frontier War (1846-1847), while Mthikrakra remained neutral for some time. Mthikrakra could not take sides with the Colony lest he incur the wrath of his people to uNkosi Maphasa's advantage. In another context, assisting the Colony would help Mthikrakra to deal with Maphasa accordingly and settle land disputes with Madolo (Mandoor) and uKumkani Sarhili, A! Ntaba! Threats generated by such strained relations did not have a cohesive effect on the abaThembu political and social order.

Having joined the Seventh Frontier War in August 1846, uNkosi Maphasa proceeded to set fire to the Imvani mission station established near uKumkani Mthikrakra's Great Place (KomKhulu). Hence, when Maphasa was attacked by a Mr Joseph Read and the Khoekhoe in

---

223 Theal, *History of South Africa*, 68.
224 Van Aswegen, *South Africa*, 215.
225 Theal, *History of South Africa*, 177.
226 Brownlee, *Transkei Native Territories*, 22; *Select Committee Reports*, A.12 – '73, 31 and 36.

November 1847, Mthikrakra, intent on winning the favour of the Colony against his rivals, openly attacked Maphasa "in the rear, seized 4,000 cattle … and utterly ruined the [aba] Thembu chief for the time".[227]

Having temporarily broken the might of uNkosi Maphasa, uKumkani Mthikrakra set out to strengthen his position. He handed over to Governor Maitland some 300 head of cattle, being a portion of cattle raided by Maphasa from the Colony. This action served as 'proof' of uKumkani Mthikrakra's fidelity to the Cape Government, and his wish to live harmoniously with it. Using Reverend J.C. Warner, a Wesleyan missionary, as interpreter, uKumkani Mthikrakra sought 'British protection', so that his lands could become part of British territory. UKumkani Mthikrakra justified his request by stating that ever since he assisted the Cape Government against uKumkani Sarhili (1809-1892)[228] and protected the missionaries and white traders during the Sixth Frontier War, he had earned more enemies. He also alluded to the fact that he was too weak to face the amaGcaleka-Xhosa.[229] Governor Maitland acquiesced in this request and soon made recommendations to the British Government to that effect. In fact, Maitland envisaged placing uKumkani Mthikrakra's territory under British magistrates and deposing chiefs of the abaThembu.

The resignation of Maitland as Governor of the Cape Colony in 1847 was ill-timed in view of his readiness to implement the acceptance of King Mthikrakra as a British subject. His successor, Sir Henry Pottinger, rejected Maitland's proposal, and found his task simply "to end the war rather than build the peace".[230] Observing this attitude of Pottinger, Earl Grey, Secretary of State for War and Colonies since 1846, replaced him with Sir Harry Smith (1787-1860) in December 1847, a position he held until March 1852.

Sir Harry Smith summoned abeNguni chiefs and kings to a meeting in King William's Town where they would take an oath of allegiance to the Queen of England in January 1848. These traditional leaders were accompanied by *amaphakathi* (councillors). At the meeting, Sir Harry Smith extracted promises of peace from each chief and king. UKumkani Mthikrakra and uNkosi Maphasa were signatories to this treaty. He declared all treaties with African kings and chiefs null and void, proclaimed the lands between the Keiskamma and the Kei Rivers as British Kaffraria to be a separate British dependency, directly ruled by Smith in his capacity as High Commissioner.[231] He annexed the ceded territory between the Fish and the Keiskamma Rivers and named it Victoria East. In Victoria East, Sir Harry Smith placed the amaMfengu settlers holding quitrent title.[232]

---

227 Wagenaar, "History of the Thembu", 17; Theal, *History of South Africa*, 289.
228 UKumkani Sarhili's *ingoma* was: *uMqolo weNamba*. His mother was Nomsa, uKumkani Hintsa's Great Wife.
229 *Select Committee Reports*, A.12 – '73, 31, 39-40.
230 Davenport, *South Africa*, 120.
231 Wagenaar, "History of the Thembu", 19.
232 Davenport, *South Africa*, 120.

Maphasa's territory was part of British Kaffraria placed under the rule of the High Commissioner and ruled on behalf of Britain. Sir Harry Smith made an arrogant gesture of treating Maphasa and Mthikrakra as his subjects and subordinates by coercing them to accept him as their *Inkosi Inkulu*.[233] This was a gross humiliation in view of the fact that Smith, being a commoner, undermined traditional leaders in the presence of their subjects. While acknowledging the separate existence of amaTshatshu, Smith placed uKumkani Mthikrakra between the colonial boundary and the Indwe River as a reward for his neutrality in the Seventh Frontier War. Under uKumkani Mthikrakra he placed ooNkosi Tyhopho, Fadana, Jumba, Khelelo, Kholobeni, Mali and Qhwesha.[234] He further promised uKumkani Mthikrakra 'protection' against Sarhili. But such 'protection' would be given only if uKumkani Mthikrakra remained between the colonial boundary and the Indwe River, and not in his lands between the Mbhashe and the Mthatha Rivers. Smith also gave *amagqobhoka* (converts) from Lesseyton station some land close by as a reward for siding with the Colony during the Seventh Frontier War.

Smith's annexation of the abaThembu territories in July 1848 and the administering of this area by a 'police force' constituted by the amaNgqika, as well as Pottinger's rejection of Maitland's proposal, strained colonial relations with the western abaThembu. Following the annexation of these territories, the missionaries, viewing the spread of Christianity as inseparably linked with the expansion of British rule, "preached loyalty to God in the same breath as loyalty to the Queen".[235] Wagenaar maintains that "the black people were introduced to two foreign abstract concepts: the invisible unknown God of the white man in heaven, and an equally invisible and unknown ruler across the sea."[236]

The fact that farmers moved into the annexed abaThembu territory, and Smith's practice of humiliating the abaThembu king and chiefs, further aggravated these relations. Smith called kings and chiefs to a meeting in Qonce (King William's Town). He put his foot on uKumkani Mthikrakra's neck, as he did with other kings and chiefs so as to illustrate their submissiveness to the British Government.[237] The abaThembu traditional leaders in particular and other southern abeNguni kings and chiefs in general never forgave this act of contempt and humiliation easily.[238] Hence, from 1848 onwards sour and stormy relations emerged between the abaThembu and the colonial authorities. Not only were the Tshatshu-abaThembu not kindly disposed to white people, they also acted quite independently of uKumkani Mthikrakra's authority.

Both uKumkani Mthikrakra's and uNkosi Maphasa's powers were broken by Smith. Realising his military and political impotence, uKumkani Mthikrakra warned his subjects to return to the

---

233 *Inkosi Inkulu* is an isiXhosa term, which means a senior chief. By calling himself *Inkosi Inkulu*, Smith regarded himself as greater than African kings and chiefs.
234 Wagenaar, "History of the Thembu", 20.
235 *Grahamstown Journal*, 24 October 1880.
236 Wagenaar, "History of the Thembu", 32.
237 *Walter Stanford Papers*, D.10, E.J. Warner's Biography Sketch of his Father.
238 Van Aswegen, *South Africa*, 217.

Mbhashe–Mthatha region so as to be far from the colonial boundaries.[239] Before the dispersal of the abaThembu, uKumkani Mthikrakra died in 1849. He was survived by his mother, uKumkanikazi Nonesi, and his heir, Prince Qheya, a minor. Although uNkosi Mathanzima, son of uKumkani Mthikrakra in the Right-Hand House, had attained maturity, uKumkanikazi Nonesi refused to have Chief Mathanzima acting for Prince Qheya.[240] At this stage, Shweni, brother of uNkosi Joyi and uKumkani Mthikrakra, shot himself owing to frustration generated by uKumkanikazi Nonesi's careless statement that Shweni was happy that his brother had died. It would appear that Shweni expected to inherit the abaThembu kingship. Intent on interfering in the abaThembu internal affairs, J.C. Warner had two regents appointed. In this way, he wished to divide abaThembuland politically. UKumkanikazi Nonesi took responsibility of the western abaThembu, while Chief Joyi ruled the Mbhashe-abaThembu. The appointmtent of two regents had no known precedent in the history of the abaThembu. Wagenaar remarks that, "not only was this an unusual situation, but it was unwarranted interference in the internal affairs of the [aba]Thembu."[241] Thus, the abaThembu were not only divided politically but were also split territorially by external forces, factors and influences. As a result, the long-term effects of this divisive action was the coming into being of Emigrant abaThembuland in 1865.

After the funeral of both Shweni, "a man greatly respected by the Cape Town authorities ... [who had] accidentally shot himself"[242] and uKumkani Mthikrakra, uKumkanikazi Nonesi refused to heed the warning of the late Mthikrakra and remained on the north-eastern border of the Cape Colony, stressing that she would not leave her child's grave so soon. UNkosi Mathanzima also remained. Even there, the abaThembu were divided for Chief-Regent Joyi moved to Nxankolo at Qumbu, then to Malephelephe at Tsolo and ultimately to Bhaziya at Mthatha. As the late king's brother, Chief-Regent Joyi, established himself at Bhaziya, Prince Qheya (A! Ngangelizwe!), son of the late uKumkani Mthikrakra, "was growing up near the Mb[h]ashe river in [aba]Thembuland proper under Chief Joyi ... far from the troubled frontier".[243]

UNkosi Jumba, son of uKumkani Ndaba in the Right-Hand House, migrated first to Qumbu and then to Mhlwazi just above the Drakensberg Mountains. Chief Mgudlwa migrated to Qhumanco, while uNkosi Mdukiswa came to the mission station at Tabase.[244] Thus, the House of Ngubengcuka was scattered within and beyond the territorial confines of abaThembuland. External challenges could with ease make terrible inroads into the abaThembu crumbling socio-economic and political threads.

---

239 Sihele, "Ngobani?", 74.
240 Ibid.
241 Wagenaar, "History of the Thembu", 22.
242 Sihele, "Ngobani?", 74.
243 Mager, "Gungubele and the Tambookie Location", 1161.
244 Sihele, "Ngobani?", 34.

The foregoing survey of the abaThembu encounters with the amaNgwane, missionaries and whites shows how external factors disrupted the abaThembu. The period of the Mfecane wars cannot be viewed as the roots of a rift within the abaThembu, but as the intensification of a split, which is traceable to power relations and conflict between uKumkani Nxeko's sons, viz. Prince Hlanga of the iNdlu eNkulu and Prince Dlomo of the iNdlu yaseKunene. Thus the Mfecane/Difaqane wars greatly caused a further rift within the abaThembu.

Similarly, the presence of white traders and missionaries in abaThembuland was also responsible for the escalation of a split within the abaThembu kingdom. These internal and external factors culminated in the territorial and social split within the abaThembu. As a result of abaThembu exposure to these influences, the abaThembu became frail, and were no longer acting and reacting in unison with external challenges.

4

THE ORIGINS OF EMIGRANT ABATHEMBULAND, 1848-1865

In this chapter, an attempt is made to examine the circumstances leading to the coming into being of Emigrant abaThembuland in 1865. In an effort to provide some context for the reader, a survey of the Eighth Frontier War of 1850-1853 and the destructive effects of the Xhosa cattle-killing movement on the abaThembu is made. The abaThembu–Gcaleka relations and whites' interference in these relations are also analysed.

However, it is important to note that there were three emigrations from the abaThembu heartland around the Clarkebury area of the Mbhashe River. The first one occurred about 1825 when uNkosi Bawana of the amaTshatshu was pushed west as far as Hewu (Whittlesea) by the first Bhaca invasions. The iNdlu eNkulu of Ngubengcuka was still ruling on the Mbhashe. UNkosi Bawana's son Maphasa established his authority over the amaNdungwana and amaGcina already living in that area, and signed the treaty with Stockenström in 1837. The second emigration took place in 1837. UKumkanikazi Nonesi and the young uKumkani Mthikrakra left the Mbhashe Great Place, and established themselves at Rode/Imvane area (Gqebenya *lali* where Mthikrakra is buried). They were again under pressure from the amaBhaca, and also from the Mnqanqeni family, which claimed the kingship. They were further persuaded by J.C. Warner, the missionary at Clarkebury and later abaThembu agent. UNkosi Maphasa could not refute their seniority, but nevertheless resented their arrival. As a result, when the Wars of the Axe (1846-1847) and Mlanjeni (1850-1853) broke out, Maphasa sided with the amaXhosa, while Mthikrakra/Nonesi joined forces on the side of the British.[245] Although, in both the above cases, we see the abaThembu emigrations, but the term 'Emigrant abaThembu' was not used until 1865 under the circumstances, which are described in this chapter.

---

245 Peires, Telephone Interview, 15 April 2020.

Between 1839 and 1853, the abaThembu helplessly witnessed "increasing interference from the Cape Colony".[246] By 1848, all the previous abaThembu relations with the colonial authorities were not conducive to peace. On the contrary, these turbid relations aroused the abaThembu hostility, distrust and suspicion. Hence, from 1848 onwards the abaThembu relations with the Colony became turbid and uneasy. The activities of missionaries, which caused divisions within the abaThembu society and the latter's gradual inclination towards the militarily superior Colony, did not only exert pressure on the abaThembu society, but also divided and weakened them to such an extent that, by 1848, uKumkani Mthikrakra warned the ruling house to move towards, and settle on, the Mbhashe–Mthatha region for fear of his people being permanently ravaged by the Colony.[247]

On the death of uKumkani Mthikrakra in 1849, abaThembu occupied the land west of amaXhosaland right from Mthatha to the present-day Komani (Queenstown). UKumkani Mthikrakra had been powerless to resist white intrusion and to withstand uKumkani Sarhili's challenges. UNkosi Maphasa was not prepared to work cooperatively with the abaThembu king. UKumkani Mthikrakra's heir, Prince Qheya, was a minor and Warner was instrumental in having abaThembuland ruled by two chief-regents, viz. uKumkanikazi Nonesi and uNkosi Joyi. Although uKumkanikazi Nonesi and uNkosi Mathanzima remained on the north-eastern border, Chief-Regent Joyi, and ooNkosi Jumba, Mgudlwa and Mdukiswa migrated in different directions, scattering within and outside the boundaries of abaThembuland. UKumkanikazi Nonesi and uNkosi Mathanzima remained sandwiched between the Indwe River and the colonial border by white farmers and the amaGcaleka-Xhosa. As a result of these strained relations, abaThembu of uNkosi Maphasa north of the Amatola joined the amaRharhabe-Xhosa during the War of Mlanjeni, known as the Eighth Frontier War (1850-1853).[248] The war, which spread to abaThembuland, was precipitated by a "severe drought in 1850, [and] resistance was mobilised through the war doctor Mlanjeni".[249] Apart from the threat of the amaGcaleka-Xhosa joining forces against the colonial forces, the Khoekhoe of the Kat River settlement, from which uNkosi Maqoma was expelled in 1829, and some subjects of uKumkanikazi Nonesi, joined forces on the side of the amaRharhabe-Xhosa.[250]

Chief-Regent Joyi and uKumkanikazi Nonesi remained loyal to the Colony. Nonesi and uNkosi Qhwesha proved this loyalty by protecting the border of Cradock district. Resenting the extension of the Cape Colony to the Keiskamma River in 1847 and the resettlement of retired English people, Khoekhoe and amaMfengu in the annexed territory between the Nxuba (Fish) and the Keiskamma Rivers, uNkosi Maphasa attacked the town of Hewu (Whittlesea) and

---

246 Wagenaar, "History of the Thembu", 16.
247 Sihele, "Ngobani?", 34.
248 Wagenaar, "History of the Thembu", 23.
249 J. Hodgson, "A Battle for Sacred Power: Christian Beginnings among the Xhosa", in R. Elphick and R. Davenport (eds), *Christianity in South Africa: A Political, Social and Cultural History* (Cape Town: David Philip, 1997), 80.
250 Mostert, *Frontiers*, 1045; Saunders (ed.), *Illustrated History of South Africa: The Real Story* (London: Reader's Digest Association, 1994), 136.

Shiloh in January to February 1851.²⁵¹ At the Battle of Imvani (White Kei River) of April 1851, the abaThembu-Xhosa troops and Khoekhoe rebels who had felt insecure at the Kat River settlement, following their rebellion against the Colony during this war, were routed by the colonial forces and "more than two hundred [ama]Xhosa and [aba]Thembu were killed".²⁵²

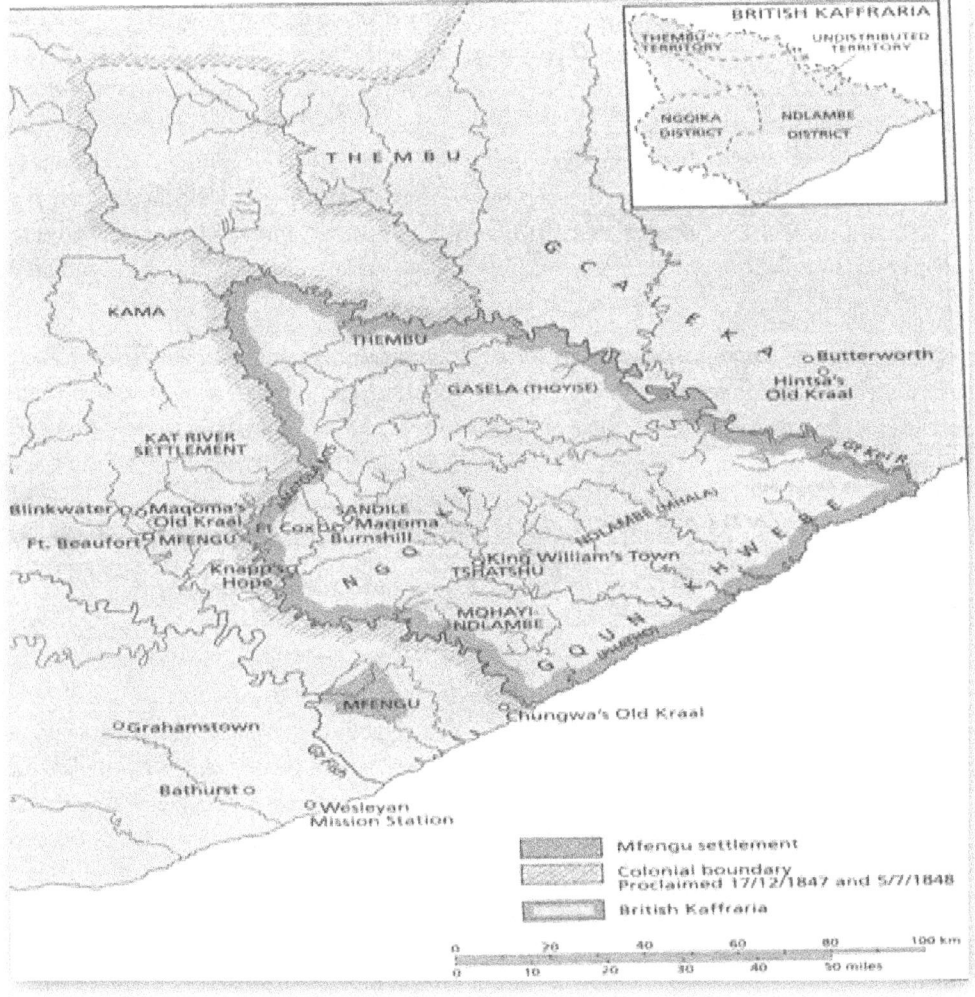

MAP 6: The Eastern Cape frontier area, 1847-1850²⁵³

In spite of her alliance with the Colony, uKumkanikazi Nonesi was attacked in January 1851 by Gideon Joubert's commando on the pretext that Gideon Joubert's forces had been attacked by a portion of uKumkanikazi Nonesi's subjects. Joubert exacted a tribute of 2,000 head of

---

251 Wagenaar, "History of the Thembu", 12.
252 Peires, *The Dead Will Arise: Nongqawuse and the Great Xhosa Cattle-Killing Movement of 1856-7* (Johannesburg: Ravan Press, 1989), 17.
253 Price, *Making Empire*, xxviii.

cattle and 150 horses. On the order of the colonial authorities, Nonesi retreated beyond the Mbhashe River.[254] However, a large number of her subjects remained faithful allies of the Cape Government, and were reportedly true to their allegiance.[255] Thus, the abaThembu sympathy towards the Colony was divided. While uKumkanikazi Nonesi refrained from siding against the Colony, a portion of her subjects joined forces against the Colony with disastrous consequences for the traditional ally of the Colony. Her collaboration with the colonial authorities did her more harm than, if any, good, as can be seen from the fact that she was instructed to evacuate her dormer lands. Had she acted in concert with Maphasa to defend the abaThembu independence, it is likely that they would have resisted colonial attacks with ease. UKumkanikazi Nonesi's collaboration and Chief-Regent Joyi's reluctance to aid Maphasa impeded such possibility and, on the contrary, led to deep historic rivalries between the abaThembu clusters. Furthermore, all participants in this war against the Colony lost land to whites. In particular, the abaThembu of Maphasa were declared by whites to have forfeited their land rights.[256]

To exacerbate the situation, calamity struck abaThembuland when in 1852 uNkosi Maphasa died of heart attack. Consequently, his death shattered the fighting spirit of his warriors. There followed a wrangle over the question of succession. At the same time, Sir George Cathcart (1794-1854) replaced Sir Harry Smith as new Governor and High Commissioner of the Cape Colony on 31 March 1852. No sooner did Sir George Cathcart arrive at the Cape than he embarked on attempts to bring the war to an end. He soon started discussing the possibility of ending hostilities with the abaThembu. White farmers, sensing that victory was imminent, strongly objected to Sir George Cathcart's move but to no avail.

The results of the War of Mlanjeni were disastrous for the abaThembu, as well as the amaRharhabe-Xhosa and the Kat River Khoekhoe. In particular, the peace terms dealt "the rebellious abaThembu of [uNkosi] Maphasa"[257] a heavy blow. UNkosi Maphasa's people were evicted from their territory north of the Amatola mountains – an area known as North Victoria since annexation by Smith in 1847. They were forced to stay across the colonial boundaries by Sir George Cathcart, Cape Governor (1851-1853). Their land was turned into 300 farms and then sold to white farmers – both Dutch and English – to promote integration. On these farms, Komani (Queenstown) was laid out in 1853 at the end of the Eighth Frontier War by Sir George Cathcart, Governor of the Cape from 1851 to 1853. Thus, Megan Voss aptly remarks that "in 1853, at the close of the war, Queenstown was formed as part of a rampart of frontier defence, in the land confiscated from the anti-colonial contingent of the abaThembu".[258] Governor Cathcart (1794-1854) felt that Komani (Queenstown) should be populated with Europeans in order to prevent the 'rebel Tambookies', "who had been expelled from returning to their

---

254 *Grahamstown Journal*, 15 March 1851.
255 *Select Committee Reports on Native Affairs*, A.12 – '73, 33 and 40.
256 Ibid., 40.
257 Milton, *Edges of War*, 223.
258 Voss, "The Making of Colonial Queenstown", 5.

land".[259] According to the 'Cathcart system', the districts of Komani (Queenstown) and Hewu (Whittlesea) were taken for commercial farms and indigenous Africans were chased into the Tambookie location (Lady Frere).

UNkosi Maphasa's adherents were settled in the colonial and newly created Tambookie[260] Location (Lady Frere) west of the Indwe River. The Tambookie location (Lady Frere) was a result of the colonial government's allocating 40,000 pardoned and 'loyal' abaThembu to a stretch of territory to the north of Komani (Queenstown). The amaMfengu allies were settled about 20 miles southwest of Queenstown in the vicinity of Kamastone Wesleyan Mission along the Oxkraal River.[261] Others were settled along the Oxkraal River near Hackney Mission of the London Missionary Society. It was in the area that Kamastone and Oxkraal Locations (amaMfengu reserves near Komani) came into being.

Both Komani (Queenstown) and the Tambookie location (Lady Frere) "were established as twin colonial projects at the end of the Seventh Frontier War",[262] on land wrested from the late uNkosi Maphasa of the amaTshatshu. Komani, writes Mager, was not only a white town, but it also "provided a locus for settler colonial commerce and magisterial control over the district that encompassed the Tambookie location [Lady Frere]."[263]

UKumkanikazi Nonesi was ordered to return from across the Mbhashe River and become the head of the displaced abaThembu, so that the displaced abaThembu were scattered amongst Nonesi's people in the Tambookie location (Lady Frere).[264] Moreover, the Tambookie location (Lady Frere) was mainly inhabited by the amaMfengu and the abaThembu who had emigrated from the Colony on the command of the Cape Government.[265] Joseph Warner was placed in the Tambookie location (Lady Frere) as a government agent assigned to the duty of commanding supreme control over the abaThembu. Nevertheless, Cathcart (1794-1854), writes Milton, "refused to break the power of the chiefs",[266] by urging Warner to act in an advisory capacity and not to act as the abaThembu magistrate. Chief-Regent Joyi had remained behind at Mbhashe with the amaHala (see Umnombo 6). In the circumstances, the House of Thembu was thus scattered and dislocated through the interference of the colonial authorities, whose sole aim was to have control over the abaThembu and other African kingdoms and chiefdoms.

---

259 Ibid., 6.
260 According to Mager, "Gungubele and the Tambookie Location", 1159, the word 'Tambookie' is the San name given to abaThembu living in Bushmanland, the territory west of the Nciba River, where uNkosi Maphasa moved with his father, Bawana, in the 1820s.
261 Voss, "The Making of Colonial Queenstown", 7.
262 Mager, "Gungubele and the Tambookie Location", 1159.
263 Ibid.
264 *Select Committee Reports on Native Affairs*, A.12 – '73, 40.
265 *Cape of Good Hope Report of Langham Dale*, General Superintendent of Education, to Cape Parliament, G.11 – '74, 11.
266 Milton, *Edges of War*, 223.

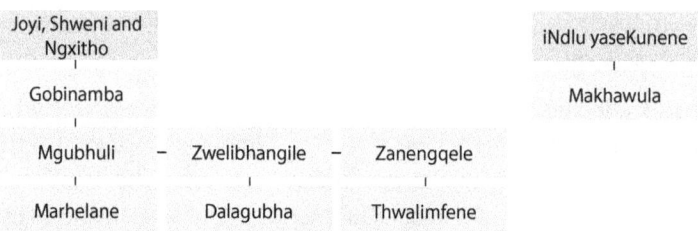

Umnombo (Genealogy) 6: The House of Joyi[267]

Not only the amaTshatshu suffered the consequences of the Eighth Frontier War. UNkosi Qhwesha of the amaNdungwana lost power to his son, Ndarhala. The ex-regent of the abaThembu kingdom, uNkosi Fadana, along with other amaNdungwana and amaTshatshu chiefs, were coerced to settle in the Tambookie location (Lady Frere). UNkosi Fadana was coerced to reside within uKumkanikazi Nonesi's political domain in the Tambookie location (Lady Frere).[268] In this way, the Eighth Frontier War left the abaThembu landless, dispossessed, dispirited and helpless. Its settlement left deep-seated scars, accentuated the schism between the abaThembu and on a wider plane did not encourage the abaThembu cohesive political unit. Even so, "a growing alienation between the [aba]Thembu and their white allies",[269] which had become apparent after 1847, remained. However, the former's might was completely broken.

The successor to Sir George Cathcart was Sir George Grey (December 1854 to January 1862), who "implemented a policy of pacification of the [ama]Xhosa through a long-term programme of socio-economic and cultural transformation".[270] Governor Grey (1812-1898) had a dream to have all the economically valuable land from the Nciba (Kei) River to Port Natal brought under British rule. Under his tenure as Cape Governor, there was "a deliberate production of a Xhosa history that depicted amaXhosa as having a barbaric past and in need of civilisation".[271] To this end, his term of office was characterised by his fervent desire "to break the power of the chiefs and destroy the tribal system",[272] and integrate Africans into the economic system of whites. According to Bundy, Governor Grey squashed the power of the chiefs by undermining the social, cultural and material plank of their authority and influence.[273]

His main purpose was to turn Africans into the servants of whites, consumers of their goods and contributors to their revenue – to be used as a source of strength and wealth to the Cape Colony.[274] No wonder then that Governor Grey encouraged and supported such agents

---

267 Author's version, 2019.
268 Mager, "Gungubele and the Tambookie Location", 1161.
269 Wagenaar, "History of the Thembu", 34.
270 Hodgson, "A Battle for Sacred Power", 83.
271 Tisani, "Continuity and Change", i.
272 Majeke, *Missionaries in Conquest*, 65.
273 C. Bundy, *The Rise and Fall of the South African Peasantry* (Cape Town: Macmillan, 1988), 50.
274 Majeke, *Missionaries in Conquest*, 66.

of white expansion as the missionaries, traders, farmers and government agents, which undermined the abaThembu kingdom.[275] The missionaries, frustrated by some abaThembu hostility to conversion, advocated British rule, and owing to their inadequate knowledge of the abaThembu philosophy of life, waged "open, illogical and unwarranted attacks"[276] on the abaThembu culture. Generally, there is no doubt that most missionaries were agents of colonial conquest,[277] and played a major role in launching an attack on African philosophy of life and traditional religion. Furthermore, some missionaries, writes Beck, were so immensely involved in commercial relations with Africans that they "abandoned forever the holy book for the account book".[278] While discerning Christianity as aligned and closely interwoven with Western civilisation, "many early African Christians, like most missionaries, regarded Christianity and African religious views as mutually exclusive and even hostile to one another".[279] However, these attacks were not the proper mode of advancing the cause of Christianity. Moreover, some chiefs realised that "once rites and customs went, [their] society would disintegrate and their power would be nullified".[280]

Determined to win Africans over to Western civilisation and Christianity, Governor Grey pursued a policy of mixed settlement of Africans and whites by filling British Kaffraria with whites, who would introduce Africans to white cultural values and lifestyles.[281] He set out to use mission stations as the best way of bringing Western civilisation closer to Africans. He encouraged the missionaries to rebuild mission stations burnt down during the wars of dispossession, known as the Frontier Wars, and to build new ones. Holding the view that missionary education was too bookish, he set out to make industrial education a cornerstone of his policy.[282] He also urged the missionaries to undertake educational programmes by assisting in the building of hospitals and agricultural and technical schools. Grey's ulterior motive behind all these exercises was to reduce "to peaceful, industrious ways the more barbarous and savage races of South Africa",[283] the abeNguni people. Here one can glean Sir George Grey's lack of clear understanding of the abeNguni way of life in viewing their *modus vivendi* and *modus operandi* as reflecting barbarism and savagery. Under these circumstances one is inclined to agree that like other abeNguni communities, the abeThembu kingdom was "undermined from within and overwhelmed from without".[284]

275 L. Thompson, "The Subjection of the African Chiefdoms, 1870-1898", in M. Wilson and L. Thompson (eds), *The Oxford History of South Africa*, vol. ii (Oxford: Oxford University Press, 1971), 251.
276 Williams, "Missionaries", 312.
277 M. Legassick, *The Struggle for the Eastern Cape, 1800-1854* (Johannesburg: KMM Publishing Co., 2010), 7; J. Mvenene, "A Social and Economic History of the African People of Gcalekaland, 1830-1913", *Historia*, vol. 59, No. 1, May 2014, 59.
278 Beck, "Bibles and Beads", 213.
279 R. Elphick, "Christianity in South African History", in R. Elphick and R. Davenport (eds), *Christianity in South Africa: A Political, Social and Cultural History* (Cape Town: David Philip, 1997), 4.
280 D. Williams, *When Races Meet* (Johannesburg: Longmans, 1967), 93.
281 Davenport, *South Africa*, 121; Milton, *Edges of War*, 225.
282 J. Hodgson, "Mission and Empire: A Case Study of Convergent Ideologies in 19th Century Southern Africa", *Journal of Theology for Southern Africa*, 38 (March 1983), 36.
283 G. Callaway, *A Shepherd of the Veld* (London: Darton and Company, 1911), 16.
284 Thompson, "African Chiefdoms", 251.

The worst was yet to come with the crossing over the Rhoda River of a destitute section of the abaThembu who settled at Hohita near uKumkani Sarhili's Great Place. Resenting this action, uKumkani Sarhili ordered the amaGcaleka to repulse the intruders. The amaGcaleka army was split into the Qawuka under Rhuneyi and the Ntshinga under Khwaza. The Qawuka division drove the abaThembu across the Rhoda River, while the Ntshinga and uKumkani Sarhili intercepted them on the other side of the river. The nature of the offensive earned the war the name *Umngqingo*.[285] This scuffle sapped the military power of the abaThembu, and, like the outbreak of the lungsickness (bovine pleuropneumonia) epidemic of 1855, which had wiped out large numbers of the abaThembu and the amaXhosa cattle,[286] it further weakened the abaThembu. The great cattle-killing movement of 1856-1857 further devastated and accentuated the schism within the House of Thembu. It caused distress, division, chaos and loss of lives. At the time, the abaThembu, like the amaXhosa, had suffered in the Eighth Frontier War (1850-1853) and had experienced the devastating results of the lungsickness of 1855. Furthermore, "the country was in the throes of a severe drought, and [uKumkani] Sarhili was desperate."[287] And it is against these circumstances that the attitude and response of the abaThembu and other southern abeNguni communities towards Nongqawuse's prophecy should be assessed. Regarding the effects of lungsickness on the amaXhosa participation on the cattle-killing, Peires argues:

> Lungsickness was a necessary cause of the [ama]Xhosa cattle-killing: without it, the movement could never have occurred ... In Xhosaland, it encountered an exceptionally battered and divided society, demoralized by the frustration of a long series of military defeats, by the social insecurity of expulsion from natal lands and pastures; by the material sufferings of migrant labour and of resettlement in cramped and ecologically deficient locations; by the new wealth of those who had climbed on the military-commercial bandwagon of settler expansionism ... The movement was further encouraged by contingent factors such as the new policies of Governor Sir George Grey, ... and the hopes raised by rumours of British defeat in the Crimean War.[288]

A young girl, Nongqawuse (1841-1898), circulated prophetic news amongst the amaXhosa and the abaThembu that, as per instruction from the *izinyanya* (ancestors), people were to kill all their cattle, destroy all the harvest, stop practising witchcraft, refrain from sowing,[289] but should clear, cleanse and enlarge their corn pits and kraals. If these instructions were carried out, so the prophecy went, there would be an abundance of corn and cattle, the dead would rise, the old people would be rejuvenated and, "on a day – subsequently designated as Wednesday, 18 February 1857 – a mighty hurricane would sweep the hated white man",[290]

---

285 Soga, *South-Eastern Bantu*, 240.
286 Hodgson, "A Battle for Sacred Power", 81.
287 Mager, "Gungubele and the Tambookie Location", 1163.
288 Peires, "The Central Beliefs of the Xhosa Cattle-Killing", *Journal of African History*, 28, 1 (1987), 45.
289 Lewis, "Materialism and Idealism", 244.
290 Du Plessis, *Christian Missions*, 296; Mager, "Gungubele and the Tambookie Location", 1163.

amaMfengu and all those who did not believe the prophesy down into the sea,[291] as wagons, clothing and ammunition would be emerging. About 200,000 cattle were killed, and approximately 25,000 Africans died as a result of starvation.[292] However, Peires points out that, "during the thirteen months of cattle-killing (April 1856 to May 1857), about 85 per cent of all [ama]Xhosa adult men killed their cattle and destroyed their corn in obedience to Nongqawuse's prophecies."[293] Peires provides an estimation of 400,000 cattle having been slaughtered and 40,000 amaXhosa who had died of starvation, while 40,000 left their homes in search of food.[294] In another context, Jack Lewis observes that mass starvation resulted in over 30,000 deaths and further concludes:

> Tens of thousands of [the ama]Xhosa streamed into the Colony to work on the farms, roads and other public works. Massive land losses resulted in the final destruction of the old [ama]Xhosa chieftaincy, the accelerated spread of commodity production, proletarisation and colonial domination.[295]

As a result of the catastrophic consequences of the delusion, "the power of the [ama]X[h]osa nation and their [aba]T[h]embu allies was destroyed".[296]

Viewed critically, the notion of mass slaughtering of cattle was not the usual and known practice amongst the abaThembu and the amaXhosa and other southern abeNguni communities. It had no known precedent in the history of African societies though it was linked with the *izinyanya* (ancestors), the pillar of strength to the abaThembu and the amaXhosa. However, some of Nongqawuse's prophecy was aligned to "[ama]Xhosa thought-patterns and beliefs, [and used] Christian symbols as carriers of sacred power".[297] Correspondingly, Peires concludes that the "beliefs and practices which seem bizarre and irrational to us appeared natural and logical to the [ama]Xhosa of the 1850s."[298] Common amongst the southern abeNguni communities was the discarding of possessed properties but this was practised when the head of a family had departed to the ancestral world. His old ornaments were abandoned and his utensils were broken and thrown away as houses and milk-sacks were cleansed.[299]

AbaThembu had had some dealings with the missionaries from whom they learnt about biblical doctrines. Undoubtedly, they had been acquainted with the story of Jesus Christ and Lazarus who rose from the dead. The missionaries had proclaimed goodness, peace and salvation; they had preached God, the devil, the creation and resurrection. In the words of

---

291 Majeke, *Missionaries in Conquest*, 71.
292 Ibid.
293 Peires, "Central Beliefs", 43.
294 Ibid.
295 Lewis, "Materialism and Idealism", 244.
296 Du Plessis, *Christian Missions*, 296.
297 Hodgson, "A Battle for Sacred Power", 81.
298 Peires, "Central Beliefs", 45.
299 Mlahleni Xundu, Interview, 16 April 1996; uNkosi Dalagubha Joyi, Interview, 7 May 1994.

Hodgson, "the emphasis on an apocalyptic resurrection of the dead showed how millennial concepts in Christianity, linked with the second coming of Christ, were realigned with [ama]Xhosa concerns."[300] Broadly speaking, the abaThembu had knowledge of "Christian doctrines such as belief in miracles, the land of milk and honey".[301] In this sense, therefore, part of Nongqawuse's message could appear to the despondent abaThembu as "the fulfilment of biblical prophecy".[302] Thus, the carrying out of the prophecy was not, as Wilson asserts, "a pagan reaction"[303] to the pressures of colonial and Christian influence, but was a logical response to "social disruption"[304] of the abeNguni. Correspondingly, Peires claims that "the movement was by no means a 'pagan reaction', but one that combined Christian and pre-Christian elements fused under the heroic leadership of the expected redeemer, the son of sifuba-sibanzi, the Broad-Chested One."[305]

In the same vein, Nosipho Majeke writes, "the Nongqawuse Cattle-Killing was missionary inspired. It was the first fruits of the subjugation of the minds of the people."[306] She aptly qualifies the cattle-killing mania as "an act of terrible faith on the part of the Xhosa and Thembu people".[307] To be more exact, loss of land, military defeats, social insecurity, increasing missionary activities, droughts of the summer of 1855-1856, lungsickness, humiliations and other frustrating experiences were responsible, though in varying degrees, for the abaThembu participation in the delusion. Furthermore, despite loss of land and colonial dispossessions, the southern abeNguni were known "for increasing populations",[308] a factor that prompted the abaThembu to strive to regain their lands, however difficult that might prove.

More promising and relieving to the desperate abaThembu was Nongqawuse's statement that the *izinyanya* (ancestors) had also referred to the sorrowful plight of the "ruin of their race from the oppression of their conquerors; and ... would no longer be silent spectators of the wrongs and insults".[309] Indeed, this message carried a ray of hope to the despondent and dispossessed southern abeNguni communities. It was a legitimate cause for iiNkosi and iiKumkani to exhort people to act in accordance with the message. It was the responsibility of the traditional leaders as national links with the *izinyanya* (ancestors) and as conductors of communal worship "for such benefits as victory, rain, fertility of lands and herds"[310] to take

---

300 Hodgson, "A Battle for Sacred Power", 81.
301 B.B. Keller, "Millenarianism and Resistance: The Xhosa Cattle-Killing", *Journal of Asian and African Studies*, 13, 1-2 (1978), 106.
302 Peires, "Central Beliefs", 56.
303 M. Wilson, "Co-operation and Conflict: The Eastern Cape Frontier", in Wilson and Thompson (eds), *Oxford History of South Africa*, vol. I, 256.
304 J. Zarwan, "The Xhosa Cattle-Killings, 1856-57", *Cahiers d' Etudes Africaines*, vol. xvi, No. 63-64, 1976, 520.
305 Peires, "Central Beliefs", 45.
306 Majeke, *Missionaries in Conquest*, 69.
307 Ibid., 70.
308 Keller, "Xhosa Cattle-Killing", 101.
309 C.P. Brownlee, *Reminiscences of Kaffir Life and History* (Lovedale: Lovedale Press, 1896), 126.
310 Williams, "Missionaries", 294.

major decisions relating to the prophecy with a view to salvaging the nation. In a letter to Colonel John Maclean (1810-1874), Chief Commissioner of British Kaffaria, Charles Brownlee (1821-1890), who was amaNgqika Commissioner, wrote: "It seems absurd that a shrewd and reasoning people like the [Africans] be led astray by such reports"[311] as were circulated amongst the amaXhosa and the abaThembu. This remark is an indication of Brownlee's inadequate knowledge of the abeNguni practices and beliefs with which the prophecy had some association. He also failed to take into account that the prophecy came when the abeNguni were despondent and morose. The abaThembu had lost land to whites before and after "the longest and most successful [ama]Xhosa resistance against European hegemony",[312] the Eighth Frontier War, which is described by Peires as not only the longest war but also as "the hardest and ugliest war ever fought over one hundred years of bloodshed on the Cape Colony's eastern frontier".[313] The Eighth Frontier War had resulted in widespread famine. As a result of loss of land and famine, the abaThembu were divided in their attitude and reaction to the prophecy. Moreover, the severe drought of 1855 had devastated crops in abaThembuland and amaXhosaland, while the lungsickness epizootic had crippled the economy of the abaThembu and further weakened chiefly power and pastoral patronage. Equally important in its effects was the abaThembu loss of lives and cattle as well as their absorption into the colonial economic system.

In another context, whites blamed African kings and chiefs for the prophecy, though the latter participated in the cattle-killing episode in the hope that they would be relieved of previous frustrations, and would regain their lost power, land and authority. Whites maintained that the prophecy was a chiefs' plot to plunge the Colony into war.[314] Under the pretext that the amaXhosa had been planning a rebellion – the myth of the so-called chiefs' plot – the colonial government confiscated the lands of several chiefs. Lewis concludes:

> The whole area from the Keiskamma to the Kei was lost [to whites]. Two hundred farms for whites of about 1 500 acres each were carved out from this land. The most senior branch of the Xhosa, the Gcaleka under chief Sarhili, nominally independent in the transKei, were driven from their land by the colonial police into a cramped location between Butterworth and the sea.[315]

However, there is no evidence to support the whites' view, and it is for that reason that Stapleton refers to it simply as "the mythological chiefs' plot".[316] Though Africans had been engaged in wars with the colonists, they had not instigated the cattle-killing nor had they wished to embroil the Cape Colony in war. Though Africans were blamed for the movement, not all Africans participated in the cattle-killing.

---

311   Brownlee, *Reminiscences*, 145.
312   Stapleton, "Jingqi Oral Tradition", 321.
313   Peires, *House of Phalo*, 12.
314   *Cape of Good Hope Government Gazette Extra-ordinary*, No. 2911: Governor's Speech, 10 March 1858, 34.
315   Lewis, "Materialism and Idealism", 244.
316   Stapleton, "Reluctant Slaughter: Rethinking Maqoma's Role in the Xhosa Cattle Killing (1853-1857)", *International Journal of African Historical Studies*, 26, 2 (1993), 368.

Nevertheless, some abaThembu chiefs participated in the cattle-killing, while others dismissed it as no more than a hollow promise devoid of sense and truth.[317] The ex-chief of amaNdungwana, Qhwesha, who had lost power to his son, Ndarhala, was *ithamba* (a believer). Chieftainess Yeliswa, the widow of the late Chief Maphasa, though initially hesitant, later joined the *amathamba* (believers). By August 1857, Yeliswa's people started to kill their cattle with young Gungubele observing the slaughter, hunger and distress.[318]

It is worth noting that like her father-in-law, the late Chief Bawana, Chieftainess Yeliswa had "a year after she settled on the Gwatyu [a tributary of the Swart Kei River], ... made contact with the Shiloh Moravians, asking them to visit her".[319] She sought to use the missionaries as "a key means of acquiring resources in the colony."[320] However, her overtures towards the establishment of a mission station on the Gwatyu[321] were in vain, as the Moravian headquarters at Herrnut, Germany, did not pay heed to Yeliswa's request.

So much for Chieftainess Yeliswa's relations with the missionaries. Chief-Regent Joyi, as *igogotya* (a non-believer) advised the amaHala not to heed the prophecy; uKumkanikazi Nonesi, who lived west of the Indwe River (later Glen Grey), failed to dissuade all western abaThembu. So, there was division of reaction – the abaThembu chiefs and commoners divided into *amathamba* (believers) and *amagogotya* (non-believers). In essence, the cattle-killing movement paved the way for abaThembu disunity and disintegration, and rendered them susceptible to colonial subjugation. As Majeke aptly remarks, "chief was divided against chief, brother against brother. Famine and fratricidal strife delivered the Africans into the hands of the White man."[322]

The ex-regent of abaThembu, Prince Xokiso, and head of about 20 homesteads, Fadana, was a leader of *amathamba*.[323] A diviner and magician of repute, Chief Fadana hoped that by leading *amathamba* he would regain the power and popularity he had lost when Prince Xokiso took over from him. The effects of Chiefs Tyhopho, Qhwesha and Chieftainess Yeliswa, the amaTshatshu regent who lived with some 15,000 followers in the Tambookie location (Lady Frere),[324] becoming believers cannot be overemphasised. The common denominator

---

317 G.G. Thozamile Matshayana, Interview, Clarkebury Village, Ngcobo, 17 April 1996; uNkosi Dalagubha Joyi, Interview, 16 April 1996.
318 Mager, "Gungubele and the Tambookie Location", 1164.
319 Ibid., 1160.
320 Ibid.
321 The word 'Gwatyu' is a war song, which was sung to propel warriors into fighting valiantly. Thus, the Gwatyu River took its name from the war song. For more on this aspect see D.L.P. Yali-Manisi, "Idabi LaseGwatyu", in P.T. Mtuze and R.H. Kaschula (eds), *Izibongo Zomthonyama* (Cape Town: Oxford University Press, 1993), 62-66; "UNkosi Sobantu Gungubele", in D.L.P. Yali-Manisi, *Yaphum' Ingqina* (Grahamstown: Institute of Social and Economic Research, Rhodes University, 1980), 91-93; A. Somana, *A Preliminary Study of the History of the Thembus of Western Thembuland* (Johannesburg: Nikel Kruse Publishers, 2010).
322 Majeke, *Missionaries in Conquest*, 71.
323 Peires, "Central Beliefs", 54.
324 Mager, "Gungubele and the Tambookie Location", 1160.

of these traditional leaders was that they had sustained losses as a result of their interaction with the colonial authorities. For example, uNkosi Maqoma had been "hounded continually by colonial raids",[325] before being expelled from the Kat River valley in 1829. UNkosi Maqoma, along with approximately 16,000 subjects, was forcefully evicted by the colonial forces from the Kat River area. His expulsion was precipitated by his attack on uNkosi Bawana's abaThembu, who had established themselves north of his area, and drove them into the colonial territory.[326] Queen Suthu, Chief Sandile's mother, as well as amaTshatshu chief Maphasa's sister, was "the first woman among the [ama]Ngqika to become Christianised, [who also] urged the fulfilling of this monstrous deed".[327] Sandile was also coerced to join the cattle-killing not only by his mother, Suthu, but also by his full brother, Prince Dondashe. However, the abaThembu regent, Chief-Regent Joyi, objected to the cattle-killing movement and supported *amagogotya*. At the suggestion of Warner, Chief Joyi visited the Tambookie location (Lady Frere) to dissuade *amathamba* from slaughtering their cattle and to refrain from planting. Chief-Regent Joyi remained there until after the 'great disappointment' in June 1857.

Once more, the interference of the government agent in the abaThembu affairs was evident, and it accentuated the schism between *amagogotya* and *amathamba*. In a bid to thwart the cattle-killing episode, Chief-Regent Joyi convened the abaThembu meeting to review the movement. However, Chief Fadana did not attend the meeting. He accelerated the movement more than ever before by insisting that Africans should slaughter all their cattle.

Furthermore, Fadana's subjects waged a massive campaign against abaThembu *amagogotya* in particular and southern abeNguni *amagogotya* in general. This move precipitated the rebellious reaction of *amagogotya* against their militant and provocative brothers and sisters – *amathamba*. UNkosi Fadana embarked on a policy of destroying cattle of non-abaThembu *amagogotya* from July 1857.[328] In August 1857, he launched an attack on Ndarhala of the amaNdungwana and took away 200 cattle from the latter. Since his invasion of Joyi in June 1857, Fadana's power rose and he also won many more of *amathamba*.

Though Chief-Regent Joyi had provided shelter to *amagogotya*, he later became disillusioned. He became hostile and negative to the starving believers owing to Fadana's provocative overtures, which manifested themselves in the latter undermining the former's authority. That conflict did not only lead to the decline of Joyi's sympathy but it also culminated in the physical conflict between Joyi and Fadana in June 1857. Following that physical conflict, the amaGcaleka-Xhosa who had taken refuge in abaThembuland, left it as it was increasingly becoming unsafe for *amagogotya*. Fadana's provocative activities were due to his quest for regaining land taken by uKumkani Hintsa (1789-1835) from his father between Bholotwa

---

325 Stapleton, "Reluctant Slaughter", 345.
326 Legassick, *Struggle for the Eastern Cape*, 30; Peires, "The British and the Cape", 484.
327 Majeke, *Missionaries in Conquest*, 71.
328 Monakali Njozela, Interview, Clarkebury Village, Ngcobo, 15 April 1996; Mlahleni Xundu, Interview, 19 April 1996.

and Indwe about thirty years previously. As a consequence, uNkosi Fadana embroiled the amaGcaleka-Xhosa in a war with the abaThembu from June to October 1857. Thereupon, Chief-Regent Joyi's support to amaGcaleka *amagogotya* came to an end. The war cost 38 abaThembu lives and Chief-Regent Joyi, who had killed Ncaphayi, uKumkani Sarhili's brother in the iNdlu yaseKunene of uKumkani Hintsa, in January 1858, came out unscathed. UKumkani Sarhili reluctantly kept a low profile "for fear of antagonizing Joyi's colonial allies".[329]

Fadana's provocative activities drew the attention of the colonial authorities who saw him as a threat to the stability and their authority. Since December 1856, abaThembu *amagogotya* had constantly called on the colonial government for military assistance against Fadana. Their call was turned down in spite of Warner's insistence that aid be given to African *amagogotya*. Following the Fadana–Joyi encounter, the Cape Parliament sent the Frontier Armed and Mounted Police (FAMP) under Commandant Walter Currie (1819-1872) to discipline Fadana. At the time, uNkosi Fadana and his subjects had sought sanctuary with uKumkani Sarhili. It was unfortunate for Fadana as the missionary H.T. Waters compelled Sarhili to expel Fadana from amaGcalekaland (the area between the Nciba and the Mbhashe Rivers). In this way, the missionary element had tried to drive a wedge into the abaThembu–Gcaleka relations much as it had torn the abaThembu apart.[330]

In another context, Reverend H.T. Waters at isiDutyini (St Mark's), an Anglican Mission Station, had sent Robert John Mullins, a 17-year-old English lad and catechist, to build a satellite station amongst Chieftainess Yeliswa's people, amaTshatshu. Mullins, who had been working as an adviser amongst Chief Ndarhala's amaNdungwana and regarded the chief as his father, was reluctant to leave Chief Ndarhala for Chieftainess Yeliswa. However, Mullins left Chief Ndarhala for Chieftainess Yeliswa's people, where he built a chapel and a boarding school.[331] Chieftainess Yeliswa's children and younger siblings of a 14-year-old Gungubele, namely Manathi, who was renamed Peter, and his sister, Nonestita, were the first boarders. Mullins described Manathi as a "very promising lad [who] kept the other boys in order".[332] For Mullins, Nonestita was suffering from nostalgia.[333] Meantime, the cattle-killing episode affected Chieftainess Yeliswa, and it brought turmoil in the Tambookie location (Lady Frere).

It is fitting to return to the plight of Chief Fadana as a result of the missionary factor in the abaThembu–Gcaleka relations during the Nongqawuse mania. Failing to find Fadana, Currie (1819-1872) launched an attack on uNkosi Qhwesha, and abaThembu and amaGcaleka *amathamba* residing in the Tambookie location (Lady Frere). Meantime, Inspector Charles Duncan Griffiths, Civil Commissioner and Resident Magistrate, successfully traced Fadana, finding him in uNkosi Fubu's country in Ngcobo. Griffiths and other colonists successfully

---

329 Peires, *The Dead Will Arise*, 279.
330 Zakade Bhuka, Interview, Gqobonco Village, Ngcobo, 19 July 1995; Monakali Njozela, Interview, 15 April 1996.
331 B. Nicholls, N. Charton and M. Knowling, *The Diary of Robert John Mullins 1883-1913* (Grahamstown, Rhodes University Department of History, 1998), 40-41.
332 Ibid., 41.
333 Ibid.

attempted to arrest Fadana before tethering him with a noose around his neck. Beaten and badly injured, Fadana was driven to Komani (Queenstown), and he and uNkosi Qhwesha were convicted by a Queenstown court of robbery. Qhwesha and Fadana were then sentenced respectively to one and seven years' hard labour for persecuting *amagogotya*.

Chieftainess Yeliswa felt the brunt of the outcomes of the failure of the cattle-killing delusion. Towards the end of 1857, Yeliswa, like uKumkanikazi Nonesi, was slumped into famine and despair. She was dependent on Mullins for food and supplies. When she could not get food from Mullins, "she was so cross on Christmas day that she did not attend the church service. But by the new year, she had cheered up somewhat and sent Mullins a gift of a sheep and a loaf of bread and asked for a shawl to go with her new dress".[334]

The end of 1857 saw Mullins, adviser to Yeliswa, leaving the Tambookie location (Lady Frere) for Britain, whereupon Reverend A.J. (John) Newton took over the running of St Peter's, replacing Mullins. St Peter's was about 500 yards from Queen Yeliswa's Great Place. St Peter's and its infrastructure is described by John Hemming as "the most credible [mission] of its kind"[335] outside of the Cape Colony. The station encompassed a chapel, school and printing press. Msheshwe, son of Somana, Chief Gungubele's brother, was educated at St Peter's. John Hemming gives a distinctly clear picture of the station as follows:

> The station consisted of a mission house with a good garden, behind which stood the church; a number of huts; small stone-built kraals, belonging to the school kaffirs; the trading stations of Messrs Thomson and Klette, (these premises being of considerable size), and a large garden enclosed by a stone and sod wall, belonging to the latter; the whole being situated in the Gwatyu stream, and lying between it and the hill on which Gungubele's huts stood.[336]

UKumkanikazi Nonesi's people were divided by the Nongqawuse debacle, as some killed their cattle and others refused to kill. Most of her people were sceptical about killing their cattle but did so out of fear of reprisals.[337] Having been invited by uKumkanikazi Nonesi to come and address the abaThembu in the Tambookie location (Lady Frere) towards the end of February 1857, Chief-Regent Joyi, who was raising the abaThembu heir on the Mbhashe River, "scolded those who had run after the delusions of the amaGcaleka [uKumkani] and advised the abaThembu to follow their own leaders lest they become 'servants' to Sarhili".[338] At the public meeting addressed by Chief-Regent Joyi, one of the attendees begged for forgiveness and made a plea for mercy that they had killed their cattle, singing the praise:

> We have been listening to a lie; we have been led astray by falsehood, and have got bewildered in the black mist ... Your children have not so far gone

---

334 Ibid., 45 and 47.
335 *Walter Stanford Papers*, D.4, 3 August 1857, Memorandum for Mr Solomon, Case of the Rev. A.J. Newton, 14.
336 Ibid.
337 Mager, "Gungubele and the Tambookie Location", 1164.
338 *Papers of Joseph Cox Warner*, Tambookie Agent, 1857-1858, J.C. Warner to Richard Southey, Resident Secretary, King William's Town, 24 February 1857.

astray that they may not be recovered; they have not all fallen; many have been wise enough not to listen to these lies; and many who have listened have only done so with one ear; the cattle are not all dead, and there is a little corn left for the children to eat ... Mercy! Mercy![339]

The results of the failure of the prophecy to produce the desired effects were disastrous for the abaThembu and other southern abeNguni communities. An example in point was an instance when the colonial forces ruthlessly attacked abaThembu *amathamba* in their campaign against Fadana. *Amagogotya* were also attacked along with *amathamba*. Starving and non-resisting, some of the abaThembu in the Tambookie location (Lady Frere) were killed, and those who survived were later evacuated by the Cape Government from their land, which was distributed amongst white settlers. This military campaign resulted in the abaThembu losing both political power and military prestige. The abaThembu's loss of cattle, from which they eked out their living, and loss of many lives, contributed to the weakness of the abaThembu. Thus, the loss of cattle and lives had been a shattering blow to the abaThembu.[340]

The resulting famine and the abaThembu's partial "dispossession by opportunistic colonial authorities"[341] further threw the abaThembu into disarray. Poverty caused them to look to whites for salvation, food, shelter and protection, losing hope in their basic economic unit. J.C. Warner advised the destitute abaThembu to seek work, that is – *ukuphangela*[342] – in road construction, "as a road linking the Tambookie location to Queenstown [Komani] was under construction".[343] Seeking work from white farmers, and in the construction of the Tambookie–Komani (Queenstown) road, the abaThembu became wage-earners and were thus further divided and scattered.[344] It is important to note that jobseekers entered the job market for the period during which they wanted sufficient money to purchase cattle they had lost during the mania. In the words of Mager, "in a post-famine context, entering the job market was seen as a short-term measure...; when an individual deemed that he had fulfilled his share [*impangelo*], he gave up work ... White farmers complained bitterly that those with sufficient to eat had no desire to work."[345] However, the 1860s saw the Tambookie location (Lady Frere) abaThembu having acquired small and large livestock and thus recovering from famine. For example, by 1864 the abaThembu returning from work had acquired no less than 16,000 properly certified sheep and goats besides cattle; the more successful reared 500 to

---

339 J.C. Warner to Richard Southey, Resident Secretary, King William's Town, 24 February 1857.
340 Thompson, "African Chiefdoms", 257; uNkosi Sindile Zwelodumo Mthikrakra, Interview, Qulugqu Village, Ngcobo, 30 December 2012.
341 Stapleton, "Reluctant Slaughter", 346.
342 In a precolonial context, *ukuphangela* means to do one's share, which implied taking part in raiding or fighting, and so receiving a share of the plunder as reward. For more on this, see Mager, "Gungubele and the Tambookie Location", 1165.
343 J.C. Warner to Richard Southey, Resident Secretary, King William's Town, 11 March 1857; 7 April 1857.
344 Thompson, "African Chiefdoms", 258.
345 *Cape of Good Hope Proceedings of and Evidence taken by Commission on Native Affairs 1865*, Joseph Cox Warner's Testimony, 11 February 1865, 82.

1,500 sheep.[346] Even so, the abaThembu survivors of the movement, by resorting to seek salvation in white towns, played into the hands of Grey who did not hesitate to exploit their circumstances "in order to impose white domination".[347]

Sir George Grey (1812-1898) had taken advantage of the prophecy, and manipulated the situation created by the prophetess, Nongqawuse. He had set out to subvert the status and power of the traditional leaders. He wanted to make traditional leaders dependent upon the support of the colonial government, and the people upon the colonial economy.[348] To that effect Governor Grey introduced resident magistrates with the traditional leaders. These magistrates were to take over some of the judicial powers from the chiefs and kings. For example, in 1856 he had induced all chiefs in British Kaffraria to accept white magistrates as having power to exact fines from their subjects. In return, these chiefs would be given annual stipends, so that, Governor Grey calculated, the economic unit of these chiefs would be money based.[349] Once having a money-based economy, chiefs and kings would become more inclined to earning wages and thus could serve as sources of labour on white farms. As a matter of fact, the payment of the traditional leaders in money compromised their dignity, as they were rendered to owe allegiance to the paymaster and be susceptible to utilisation towards the betrayal of his subjects.[350] Majeke aptly notes that "the money payment was supposed to be a convenient substitute for the revenue derived from fines, which the chief would lose if cases were tried by a White magistrate. But by submitting to such an arrangement he lost very much more than his revenue. He lost his very birthright, his chieftainship."[351]

Governor Grey had also advocated mixed African-and-white settlement in British Kaffraria so as to change the African outlook on life, thereby adopting civilisation by mingling. He further encouraged missionary work as a stimulus to break chiefly power. The cattle-killing movement and its outcomes provided the fertile ground for the realisation of Grey's objectives, viz. to break the power of the traditional leaders by destroying the tribal system, "a task for which he had received ample training, for he had just come from the subjugation of the Maoris of New Zealand by methods that were to become familiar in his new sphere of colonial activity".[352] It also served to accelerate the erosion of chiefly power.[353] The death of so many cattle made it impossible for traditional leaders to use pastoral patronage in the control of their people. Overall, the cattle-killing extremely weakened amaXhosa and abaThembu. As Majeke neatly puts it, "in the Cape Colony, however, the military power of the amaXhosa and the abaThembu

---

346 Ibid.
347 Peires, "Nongqawuse Catastrophe", 48.
348 Lewis, "Materialism and Idealism", 254.
349 Majeke, *Missionaries in Conquest*, 66.
350 Ibid., 67.
351 Ibid.
352 Ibid., 65.
353 Stapleton, "Reluctant Slaughter", 354, 356, 365 and 368.

had been broken; a vast labour force had been acquired and the Europeans could look forward to a period of unprecedented prosperity",[354] as a result of the Nongqawuse delusion.

Having dealt Fadana a heavy blow, Grey turned on Sarhili, who, the colonial authorities so alleged, had masterminded and enforced the cattle killing. Indeed, uKumkani Sarhili and uNkosi Mhala[355] (the latter, died in 1875) were regarded as "the two foremost supporters of the cattle-killing".[356] It was alleged that Sarhili had "plotted against the colony in bringing about the cattle-killing in spite of warnings"[357] by Governor Grey. With the purpose of expelling "Sarhili and the [ama]Gcaleka-Xhosa beyond the Mbhashe River so that by being at so great a distance from us ... he would no longer be capable of annoying us in the manner he has heretofore done."[358] Grey commanded Currie (1819-1872) to launch an attack on Sarhili. Currie enlisted the support of Major Gawler's police and Chief-Regent Joyi's abaThembu who had not participated in the movement,[359] to drive uKumkani Sarhili, so that Grey could with ease remodel amaGcalekaland, which was characterised by the colonial government's efforts to bring amaGcaleka under colonial rule by crushing the power of the traditional leaders and undermining as 'heathen' their culture, customs and traditions,[360] into British image. To that effect Grey was to execute this herculean task by establishing white settlement in Sarhili's political domain. This was an example of Grey playing one kingdom against the other with the purpose of realising his dreams. Joyi's abaThembu entered amaGcalekaland "from its north-eastern corner near Hohita"[361] in a bid to attack and cripple Sarhili. After the encounter, Sarhili lost 500 head of cattle to Currie, 70 cattle (calves excluded) and 4 horses to Gawler. Eighty-three amaXhosa lay dead. Sarhili was banished to Bomvanaland, Chief Moni's territory, in February 1858.

Thus, the aftermath of the Nongqawuse incident saw Governor Sir George Grey driving King Sarhili across the Mbhashe with a view to opening these lands for white settlement.[362] However, Governor Grey was succeeded by Governor Wodehouse, whose plans for white settlement were turned down by the British Government in London, which decided that white settlement should stop at the Nciba River. As a result, the whole country remained vacant between 1858 and 1864, and was patrolled by the "Frontier Armed Police" commanded by Sir Walter Currie (1819-1872). Idutywa Reserve was set aside for the *amagogotya* under ooNkosi Sigidi and Smith Mhala. However, uNkosi Mhala, writes the historian J.B. Peires, "was a strong advocate of the cattle-killing".[363] Meanwhile, the amaGcaleka were still homeless, destabilising

---

354 Majeke, *Missionaries in Conquest*, 74-75.
355 UNkosi Mhala was the brother of uNkosi Mdushane (d. 1829) and son of uNkosi Ndlambe (d. 1828).
356 Peires, "Central Beliefs", 60.
357 *Government Gazette*, 10 March 1858, 34.
358 Ibid., 41-42.
359 *Select Committee Reports on Native Affairs*, A.12 – '73, 33 and 35.
360 Mvenene, "African People of Gcalekaland", 59.
361 Peires, *The Dead Will Arise*, 284.
362 Peires, Telephone Interview, 30 July 2018.
363 Peires, "Central Beliefs", 49.

the Cape frontier. Wodehouse agreed for them to settle in Gatyana and Centane. The north part of amaGcalekaland, the present-day Cofimvaba and Xhalanga, was allocated to the abaThembu under uNkosi Mathanzima (alias Rhaxothi).[364]

Having been forced off his land at iSidutyini (St Mark's), Sarhili spent a fugitive life of eight years in forced exile.[365] He temporarily settled at Bholotwa. However, he was thoroughly expelled and chased across the Mbhashe River, living as a refugee for about eight years before being allowed back to Gatyana and Centane in 1865.[366] His land was then given to the abaThembu "from whom far more was expected than from Sarhili",[367] who was dubbed the troublemaker. Thenceforth, the Cape Government always stressed that the abaThembu had not won Sarhili's land "by their own arms, but had obtained it from the Government".[368] It would appear that the abaThembu had to pay a huge price for being given iSidutyini, near Sarhili's Great Place of Hohita, by, inter alia, collaborating with the Cape Government against other African societies. The AbaThembu had to accept the British officials as their head and denounce the authority of their traditional leaders. For example, Chief Mathanzima had to become independent of King Ngangelizwe; Ndarhala was to have authority over his father, Qhwesha, at Hohita.[369] Thus, the colonial authorities successfully played one traditional leader against the other, son against father and relative against the other.

No sooner did uKumkani Sarhili settle at Bholotwa than uNkosi Mphendukana, A! Mnqanqeni! stole amaGcaleka's horses.[370] Out of jealousy and greed, stimulated by the effects of the cattle-killing, Joyi "set out to commandeer Sarhili's horses for himself".[371] This precipitated the beginning of the second offensive whereupon Joyi was cornered at the Mgwali River near Clarkebury. Chief-Regent Joyi was captured though he was soon released by uKumkani Sarhili. The physical conflict between these two kingdoms further served to weaken the abaThembu. These two kingdoms could not jointly face the colonial forces, as they were not united owing to petty quarrels. They had played into the hands of their foes.

In a bid to accelerate his assault on kingship and chiefship, Governor Grey revived his policy of urging missionaries to undertake educational programmes. Hence the missionaries gained an increasingly wide hearing and exercised "their various functions on a much larger scale than before".[372] As a consequence, the abaThembu became more seriously impaired culturally, religiously, politically, militarily and economically. Upon the renewal of interest in missions' building, the All Saints' Mission was in 1861 begun by Reverend J. Gordon amongst the amaQwathi of uNkosi Fubu. It was built on the lower slopes of Khalinyanga Mountains. It was

---

364 Peires, Telephone Interview, 5 September 2018.
365 *Cape of Good Hope Debates in the Legislative Council*, 9 April 1886, 10.
366 Peires, Telephone Interview, 5 September 2018.
367 *Blue Book on Native Affairs*, G.27 – '74, 136.
368 Ibid.
369 Ibid.
370 UNkosi Mnqanqeni was uKumkani Sarhili's brother-in-law through his (Sarhili's) Great Wife.
371 Soga, *South-Eastern Bantu*, 247.
372 Majeke, *Missionaries*, 75.

a common feature of the nineteenth-century chiefs and kings to "receive missionaries for a variety of reasons, the least significant of which were theological".[373] UNkosi Fubu and his son, Dalasile, were no exception. UNkosi Fubu attended Church when he sought protection from uKumkani Sarhili.[374] UNkosi Dalasile used to pay regular visits to the mission to enjoy a slice of plum pudding and coffee.[375] Every Sunday of the chief's attendance at Church, there was a prayer for the Queen of England, followed by that for the chief of the amaQwathi.

After the cattle-killing movement, the commoners, chiefs and kings were torn apart more than ever before. Chiefs were torn from chiefs, parents from children, and husbands from wives as they had differed in their response, reaction and resistance to the prophecy. There was a period of uncertainty, mistrust, tension, hopelessness and despair. Those who survived were used by the Cape Government as sources of labour. *Amagogotya* were subjected to European magistrates and were placed in villages "into which no newcomers are admitted without the consent of the Government previously obtained".[376] They were settled at Dutywa by Cape Governor Grey. A Transkeian special magistrate was stationed there to exercise authority over *amagogotya*. Thus, their refusal to slaughter their cattle did not spare them any subjection to European control. To prevent any return of Sarhili, the Cape Government placed 'loyal' Africans along the banks of the Mbhashe River to be under white magistrates.

One other notable incident illustrating this division was when Chief-Regent Joyi and uNkosi Gqirhana (Mditshwa) of the Qweqwe amaMpondomise went to war in 1860 following mutual cattle-raiding activities. UNkosi Gqirhana had taken up residence west of the Mthatha River, at Cicirha and Zimbane, following a war with Mhlontlo, his nephew, over chieftainship. Having assisted Currie (1819-1872) against Sarhili in 1858, Chief-Regent Joyi, on being attacked by Mditshwa, sought the protection of amaGcaleka by offering Sarhili 4,000 head of cattle. UKumkani Sarhili reacted to the offer by seizing more cattle. Thus, Joyi had to face Sarhili and Mditshwa simultaneously. The Cape Government stood aloof as it had abrogated all treaties with the abaThembu chiefs. The abaThembu also remained aloof, and as a result of their non-commital attitude, the amaHala retreated to Qunu. However, the amaNqabe, the amaHegebe and the amaXesibe together with the abaThembu living between the Darhabe and the sea came to the rescue of Joyi. On their arrival, they found the amaMpondomise having evacuated the disputed land and moved to Tsolo, which had since become "the main position of Gqirhana's (Mditshwa's) [ama]Mpondomise".[377] In another vein, the amaGcaleka-Xhosa, who had taken refuge at Mngazana rather than assisting Joyi, captured the abaThembu cattle as the abaThembu were concentrating their energies on retaliating against the amaMpondomise. These cattle were taken in the rear and absence of their owners,

---

373 J.S. Galbraith, *Reluctant Empire* (Los Angeles: Greenwood, 1963), 95.
374 S. Green, *The First Hundred Years, 1873-1973: The Story of the Diocese of St John's in South Africa* (Umtata: Paul Mission Press, 1974), 38.
375 Ibid.
376 *Government Gazette*, 10 March 1858, 40 and 42.
377 Soga, *South-Eastern Bantu*, 481; uNkosi Zwelidumile Joyi, Interview, Bhaziya Village, Mthatha, 18 April 1996; Bhuka, Interview, 14 July 1995.

the abaThembu. For that reason, they are appropriately termed the cattle of *Umtsheko*.[378] However, he was faithful to the Cape Government, and like his forefathers, he was "prepared at any time to support government against its enemies".[379]

The year 1862 saw Chief-Regent Joyi expressing his wish to Currie to have his people become British subjects. This was generated by his fear that the amaGcaleka might launch an attack on the abaThembu. He wanted to prevent this looming invasion. In 1862, Prince Qheya, along with a 20-year-old Gungubele, heir to the amaTshatshu throne, and several of their agemates, attended a manhood lodge, underwent instruction and circumcision and graduated into manhood.[380] Before Prince Gungubele could assume chieftainship, the amaTshatshu mounted their horses, rode and visited the magistrate in Komani (Queenstown), John Hemming, to seek his approval for the installation of Gungubele. But to no avail as Hemming refused to formalise Gungubele's traditional leadership. Meantime, J.C. Warner, a government agent, was in full control in the Tambookie location (Lady Frere), using chiefs and headmen to keep order. He appointed Prince Gungubele as headman in charge of approximately 400 families residing on the Gwatyu, and later requested that uNkosikazi (iNkosi's wife) Yeliswa's authority and power be transferred to her son, Gungubele. In spite of acceding to Warner's request, the colonial government did not recognise the amaTshatshu chieftaincy.[381] UNkosi Gungubele's iKomkhulu (Great Place) was securely situated on top of a hill, which was

> about 200 feet high, was rugged in the extreme, covered with boulders of all sizes from that of a small house down to that of a cannonball, with trees and bushes pretty thickly scattered about it. The summit of this hill, on which stood Gungubele's huts and cattle kraals, is flat, and the hill forms a spur from the mountain dividing the country occupied by Gungubele from that of Vizi [an elderly chief], and is approached by two rugged footpaths.[382]

In 1863, Prince Qheya, who had come of age in 1859,[383] assumed power as the abaThembu king and took the name Ngangelizwe. He, however, did not relocate to the Tambookie location (Lady Frere). On his induction ceremony in Cacadu (Glen Grey), uKumkani Ngangelizwe was presented with a sum of £50 by J.C. Warner on behalf of the colonial government as a gesture of friendship. Warner promised Ngangelizwe a stipend of £52 a year provided he remained faithful to the Cape Government.[384] Warner and Reverend Hargreaves (uHagile) put it to Ngangelizwe that Cacadu (Glen Grey) residents were to interact with him through Warner, the government agent in Cacadu (Glen Grey). In this fashion, Ngangelizwe was perceived by Goverrner Philip

---

378 *Umtsheko* is a Xhosa noun that refers to the loose excreta from a loose stomach.
379 *Select Committee Report on Native Affairs*, A.12 – '73, 133.
380 Mager, "Gungubele and the Tambookie Location", 1168.
381 Ibid.
382 John Hemming, "A Narrative of the Proceedings in the Tambookie Location during the Kafir War of 1877-78", *The Cape Quarterly Review* incorporated in the *Cape Monthly Review*, 2, 6, January 1883, 100-101.
383 Mager, "Gungubele and the Tambookie Location", 1163.
384 Wagenaar, "History of the Thembu", 239; *Blue Book on Native Affairs*, 1885, 28.

Wodehouse as a bulwark against uKumkani Sarhili and as a potential ally against other African chiefdoms and kingdoms. Also, Joyi urged Ngangelizwe to maintain friendly relations with the Cape Government for fear of the dreaded amaGcaleka under uKumkani Sarhili, the amaQwathi of uNkosi Dalasile and the amaMpondo of uNkosi Nkqwiliso.

UNkosi Dalasile, though living in the abaThembu territorial domain, was disinclined to submit to uKumkani Ngangelizwe. The young and inexperienced abaThembu king initially contemplated embarking upon expansionism, but later abandoned his plans for fear of the colonial government, which aimed at undermining the abaThembu military potential. Having had scriptural lessons from Reverend Peter Hargreaves (uHagile) who "exerted a remarkable influence over the [aba]Thembu"[385] during his twenty-four-year stay at Clarkebury Mission station since 1858, Ngangelizwe developed an appetite for Christianity. Also, uKumkani Mthikrakra had entrusted the education of Prince Ngangelizwe to J.C. Warner.[386] Owing to monarchical commitments, however, Ngangelizwe's time was used more on titular responsibilities. The abaThembu being divided between *amagqobhoka* and *amaqaba* inveighed heavily against their king aligning himself with the reactionary Christianity.

Under these circumstances, uKumkani Ngangelizwe, in a bid to alleviate the threat posed by the amaGcaleka-Xhosa, the amaQwathi, the amaMpondo and whites, generously granted land to the amaMfengu of uNkosi Menziwa on the east bank of the Mbhashe River to act as a human buffer zone against outside attacks.[387] UNkosi Menziwa had taken refuge in abaThembuland during Mthikrakra's tenure as king. As though that was not enough, Ngangelizwe allocated farms on lease to whites in Mthatha in the hope that these farmers would serve as a buffer between him and the amaMpondo.[388] The area in which Ngangelizwe placed white farmers in return for benevolent relations was "one of the best parts of Ngangelizwe's territory".[389] This part later developed and became the town of Mthatha. Notwithstanding Ngangelizwe's generosity, his scheme was ineffectual as whites never came to his military aid in the ensuing conflict with other African kingdoms. The amaMfengu and whites were later to challenge the authority of the abaThembu king.

In 1864, Sir Philip Wodehouse, Cape Governor and High Commissioner, devised a scheme to settle the abaThembu east of the Tsomo River. Wodehouse was supported by frontier farmers, Richard Southey, the colonial secretary, and J.C. Warner, the colonial agent amongst the abaThembu. Intent on removing abaThembu from the Tambookie location (Lady Frere) and making place for white farmers, Warner vigorously induced these abaThembu chiefs, including uKumkanikazi Nonesi, to leave the Tambookie location (Lady Frere) and settle

---

385 Mears, *Clarkebury*, 21.
386 *Walter Stanford Papers*, D.10, E.J. Warner's Manuscript.
387 *Blue Book on Native Affairs*, 1885, 28.
388 W.D. Hammond-Tooke, "The 'Other Side' of Frontier History: A Model of Cape Nguni Political Process", in L. Thompson (ed.), *African Societies in Southern Africa* (London: Heinemann, 1978), 241-242; Phongomile S. Fadana, Interview, Mhlophekazi Village, Ngcobo, 27 August 1994.
389 *Select Committee Report on Native Affairs*, A.12 – '73, 34.

across the Indwe River into the land that had been confiscated from uKumkani Sarhili, after the Nongqawuse disaster.[390] Opponents of emigration were threatened with loss of land rights and the imposition of British rule on the opponents of emigration. Furthermore, Richard Southey and Wodehouse "offered the inducement that those [chiefs] who moved [across the Indwe River] would be allowed to live without interference from magistrates and free from taxation".[391]

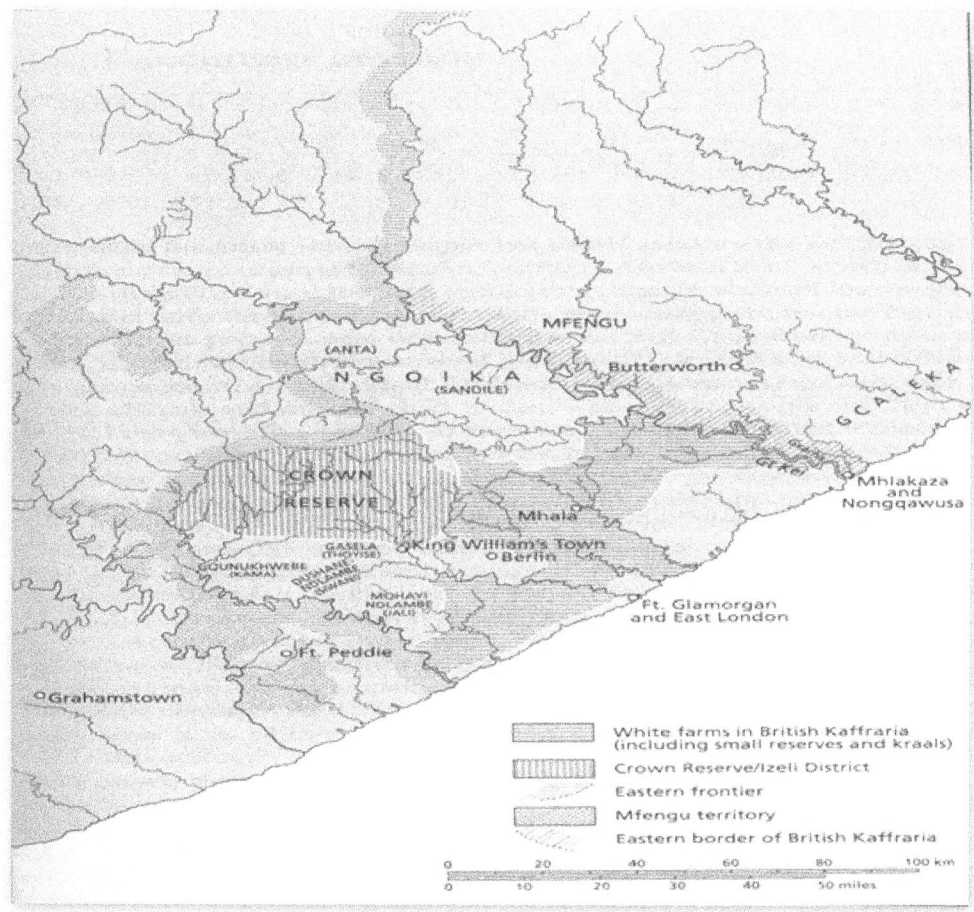

MAP 7: The Eastern Cape frontier area, 1858-1866[392]

---

390 Mager, "Gungubele and the Tambookie Location", 1168.
391 Ibid.
392 Price, *Making Empire*, xxix.

Rather than succumb to these threats, the abaThembu chiefs and Nonesi insisted that they be granted additional land between the Tsomo and the Indwe Rivers. Then Wodehouse extended the offer by making Cacadu, Xhalanga (both parts of Lady Frere) and St Mark's (iSidutyini at Cofimvaba) part of the offer. Nevertheless, there was looming danger in that arrangement because Cala and Cofimvaba had been uKumkani Sarhili's lands before he was forced to move to Bomvanaland in 1858.[393] The abaThembu occupation of these lands would, as it did, naturally escalate the abaThembu-Gcaleka conflict for some years to come. However, only four abaThembu minor chiefs, viz. Mathanzima of the amaHala, Ndarhala of the amaNdungwana, Gecelo (son of Tyhopho) of the amaGcina and Sitokhwe (son of Ndlela) of the amaQwathi moved to and occupied Cacadu, Xhalanga and iSidutyini, establishing Emigrant abaThembuland.[394] It was only these four chiefs who were properly called the Emigrant abaThembu. UNkosi Mathanzima assumed seniority, because he was the only chief of the Hala line; the others were Gcina, Ndungwana and Qwathi.[395] There they were treated by the colonial authorities as independent rulers. Furthermore, they received yearly allowances from the colonial government; their subjects were exempt from paying taxes to the colonial treasury. They collected *isizi*[396] and other dues from their subjects according to tradition. One of the promises made by the British was that European law would not be applied in Emigrant AbaThembuland and that traditional leadership would be allowed, whereas traditional leadership would be totally abolished in Tambookie location (Lady Frere), and chiefs no longer recognised.

Thus, these chiefs obtained the upper tract of Sarhili's erstwhile country, which came to be known as Emigrant abaThembuland.[397] Emigrant abaThembuland had its capital at Southeyville (Lubisi). It turned out too big to be handled by one magistrate, and it was later divided into two: St Mark's (Cofimvaba) and Xhalanga (Cala).

Even though Mathanzima, Sitokhwe Ndlela, Gecelo and Ndarhala had left the Tambookie location, however, uNkosi Gungubele (son of Maphasa) and uKumkanikazi Nonesi, regent for the abaThembu paramount, remained at the Tambookie location (Lady Frere). Richard banished uKumkanikazi Nonesi to amaMpondoland, and cancelled title to her farm on the Imvani, while uNkosi Gungubele's followers occupied the land vacated by his erstwhile neighbour, uNkosi Ndarhala.

---

393 Bongani Sithole, Interview, Mpandela Village, Mthatha, 19 April 1996; uNkosi Zwelidumile Joyi, Interview, Bhaziya Village, Mthatha, 18 April 1996; G.G. Thozamile Matshayana, Interview, Ngcobo District, 17 April 1996; Peires, Telephone Interview, 15 April 2020.
394 Mager, "Gungubele and the Tambookie Location", 1168.
395 Bongani Sithole, Interview, Mpandela Village, Mthatha, 19 April 1996; Peires, Telephone Interview, 15 April 2020.
396 *Isizi* refers to fines paid to the chief for murder, assault and other offences considered criminal, as distinguished from civil. For the amaMpondo, it also means an ox paid to the iNkosi or iKumkani when the death of a man is reported by his relatives, to console him for the loss of a subject. See *Blue Book on Native Affairs*, 1885, 26.
397 *Blue Book on Native Affairs*, G.27 – '74, 135.

It was a heavy blow to the abaThembu that on being given Sarhili's land, they were to acknowledge the headship of British officials, while E.J. Warner (being stationed at Southeyville) had become the Tambookie agent to be recognised as representing the British Government in Emigrant abaThembuland. E.J. Warner was to serve as the medium of communication between chiefs and the colonial government, using his influence in controlling the relationship between the chiefs.[398] It was also their (abaThembu) condition of occupation that they were to acknowledge the independence of Mathanzima from Ngangelizwe. This was the extremely high price the abaThembu had to pay.[399]

From these partly forced migrations and retention of land, it is deducible that Emigrant abaThembu, unlike amaGcaleka-Xhosa, did not lose much land to white farmers.[400] On the contrary, the abaThembu territory was extended from the Mthatha River to the Nciba (Kei) River. Nevertheless, the abaThembu were thus further subdivided and scattered. Western civilisation and revolutionary Christianity had penetrated abaThembu traditional beliefs and practices, which had a cohesive impact on the abaThembu socio-economic and political constitution. The colonial authorities had already emasculated chiefly power and control by exploiting inter- and extra-tribal rivalries, divisions and tensions.

In 1865, uKumkani Sarhili, having spent eight years in exile, was allowed back to part of his former territory at Hohita by Wodehouse, allowing them to settle in Gatyana and Centane, while the abaThembu continued to occupy the north part of amaGcalekaland (Cofimvaba and Xhalanga) under the original uNkosi Mathanzima (or Rhaxothi).[401] Precisely after 1865, Sarhili's land was split four ways: amaGcaleka returning to Gatyana and Centane; Dutywa reserved for *amagogotya*; amaMfengu occupied Gcuwa, Ngqamakhwe and Tsomo; abaThembu settled in Cofimvaba and Xhalanga.

UKumkani Sarhili's conditions of re-occupation of his former land were, inter alia, that never again could he stir up "trouble and unrest upon the extreme Eastern border".[402] As Lieutenant-General H. Torrens put it:

> The Gcaleka chief, Kreli, after a fugitive life of eight years, has at length, at his own request, been allocated upon the conditions imposed by my Ministers, within colonial territory, so that a grave source of trouble and unrest upon the extreme Eastern border may be regarded as closed.[403]

At the time, some abaThembu from west of the Indwe River had been induced to move to, and settle near, Hohita. This was intended to play the abaThembu king against the amaGcaleka-Xhosa king by the colonial government. Prompted by a desire to bring relief to

---

398 *Blue Book on Native Affairs*, 1885, 26.
399 *Blue Book on Native Affairs*, G.27 – '74, 136.
400 Davenport, *South Africa*, 57.
401 Peires, Telephone Interview, 5 September 2018.
402 *Cape Legislative Council Debates*, 9 April 1886, 10.
403 Ibid.

the congestion in amaMfengu areas in the Ciskei, Wodehouse also compelled amaMfengu to leave Kamastone, Oxkraal and Ngqushwa (Peddie) for Hohita. Also, Wodehouse planned for the amaNgqika under uNkosi Sandile to settle around Gcuwa (Butterworth), intending to settle their lands with white farmers. But Sandile refused, not only knowing that King Sarhili was his senior brother, but also because "he was supposedly afraid to live beyond the reach of the British protection".[404] This created a crisis for Governor Wodehouse, because the amaGcaleka were already on their way home, and he was fearful that they would enter Gcuwa.[405]

Governor Wodehouse, therefore, authorised Sir Walter Currie, the Police Commander, to recruit amaMfengu to settle the lands between the amaGcaleka and uNkosi Mathanzima's abaThembu. AmaMfengu were attracted by the lands, but they were also beginning to feel the pressure of white government, especially regarding a new law that they had to carry 'certificates of citizenship' (passes). The situation was especially bad in Fort Beaufort where the iNkosi of the amaMfengu, Zazela, refused and clashed with the white magistrate.

The circumstances leading to the introduction of passes deserves explanation. As far back as 29 June 1857, the Cape legislature passed two acts to deter the massive and rapid increase of the amaMfengu in British Kaffraria. Act No. 23, the first act, reaffirmed the prohibition on 'Kafirs' and 'other native foreigners' entering the Colony without passes and provided up to twelve months' hard labour as the penalty for contravening this regulation.[406]

The second, Act No. 24, recognised the possibility that 'Colonial Fingoes' could be mistaken for other Africans without passes and provided them with certificates of citizenship. Possession of certificates guaranteed the right to own land.[407] In this connection, Lewis regards these regulations as marking the beginning of South Africa's first effective pass system.[408]

The year 1864 saw the colonial parliament passing Act No. 17, which prescribed that amaMfengu citizenship certificates be renewed on a yearly basis.[409] Being antagonised by the Act, as they intepreted it as a ploy to force them off the land and out of the Colony itself, amaMfengu in Somerset East and Bedford refused to accept the certificates in January 1865. UNkosi Zazela, who was influential amongst the amaMfengu, was leading the defiance campaign. He refused to obey the new regulation, but later on, he reluctantly acquiesced

---

404 Stapleton, "The Expansion of a Pseudo-Ethnicity in the Eastern Cape", 236.
405 Peires, Telephone Interview, 5 September 2018.
406 Stapleton, "The Expansion of a Pseudo-Ethnicity in the Eastern Cape", 241.
407 *Cape Colonial Statute* (hereafter CCS), An Act for More Effectually Preventing Kaffirs from Entering the Colony without Passes, No. 23 (1857); CCS, An Act for Preventing Colonial Fingoes, and Certain Other Subjects of Her Majesty, from being Mistaken for Kaffirs, and Thereby Harassed and Aggrieved, No. 24 (1857).
408 J. Lewis, "An Economic History of the Ciskei, 1848-1900" (PhD. Thesis, University of Cape Town, 1984), 519.
409 CCS, An Act for Amending the Law Regarding Certificates of Citizenship, No. 17 (1864).

in the demands of the law due to the fact that he was completely dependent upon the administration for his salary and authority.[410]

In June 1865, uNkosi Mavuso and an armed party of 2,000 male amaMfengu crossed the Nciba River and inspected the land east of the Nciba River for its suitability as a settlement area. On returning to the Ciskei, uNkosi Mavuso declared that he was satisfied with the land they were to occupy in the former Transkei, and "gave the names of sixteen other headmen from Fort Beaufort, Victoria, former British Kaffraria and Oxkraal who had agreed to move".[411] Surprisingly, uNkosi Mavuso did not migrate to the former Transkei; "several of the Peddie [Ngqushwa] chiefs refuse[d] to move".[412] In July 1865, a considerable number of amaMfengu moved from the less densely populated districts of eDikeni (Alice) and Fort Beaufort, mounted and armed with guns, apparently quite pleased and proud of the prospect before them.[413] Furthemore, some amaMfengu from Kamastone migrated through Komani heading for the former Transkei, "accompanied by 5 wagons filled with grain and produce, about 1,000 sheep and 100 cattle".[414]

Even though 40,000 amaMfengu trekked from the Colony,[415] many of the senior amaMfengu chiefs of eDikeni (Alice) and Ngqushwa (Peddie), like Mabandla and Njokweni, declined to move on to uKumkani Sarhili's land. Those who moved were mostly of lesser status, and whose chieftainships were not being recognised in British Kaffraria,[416] which was annexed in March 1865 to the Cape Colony to facilitate the administration of land and labour. These chiefs considered migration as providing an opportunity to acquire more land, cattle, power and influence.[417] Under these circumstances, Captain Veldtman Bhikitsha, who had assisted Sir Walter Currie in the recruitment and settlement processes, rose to prominence. A prominent and the most influential amaMfengu headman in Gcuwa (Butterworth),[418] Bhikitsha did not only assist amaMfengu headmen to embark on a vicious campaign of land grabbing, but he was also a veteran of many campaigns against the amaXhosa chiefdoms and a government-appointed chief, acquiring the largest share.[419]

---

410 *Cape Parliamentary Paper* (hereafter CPP), Return Showing the Number of Titles of Land Issued to Fingoes and Correspondence Between the Government and the Resident Magistrate of Fort Beaufort on the Refusal of Zazela and His Tribe to take Out New Certificates, A56 (1865).
411 Stapleton, "The Expansion of a Pseudo-Ethnicity in the Eastern Cape", 245.
412 *Grahamstown Journal*, 26 June 1865.
413 Ibid.
414 *Eastern Province Herald*, 8 and 11 July 1865.
415 Stapleton, "The Expansion of a Pseudo-Ethnicity in the Eastern Cape", 237.
416 Peires, Telephone Interview, 30 July 2018.
417 Stapleton, "The Expansion of a Pseudo-Ethnicity in the Eastern Cape", 245.
418 W. Beinart and C. Bundy, *Hidden Struggles in Rural South Africa: Politics and Popular Movements in the Transkei and Eastern Cape, 1890-1930* (Johannesburg: Ravan Press, 1987), 93.
419 CPP, Correspondence with Reference to the Principles, Conditions and Detailed Arrangements on Which the Fingo Exodus has been Carried Out, A14 (1867), Currie to Colonial Secretary, 28 July 1865, 5.

At first, there was something like chaos, because the entire legal status of the amaMfengu settlement was in doubt, and Captain Charles Cobbe, the first magistrate, was a drunkard, who could not speak isiXhosa and often resorted to the whip. Cobbe was blamed for the regression of amaMfengu to their 'tribal' and 'barbaric' practices on arriving in the former Transkei.[420] It was only when the capable Captain Matthew Blyth was appointed in 1869 as the magistrate that the situation stabilised, after whom the school of Blythswood was named. The amaMfengu's experience of living in the former Transkei steered them onto the path towards 'civilisation'.[421] This marked the beginning of the education and agricultural progress for which amaMfengu became well-known and formed the peasantry made famous by Colin Bundy.[422]

The amaMfengu removal and exodus from west of the Nciba River was based on the myth of the 'empty' land. As Stapleton observes, "a fundamental tenet of the orthodox version of the exodus is that all of former [ama]Gcalekaland was uninhabited"[423] after 1858. Yet, not all amaGcaleka had left Gcalekaland in 1858; many might have been in hiding.

Thus, Sarhili eventually settled "on a small coastal strip of 1,000 square miles"[424] along the coast between the Nciba and the Mbhashe Rivers, which was equivalent to a third of his erstwhile territory. UKumkani Sarhili's discontent was therefore justified, considering land losses sustained by his people. The enmity between the amaGcaleka-Xhosa and the amaMfengu having started in 1835 when the latter, with the military assistance of the Cape Government and the spiritual support of Reverend John Ayliff (1797-1862), ran deep. Reverend John Ayliff, maintains Peires, had "espoused the cause of the beaten [ama]Mfengu refugees among the [ama]Xhosa and protected them against the authority of his host, the [ama]Xhosa king Hintsa."[425] A yawning gap between Sarhili and the abaThembu stretched even further, with catastrophic consequences for the southern abeNguni communities. External factors having been responsible for such unhealthy atmosphere escalated unfriendly relations between the abaThembu and amaGcaleka-Xhosa, and within the abaThembu themselves.

From the above account, it is abundantly clear that by 1865 the abaThembu occupied the greater part of lands from which uKumkani Sarhili had been evicted. AbaThembu had also been evicted from part of the Tambookie location (Lady Frere) through the influence of white farmers who "maintained that the [aba]Thembu posed a threat to the stability of the area".[426] However, the coming into being of Emigrant abaThembuland was a gradual

---

420 Theal, *History of South Africa since 1795*, vol. v. (London, 1908), 53.
421 Ibid., 44-69; John Ayliff and Joseph Whiteside, *History of the Abambo* (otherwise known as Fingoes) (Butterworth, 1912), 60-62.
422 Bundy, *The Rise and Fall*, 57.
423 Stapleton, "The Expansion of a Pseudo-Ethnicity in the Eastern Cape", 246.
424 C.G. Coetzee, "The Ciskei: Historical Background", in W.C. Els, E.J. de Jager, C.G. Coetzee, O.F. Raum, G.C. Oosthuizen, P.A. Duminy, D.L. Brown, J.H. Smith and C.C. Holdt, *The Ciskei: A Bantu Homeland* (Fort Hare: Fort Hare University Press, 1970), 84.
425 Peires, "The British and the Cape", 488.
426 Wagenaar, "History of the Thembu", 73.

process. Internal and external forces at work were responsible for this division within the House of Ngubengcuka (abaThembu). For example, the appointment of two chief-regents in abaThembuland, the abaThembu divisive attitudes towards, and reaction to, the colonists as well as the cattle-killing mania all contributed to the division of abaThembuland. So did the abaThembu clash with the amaGcaleka-Xhosa, amaMpondo of uNkosi Ndamase, eldest son of Faku, and amaMpondomise of uNkosi Mditshwa. The white man's quest for land, Governor Grey's renewal of missionary activities resulting in uKumkani Ngangelizwe being converted to Christianity, much against the will of his people, and the missionary assault on traditionalism also culminated in the emergence of Emigrant abaThembuland in 1865.

5

THE DIVISION OF ABATHEMBULAND INTO MAGISTERIAL DISTRICTS, 1865-1881

UKumkani Sarhili had been allowed by Governor Wodehouse to re-occupy a third of his former territory in 1865. The greater part of his erstwhile territory had been granted to the emigrant abaThembu under ooNkosi Mathanzima, Ndarhala, Gecelo and Sitokhwe Ndlela. This area was thenceforth termed Emigrant abaThembuland. In a bid to diminish Ngangelizwe's power and to implement the policy of divide-and-rule, the Cape Government recognised the independence of these chiefs in Emigrant abaThembuland. It was non-traditional and divisive that abaThembu Agent Warner (1852-1865), impressed upon these chiefs that Mathanzima, though by rank and birth junior to Ngangelizwe, was to be independent of the uKumkani of the abaThembu, Ngangelizwe; that Ndarhala was to rule independently of his father, Qhwesha, who had fought in the War of Mlanjeni.[427] What was more, uKumkanikazi Nonesi was banished to amaMpondoland following Mathanzima's report to the Cape Government that "Nonesi desired to take possession of several kraals in Mathanzima's location".[428] The Cape Government's recognition of Emigrant abaThembu chiefs and non-recognition of uKumkani Ngangelizwe's supremacy were to destroy abaThembu unity and to sow seeds of antagonism amongst abaThembu traditional leaders. Indeed, it was Warner's objective to have "the two [aba]Thembu sections ... divided into two separate antagonistic blocs".[429] This arrangement precipitated unfriendly relations between the abaThembu and amaGcaleka-Xhosa. And more was to flow from these strained relations.

In spite of strained abaThembu–Gcaleka relations owing to inter-tribal tensions and extra-tribal relations, uKumkani Ngangelizwe married Princess Nomkhafulo,

---

427 *Blue Book on Native Affairs*, G.27 – '74, 136; Mager, "Gungubele and the Tambookie Location", 1161.
428 *Blue Book on Native Affairs*, G.27 – '74, 136.
429 Wagenaar, "History of the Thembu", 242.

uKumkani Sarhili's daughter, in 1866 as his Great Wife. Princess Nomkhafulo then took the name Novili. Princess Nongxokozelo, the daughter of uNkosi Ncaphayi, uKumkani Hintsa's Right-Hand House son, became uKumkanikazi Novili's *impelesi* (attendant).[430] The purpose of this marriage was diplomatic. It was intended to effect, foster and retain good neighbourliness between the abaThembu and amaGcaleka-Xhosa. *Lobola* was paid by the abaThembu and so it was a communal undertaking. *Lobola*, which has no English equivalent, was practised for a fruitful marriage.[431] The term *lobola* had – and still has – diverse meanings. According to Nomalanga Mkhize, "lobola is a form of compensation to the bride's family because of the kind of talent and creative labour energy that her family transfers to another family."[432] She goes on to state, "These days of course lobola is complicated by the capitalist economy, the reality that most young men just do not have the means to meet a hefty cost, and the young couple still has to contend with the costs of a formal wedding."[433]

Being the traditional means of transaction between these kingdoms, *lobola* was to cement kinship threads between the amaGcaleka-Xhosa and abaThembu. And, if they remained untampered with, these kinship ties would strengthen these kingdoms. Unfortunately, the abaThembu were already divided by external forces, and furthermore the Cape Government soon interfered in abaThembu–Gcaleka relations. Though the marriage was to enhance King Ngangelizwe's traditional autonomous hegemony, factors counterproductive to maintaining strong and healthy ties between these kingdoms soon set in. European interference in these relations had devastating consequences for the abaThembu and amaGcaleka. As a result of the Cape Government's interference, these two kingdoms were never united. Worse still, there emerged divisions within the abaThembu themselves.

European Interference in the abaThembu-Gcaleka Relations, 1866-1875

The customary union between uKumkani Ngangelizwe and Princess Nomkhafulo initially appeared to be a natural formula to ease tensions between uKumkani Sarhili's amaGcaleka and uKumkani Ngangelizwe's abaThembu. It soon proved to be a truce as a result of the colonial government's interference in abaThembu–Gcaleka internal relations. This interference can be seen in relation to the colonial government's settling of Emigrant abaThembu in uKumkani Sarhili's erstwhile territory. This resettlement scheme was more destructive than curative on amaGcaleka–Thembu tensions. Furthermore, the emigration of 1865 had brought about the breaking down of cordial relations between the abaThembu and ama-Gcaleka–Xhosa.

---

430 S.E.K. Mqhayi, "USarhili", in W.G. Bennie (ed.), *The Stewart Xhosa Readers Standard vi* (Lovedale: Lovedale Press, 1970), 103; MSC 57, 26 (21), *Statement of Elias Xelo*, March 1882, 1; Saunders, *The Annexation of the Transkeian Territories: Archives Year Book 1976* (Pretoria: Government Printer, 1978), 46-47.
431 Callinicos, *A People's History of South Africa*, vol. 1, 3.
432 Nomalanga Mkhize, *Lobola* and its Many Diverse Meanings, *Daily Dispatch*, 16 April 2019, 9.
433 Ibid.

uKumkani Ngangelizwe's granting to certain Afrikaner and abeSuthu families of land along the Tsomo River in Emigrant abaThembuland in 1867 led to conflict between the abaThembu king and Warner (British Resident, 1865-1869). Moreover, uNkosi Mathanzima had complained to Warner of uKumkani Ngangelizwe's attempt to undermine his authority in Emigrant abaThembuland.[434] Warner saw this looming conflict between the sons of uKumkani Mthikrakra as an opportunity to be used to divide these traditional but unequal leaders. He sought to represent uKumkani Ngangelizwe as a tyrant from whose authority uNkosi Mathanzima and other lesser chiefs should secede and seek 'British protection'. In this issue, it became clear that the Cape Government was determined to interfere in abaThembu affairs with the purpose of dividing and controlling the abaThembu. Having used Ngangelizwe's action as a justification for the Cape Government's interference in the abaThembu affairs, Warner proceeded to humiliate uKumkani Ngangelizwe who had been opposed to the abaThembu emigration of 1865.[435]

Warner displayed contempt for the abaThembu king by expelling from Emigrant abaThembuland farmers who, on Ngangelizwe's concession, had resided around the Tsomo River. This was meant to diminish the status of the abaThembu king in the eyes of these farmers. He further put it to the abaThembu king that he had no legal jurisdiction over the Emigrant abaThembu and that he was only their nominal head. This was to precipitate, exacerbate and further widen the gulf between the abaThembu king and the Emigrant abaThembu. He also put it to Ngangelizwe that the Emigrant abaThembu chiefs, and not the king, had been granted legal title to their land. This was to reverse abaThembu communal land ownership and to replace it with the title system. He went on to threaten the abaThembu king that his incessant interference in Emigrant abaThembu affairs would result in the Cape Government withdrawing his annual stipend.[436] To these threats by Warner, Richard Southey, Cape Colonial Secretary, objected as they would probably enrage the Cape Government. Hence, on realising the ineffectiveness and futility of Warner's attempts to present Ngangelizwe in a dark light, Governor Wodehouse commanded Warner to resign as British resident in the former Transkeian territories, on the pretext of financial constraints. This move by the Cape Government was tantamount to "turning the tables on Warner",[437] who retired in 1870.

Not only did uKumkani Ngangelizwe face problems emanating from uNkosi Mathanzima's quest for independent authority but he had to contend with setbacks created by his uncle, uNkosi Mnqanqeni. Mnqanqeni had remained at the Mbhashe area when King Mthikrakra, his brother, was at the Imvani (White Kei). The colonial government accorded uNkosi Mnqanqeni recognition as a chief. Thus, both Mnqanqeni and Mathanzima were given recognition by the colonial authorities, while uKumkani Ngangelizwe was being undermined. It is worth noting that uKumkani Ngangelizwe's "activities and experiences showed that his embrace of colonial

---

434 Sizakele Matiwane, Interview, 29 June 1995; Monakali Njozela, Interview, 17 June 1997.
435 Mncedi Phondolwendlovu Nyoka, Interview, Tyhalarha Village, Mthatha, 7 September 1994.
436 Wagenaar, "History of the Thembu", 243.
437 Davenport, *South Africa*, 124.

law came about as a result of induced compliance"[438] by the Cape Government. Yekela opines that "the induced consent brought forth benefits like the house that the government built for Ngangelizwe on the site of the Wellington prison in Mthatha, [which] gave [his son] Dalindyebo an invaluable opportunity to attend St John's Missionary school."[439]

Such acts were not conducive to unity, but were intended to play one traditional leader against the other. Worse still, Chief Mnqanqeni vainly tried to break away from the king's authority. In 1870, he gained the support of other chiefs at the expense of the king. Further, uNkosi Dalasile of amaQwathi in Ngcobo also despised Ngangelizwe. Though nominally subordinate to Ngangelizwe, Dalasile had "as great, if not a greater, number of adherents than Ngangelizwe".[440] Ngangelizwe's settling on the east banks of the Mbhashe River of the amaZizi under Menziwa, and white farmers in the Slang River area in 1869 did not consolidate his kingdom. Thus, his attempt to strengthen his kingdom and to check Dalasile's might did not have the desired effects. Owing to Warner's attempts to drive a wedge between Mathanzima, on the one hand, and Ngangelizwe and Nonesi, on the other, the abaThembu became too weak to militarily face Dalasile's amaQwathi.[441]

While the split was already evident in the House of uKumkani Ngubengcuka, Ngangelizwe exacerbated matters by severely beating his Great Wife, uKumkanikazi Novili, in 1870 (see Umnombo 7: The House of Ngangelizwe). When uKumkanikazi Novili fled to her father, uKumkani Sarhili, to report the matter, "Kreli [Sarhili] had already heard that Gangelizwe [Ngangelizwe] had broken Novili's leg whilst beating her".[442] So angry was Sarhili that he wanted to punish Ngangelizwe.[443] UKumkani Sarhili sent messengers to his son-in-law, uKumkani Ngangelizwe, expressing that "I intend to report this matter to government and get permission to punish you."[444] Following uKumkani Sarhili apprising the colonial government of his intention to punish Ngangelizwe, the government warned "however, that he was not to attack mission stations nor molest British subjects".[445]

Sensing a looming danger for the Colony, E.J. Warner, the abaThembu Agent, warned that attempts should be made to prevent any assistance given to Ngangelizwe either by the amaMfengu of uNkosi Menziwa or Emigrant abaThembu. Warner thought this would lead to the amaRharhabe-Xhosa aiding uKumkani Sarhili. He reasoned that the involvement of amaRharhabe-Xhosa would then embroil the whole of the former Transkei in war and "would very probably bring on a colonial war".[446] James Ayliff, Civil Commissioner, had even alleged

---

438 Yekela, "Unity and Division", 43.
439 Ibid.
440 *Blue Book on Natives Affairs*, G.27 – '74, 137.
441 UNkosi Jonginyaniso Mthikrakra, Interview, Sithebe Village, Mthatha, 29 April 1994; Bongani Sithole, Interview, Mpandela Village, Mthatha, 19 April 1996.
442 MSC 57, 26(21), *Statement of Elias Xelo*, Councillor of uKumkani Ngangelizwe, 31 March 1882.
443 Master, "Thembuland", 64; MSC 57, 26(21), *Statement of Elias Xelo*, Councillor of uKumkani Ngangelizwe, 31 March 1882.
444 MSC 57, 26(21), *Statement of Elias Xelo*, Councillor of uKumkani Ngangelizwe, 31 March 1882.
445 Ibid.
446 *Select Committee Report on Native Affairs*, A.12 – '73, 181.

that uNkosi Sitokhwe had shown willingness to aid Ngangelizwe, and also that amaRharhabe-Xhosa intended to support Sarhili "even if that would lead them to hostilities with the English".[447] It is not far-fetched to point out that even though the abaThembu–Gcaleka war would probably involve the Colony, the prevention of the abaThembu and amaMfengu from uniting against the amaGcaleka-Xhosa could be seen as a strategy to keep them apart so that they could never rise against the Colony. Similarly, the fear that a united abaThembu-Mfengu war against amaGcaleka-Xhosa would lead to a united amaXhosa rallying behind uKumkani Sarhili could be viewed in the context of the government's tradition of ensuring that southern abeNguni kingdoms remained disjointed.

Umnombo (Genealogy) 7: The House of Ngangelizwe[448]

Ngangelizwe	iNdlu yaseKunene	iQadi of (iNdlu eNkulu)	iQadi of iNdlu yaseKunene
Dalindyebo	Thwalikhulu	Silimela	Ndumiso
Jongilizwe	Gqoloma	Busobengwe	Dinizulu
Jonguhlanga	Mgcawezulu	Nkosana	Vulindlela
Zwelibanzi		Ntsika	

The Cape Government intervened in the abaThembu-Gcaleka affair by persuading Sarhili to accept forty head of cattle as a compensation for the injuries inflicted on his daughter. The Cape Government in so reacting wished to prevent Sarhili gaining victory over the abaThembu and thereby securing their land. This would enable him to challenge the government and seek land he had lost after the Nongqawuse debacle. This intervention, therefore, was not meant solely to salvage Ngangelizwe but to maintain the balance of power, so that the government could manipulate the abaThembu king. Fear of Sarhili, who was militarily stronger than Ngangelizwe and resented Ngangelizwe's beating of Nomkhafulo, prompted Ngangelizwe to ask E.B. Chalmers, Resident with Ngangelizwe, to cede abaThembuland to the British Government in 1872. However, uNkosi Dalasile objected to the extension of white control to abaThembuland in spite of Ngangelizwe's reiteration of his desire not only to be taken as a British subject but also to "surrender his [kingship] to the British Government".[449] Hence, it failed for the time being.

As a result of Ngangelizwe's brutal attack on his wife, war broke out between the abaThembu and the amaGcaleka-Xhosa in 1872, as uKumkani Sarhili and his heir by his Great Wife, uKumkanikazi Nohute, Prince Sigcawu, launched an attack on abaThembuland.[450] In spite of the abaThembu–Gcaleka war of September to October 1872 in which King Ngangelizwe's might was broken, King Ngangelizwe risked another step by ordering his *iphakathi*

---

447 Ibid.
448 Author's version, 2019.
449 *Blue Book on Native Affairs*, G.27 – '74, 137; *Select Committee Report on Native Affairs*, A.12 – '73, 180.
450 *Blue Book on Native Affairs*, 1885, 29.

(councillor), Ndevu, to kill Nongxokozelo in 1875. Ngangelizwe gave this order owing to his "fit of uncontrollable passion".[451] Ngangelizwe was dependent for military support on Menziwa's amaMfengu along the Mbhashe River, Dalasile's amaQwathi at Ngcobo and the Jumba's abaThembu near the Tsomo River. However, uNkosi Menziwa, who had been instrumental in halting the amaGcaleka attack on the abaThembu in 1872, then publicly announced his future neutrality should war break out between Ngangelizwe and Sarhili. He deemed it unfair that Ngangelizwe had caused the death of Nongxokozelo, but in fear of uKumkani Ngangelizwe, he fled to the Dutywa Reserve.[452] On 5 August 1875, uNkosi Menziwa and his subjects (approximately 600 in number) crossed the Mbhashe River.[453] Cape Governor Barkly (1870-1877) along with Brownlee, Secretary for Native Affairs (1872-1878), ordered the return of Menziwa with the aim of preventing Sarhili from gaining more military power over the abaThembu and thereby dominating the area.[454] It is logical to point out that the colonial government was all out to prevent any situation, which would lead to any of the southern abeNguni kingdoms becoming so strong as to challenge the Colony. All it wanted was to prop up the abaThembu so as to be in a position to resist Sarhili, so that Sarhili could never be militarily strong enough as to present a threat and challenge to the Cape Government.

Meanwhile, uKumkani Ngangelizwe and some abaThembu fled to Clarkebury Mission and hid in the kitchen.[455] Reverend Hargreaves, a Wesleyan missionary who stayed at Clarkebury for twenty-four years (1858-1882), successfully persuaded uKumkani Sarhili to desist from further attacks, claiming that this would disturb uKumkanikazi Victoria of England. Hargreaves begged uKumkani Sarhili to return to his country across the Mbhashe. UNkosi Mgudlwa expressed his exasperation at uKumkani Ngangelizwe's behaviour, saying that "ever since you became a chief we have had no rest. You ill-use your wives".[456] Following uKumkani Sarhili's departure, uKumkani Ngangelizwe and the abaThembu came out of their hiding places to applaud Reverend Hargreaves.[457] Thus, uKumkani Ngangelizwe's military weakness to face the amaGcaleka army was responsible for the abaThembu seeking 'protection' from Hargreaves, who sought to evangelise them. For being given shelter and protection by Reverend Hargreaves, however, the abaThembu had to show allegiance to the mission station by aligning themselves with Christianity. Thus, the weaker the nation, the more likely it would be inclined to align itself with Christianity.

---

451 Saunders, *Annexation*, 47.
452 Soga, *South-Eastern Bantu*, 252.
453 *Blue Book on Native Affairs*, 1885, 30.
454 J.C. Molteno Papers: Barkly to Molteno, 2 September 1875.
455 W.T. Brownlee, *Reminiscences of a Transkeian* (Pietermaritzburg: Shuter and Shooter, 1975), 72.
456 MSC 57, 26(21), *Statement of Elias Xelo*, Councillor of uKumkani Ngangelizwe, 31 March 1882.
457 Mears, *Clarkebury*, 23; *Statement of Xelo*, 10.

Viewed critically, the Cape Government used the brutal attack of uKumkani Ngangelizwe on uKumkanikazi Novili and the death of Nongxokozelo to further its own interests of driving a wedge between these two kingdoms so as to weaken them. The abaThembu king's power was thoroughly subjected to the political pressures of the time. These incidents were used to force uKumkani Ngangelizwe into the orbit of the Cape Government. The Cape Government was out to tear these kingdoms apart and to sap the military strength of Sarhili. So Sarhili and Ngangelizwe, being torn apart owing to their petty quarrels, would then have to face their enemy individually. Vilified by the Cape Government, Ngangelizwe approved of Reverend Hargreaves' insistence that he ask for 'British protection'. Though promised by William Wright, a Resident with Ngangelizwe, that he would be paid £200 annually if he changed his behaviour, Ngangelizwe was deposed by the Cape Government as the abaThembu king in 1875. Thus, the Nongxokozelo affair "gave the Cape Government the opportunity of interfering in abaThembuland's internal affairs and … led directly to the deposing of Ngangelizwe as chief in 1875".[458] However, he was reinstated as king in 1876, as the colonial government could not renounce abaThembu allegiance to their king. It was a result of the abaThembu strong aversion to the deposing of their king, that at the close of 1876 Ngangelizwe's authority was inevitably restored. Even uNkosi Mathanzima had openly shown disgust at the deposition of Ngangelizwe. This could mean that in spite of apparent divisions, disputes and tensions, the abaThembu had a desire for cohesion and unity. UNkosi Dalasile also accepted 'British protection' in 1875 as a result of a missionary influence at All Saints Mission. However, Dalasile insisted that "his people should not be mixed with others, but should have a separate magistrate."[459] However, this never happened.

The abaThembu conditions of 'British protection' as were drafted by Reverend Hargreaves were deliberately designed to diminish the power of the abaThembu king, who had just been reinstated as king in 1876. His ulterior motive was to facilitate the spread of Christianity amongst the abaThembu, so that the traditional leaders lost power, prestige and authority to white magistrates. Even though the traditional leaders' judicial power was retained, it was however subject to the right of appeal to white magistrates.

During the 1870s, the Cape Government exploited tribal rivalries, divisions and tensions to realise its objectives of diminishing and eroding chiefly and kingship power. Hence, the appointment in May 1873 of William Fynn, successor to E.J. Warner, as abaThembu Agent and of William Wright as Resident with Ngangelizwe. Fynn was succeeded by Charles J. Levey in December 1875. Amongst other things, a Resident served as a diplomatic representative of the Cape Government. After 1872, the Cape ministry set out to swallow up tribal lands by extending white control. Attempts were made to drive a wedge within and between African kingdoms and chiefdoms.

---

458 Wagenaar, "History of the Thembu", 246.
459 Brownlee, *Native Territories*, 31.

The Weakening of the Ties between the East and the West, 1875-1877

The abaThembu-Gcaleka conflict aside, disunity between the Mbhashe abaThembu and the Emigrant abaThembu was also apparent. Also conspicuous was the division within the Emigrant abaThembu chiefs. And here again the Cape Government widened the gulf even further. For example, in 1869, Edward A. Judge became a civil commissioner and magistrate in Komani (Queenstown) and used headmen as court messengers. As they worked harmoniously with the colonial government, headmen were also used in capturing thieves and recovering stolen cattle.[460] As one magistrate remarked, "the condition of the police remains almost unchanged. The headmen, however, have done good service in capturing thieves and recovering stolen stock"[461] in the District of isiDutyini (Saint Mark's). It was even suggested that a police station be established as uKumkani Ngangelizwe would gladly accept that.[462]

To deal chiefs and king yet another blow, Judge embarked on the process of surveying the location and issuing title deeds to well-to-do men.[463] Ownership of title deeds was an entitlement to the status of headmanship. Judge divided Cacadu (Glen Grey) into wards, each to be under a headman. He sought headmen to deal directly with the colonial government through white magistrates.[464] The survey of Glen Grey and the appointment of headmen was cause for anger amongst abaThembu chiefs and their king. Showing aversion to the appointment of headmen, uNkosi Gungubele of the amaTshatshu put it to the government that as a chief he had a right to appoint headmen in his area of jurisdiction, eGwatyu.[465] However, the Cape Government continued appointing headmen without the consent of the amaTshatshu chief. Judge, who was determined to eradicate chieftainship in Cacadu (Glen Grey), was intent on incorporating Glen Grey into the colonial economy by encouraging young men to go out and seek work to earn cash and buy livestock and promoting payment of a hut tax, "which would maintain his proposed system of administration and augment the state coffers."[466] A hut tax was imposed in 1869.

Prior to 1870, J.C. Warner had driven a wedge between uNkosi Mathanzima and uKumkani Ngangellizwe and between uNkosi Mathanzima and uKumkanikazi Nonesi. Warner attributed every dispute in abaThembuland to either Ngangelizwe or Nonesi. He befriended Mathanzima who sought to be independent from Nonesi and Ngangelizwe. Warner also worked towards weakening Mathanzima by, inter alia, escalating conflict between these traditional leaders, so that they would not act in unison against the colonial government.

---

460 *Blue Book on Native Affairs*, G.27 – '74, 59.
461 *Cape of Good Hope Blue Book on Native Affairs, 1887-1894*, H.H. Bunn, Resident Magistrate St Mark's District, 31 December 1893, 64.
462 *Select Committee Report on Native Affairs*, A.12 – '73, 131.
463 Mager, "Gungubele and the Tambookie Location", 1170.
464 Macquarrie, *Sir Walter Stanford*, vol. i, 32.
465 *Cape of Good Hope Blue Book on Native Affairs 1878*, G.17 – '78, John Hemming, Civil Commissioner, to the Honourable J.X. Merriman, Commissioner of Crown Lands, & C, 5 December 1877, 193.
466 R. Bouch, "Glen Grey before Cecil Rhodes: How a Crisis of Local Colonial Authority Led to the Glen Grey Act of 1894", *Canadian Journal of African Studies*, 27, 1 (1993), 6.

Owing to Warner's influence, uNkosi Mathanzima became the senior chief in Emigrant abaThembuland. He gained authority over the area from which Afrikaner families established by uKumkani Ngangelizwe along the Tsomo River had been removed by the Cape Government. This was a clear indication that Warner was determined to play abaThembu chiefs and their king against one another in the pursuit of the colonial government's divide-and-rule policy. Though this action infuriated uKumkani Ngangelizwe's uncle, uNkosi Mnqanqeni, and his brothers, Siqungathi and Mbambonduna, Warner proceeded to allay their fears by encouraging them to settle in Emigrant abaThembuland under uNkosi Mathanzima. Hence, by 1875, Mathanzima had emerged as prominent abaThembu ruler, while Ukumkani Ngangelizwe was deposed.

In 1871, the colonial government divided Emigrant abaThembuland, an area not larger than an ordinary magistracy in the Colony, into the northern and southern parts.[467] The former portion was given to Dordrecht and the latter to Komani (Queenstown). Komani was further divided into 104 farms of from 1,500 to 2,000 morgen each. Eleven of these farms were given to loyal abaThembu chiefs and headmen. Senior headmen were appointed to assist in the management of these farms. Thus, the colonial government "had succeeded in destroying the influence of the traditional leaders over the colonial Tambookies"[468] by interfering with their rule in an attempt to make them better servants of the farmers. Also contributing to the erosion of chiefly power and division within the abaThembu were ooNkosi Sitokhwe's and Gecelo's applications for their own separate locations in Cacadu (Glen Grey). UNkosi Mathanzima, who had gained huge territory, including Ngangelizwe's territory east of the Tsomo River, sought a united Emigrant abaThembuland. Warner could not support Mathanzima in this venture, as that would enhance the latter's hegemony.

Another slap in the face of the traditional leaders was the colonial government's determination to have Ngangelizwe isolated. For instance, Charles Brownlee (1821-1890), British resident, insisted in 1873 that uKumkani Ngangelizwe should be kept in check so as not to ally with uNkosi Mhlontlo of the amaMpondomise. He expressed fear that such an alliance, if it ever took place, would result in disturbances and war.[469] He further recommended that Ngangelizwe be taken as British subject.

Following Hargreaves' drawing up of the terms of abaThembu conditions of cession to the Cape Colony on behalf of uKumkani Ngangelizwe in 1875, J.C. Molteno, Prime Minister of the Cape Colony and Colonial Secretary (1872-1878), passed the Annexation Bill in the Cape Parliament in June 1876. This Bill gave rise to the introduction of magisterial rule, and further division of abaThembuland into magisterial districts. The introduction of magisterial rule and the appointment of headmen were strategies to extend and strengthen white

---

467 *Blue Book on Native Affairs*, G.8 – '83, 14.
468 *Blue Book on Native Affairs*, G.27 – '74, 61.
469 Ibid., 67 and 77.

control in abaThembuland.⁴⁷⁰ In 1876, abaThembuland Proper was divided into four judicial districts, viz. The magistracy of Mjanyana under William Wright, the magistracy of Mthatha under Major J.F. Boyes, the magistracy of Ngcobo under W.E. Stanford and the magistracy of Mqanduli under Reverend John H. Scott. Wright was also the Chief Magistrate. Both Ngangelizwe and abaThembu chiefs were subservient to these magistrates. Ngangelizwe, Emigrant abaThembu chiefs and headmen became kindly disposed towards the Cape Government. They assisted Wright in uprooting witchcraft and fighting thieving.⁴⁷¹ Hence, the Chief Magistrate and successor to William Wright, H. Elliot, apprised the Emigrant abaThembu chiefs of uKumkani Ngangelizwe's repentance and loyalty to the Cape Government in 1878.

Furthermore, in 1877, Emigrant abaThembuland was further divided into the districts of iSidutyini (St Mark's) and Xhalanga, each under a separate magistrate, viz. Charles J. Levey and W.G. Cumming respectively.⁴⁷² W. Ayliff, Secretary for Native Affairs, met ooNkosi Mathanzima, Ndarhala, Gecelo and Sitokhwe at Cofimvaba and informed them about these new developments. With the creation of the chief magistracy of abaThembuland (including amaBomvanaland and Emigrant abaThembuland) in 1878 under the High Commissioner, Emigrant abaThembuland and abaThembuland Proper came to be under one Chief Magistrate, viz. Major Elliot. However, Emigrant abaThembu chiefs were discontented as they had migrated from the Tambookie location (Lady Frere) in 1865 hoping to have full authority and independence from Nonesi and Ngangelizwe. Their objection was to no avail.

In another context, Levey, resident magistrate in Emigrant abaThembuland, clashed with uNkosi Mathanzima owing to the former's attempt to weaken Emigrant abaThembu chiefs.⁴⁷³ For instance, Levey had cut off uNkosi Sitokhwe's annual stipend, consequential upon a clash between Sitokhwe and uNkosi Gecelo, which culminated in a battle between their clans in August 1874. OoNkosi Gecelo and Sitokhwe were each fined 50 head of cattle. Charles Brownlee, the Secretary for Native Affairs, addressing the abaThembu agent, Fynn, in 1874 made the following remarks:

> Government cannot allow the Emigrant Tambookie Location to be the arena for bloodshed, neither can the Emigrant Tambookies be allowed to pass by the Tambookie Agent and disregard his word. If war and bloodshed and the wishes of Government as expressed by you are disregarded, then Government will be necessitated to deal with the transgressors as it did with Kreli, and as they prove themselves unworthy of the kindness they have received from Government then others must be put into their place who will live in peace and regard and obey the orders of Government.⁴⁷⁴

---

470 Saunders, "The Annexation of the Transkei", in Saunders and Derricourt (eds), *Beyond the Cape Frontier*, 186.
471 *Blue Book on Native Affairs*, G.27 – '74, 47 and 62.
472 *Blue Book on Native Affairs*, G.8 – '83, 14; *Queenstown Free Press*, 26 January 1878.
473 *Queenstown Free Press*, 26 January 1878.
474 *Blue Book on Native Affairs*, 1885, 27.

In spite of these threats by the colonial government, the year 1877 saw uNkosi Sitokhwe, who was represented as "a turbulent character, always ready for a quarrel with anybody",[475] being accused by Brownlee of showing eagerness to brew trouble, upon which Brownlee threatened to reduce his allowance from £50 to £24 per annum. Hence, at a meeting with the Chief Magistrate in 1879, UNkosi Mathanzima impressed upon the Chief Magistrate that the Cape Government should stop taking away chiefs' traditional political rights and privileges. Subsequently, Elliot, determined to erode chiefly power by depriving them of their judicial authority, reprimanded Mathanzima for having fined an officer, Booy Solomon, who had defied the chief's summons to the Great Place.[476] He further warned Mathanzima that if he continued rendering Emigrant abaThembuland ungovernable, a suitable candidate would be secured. This was an attempt to weaken uNkosi Mathanzima and to replace him with a government-paid headman, something which was sure to create further conflict and division within the abaThembu.

THE TROUBLED YEARS, 1877-1881

At the commencement of the Ninth War of dispossession, followed by the Battle of Centane on 7 February 1878, about 7,000 amaXhosa warriors inflicted an attack on approximately 1,000 European and amaMfengu soldiers, who were under the command of Captain Upcher. Having found shelter in the rough earthern fort established proximal to Moldenhauer's Hill Store, the European and amaMfengu soldiers suffered onslaught from the amaXhosa warriors who had been doctored by the traditional doctor, Xhitho, who had made incisions on their foreheads to strengthen and make the warriors "invulnerable to the bullets from the guns of the enemy."[477]

The doctoring of the warriors by Xhitho inspired uKumkani Sarhili, A! Ntaba! and uNkosi Sandile, A! Mgolombane! to steer the warriors into fierce action in the hope that they would inflict a total defeat on the colonial government troops. The warriors were equally motivated. The traditional leaders and the warriors never imagined any possibility of a defeat, as they pinned their hopes on the magical power of Xhitho, who was both a famous traditional doctor of repute and *itola*, a war doctor.[478] The practice of doctoring amaXhosa warriors was not a new phenomenon. Based on the strong, sincere belief in witchcraft and sorcery, the doctoring of fighters was practised by the prophets Nxele and Mlanjeni in 1819 and 1850-1853 respectively to protect the army against colonists' bullets.[479]

Nxele, the prophet of 1818-1819, had called on the amaXhosa to leave their evil ways so that the earth might be made 'right' (-*lunga*) again.[480] The amaXhosa were, however, defeated in the Fifth Frontier War (1818-1819). Nxele was thenceforth imprisoned on Robben Island,

---

475 Ibid.
476 Wagenaar, "History of the Thembu", 265.
477 J. Coulter, *They Lived in Africa* (Port Elizabeth, 1988), 16.
478 Ibid.
479 Lewis, "Materialism and Idealism", 244-268.
480 Peires, "Central Beliefs", 48.

where he died. He drowned as he attempted to escape. Hence, he never returned from Robben Island.[481] Mlanjeni, the war doctor and witchfinder, circulated the news that Nxele was still alive during the Frontier War of 1850-1853. So much for Nxele and Mlanjeni.

Using his popularity as *itola*, Xhitho imbued the brave warriors to plunge into the battle by conducting "special ceremonies to make the warriors believe in their strength and ability to conquer all before them."[482] No sooner did Xhitho doctor the warriors than the latter were goaded into inflicting onslaught on the enemy, brandishing assegais, "shouting blood-curdling war cries and stamping their feet as they carried their ox-hide shields before them."[483]

In spite of Xhitho having fortified the warriors against the enemies, and making them immune to the soldiers' guns and bullets, the amaXhosa warriors were gunned down by the soldiers, much to the chagrin of uKumkani Sarhili and uNkosi Sandile. As a consequence, 300 amaXhosa warriors were killed. Only two soldiers were lost by the colonial forces.[484] The Battle of Centane ended the Ninth War of dispossession. As Sandile and his amaNgqika fled across the Nciba River, Sarhili and his amaGcaleka initially hid in the forests and hills and eventually surrendered.[485] Sarhili's followers were resettled in Gatyana (Willowvale).

UNkosi Sandile had, on 15 January 1878, been the object of attack by colonial troops at Lujilo before crossing the Nciba River to rescue uKumkani Sarhili. During a period of three days' fighting, the troops captured many cattle from Sandile and his followers, but were determined to make further inroads, as the troops had heard that the bulk of the cattle were to be found at Bholo and Qwanti.[486] While the colonial troops still pondered the capturing of more cattle, Sandile "slipped down the bed of the Kei River and, crossing over into amaGcalekaland, joined forces with Sar[h]ili for a few weeks."[487] After suffering a crushing defeat at the Battle of Centane, uNkosi Sandile and his followers returned to amaNgqikaland and landed at Amatola Mountains, "where from time to time they were fired upon, and where it is reported that in the month of May or June Sandili was killed."[488] Two of his sons, Gonya and Mathanzima, were marooned and captured by Levey at uNkosi Sitokhwe's Great Place (Komkhulu), where they were in hiding. UNkosi Sitokhwe's action could be attributed to the fact that his Great Wife was a sister of the two chiefs.[489]

Sir Bartle Frere issued a proclamation that the people who had been involved in the War surrender themselves. Most of the rebels were in hiding in the bush in various parts of amaGcalekaland and amaNgqikaland. However, the rebels feared to deliver themselves up

---

481 Ibid., 59.
482 Coulter, *Africa*, 16.
483 Ibid.
484 Ibid., 17; T.V. Bulpin, *Discovering Southern Africa* (Cape Town: T.V. Bulpin Publishers, 1980), 375.
485 Coulter, *Africa*, 17; Bulpin, *Southern Africa*, 376.
486 PR 1272, James M. Auld, 'Reminiscences', in *Blythswood Review*, December 1924, 137.
487 Auld, 'Reminiscences', in *Blythswood Review*, December 1924, 137.
488 Ibid.
489 *Blue Book on Native Affairs*, 1885, 27.

as more than one lieutenant had revealed to Reverend James Auld, who was a minister at Mgwali Mission, that "the rebels know that when they come within our reach they have little mercy to expect".[490]

Auld reported this horrible message to the Secretary for Native Affairs, Charles Brownlee (1821-1890), who was stationed at the trading station just outside Mgwali Mission. At Mgwali Mission, there was a representative of the Magistrate, Mr William Cumming, to whom matters relating to patrolling and harbouring of rebels were to be reported. Auld spotted the questionable acts of mercilessness being inflicted upon the rebels in the camp on a certain Sunday morning. On inspecting how one of the patrolling soldiers from one of the camps, established over the territory from which the troops went out doing patrol work, Auld offers a blood-curdling account of what he witnessed:

> Coming up to them [patrols] at a large kraal, I found the Fingo levies, some 30 or 40 men, drawn up in line; in front of these, also in line, 8 or 10 white men; in front of them again the men of the kraal, some 15 or 20; and in front of these stood a prisoner with a riem round his neck! The women and children of the kraal had been called out of the huts and were standing on one side.[491]

These colonial men were on a search to find out if the owners of the kraal were not harbouring rebels. White men entered the huts and made a search without finding any rebels. The search for rebels was carried out notwithstanding the governor's proclamation giving permission to rebels to surrender themselves. In another kraal, the amaMfengu troops entered the hut, and were allowed by a white officer to "help themselves to men and women's clothing, to hatchets and various other things."[492]

However, Auld reported the matter to the Secretary for Native Affairs, who had the issue brought before a court. The officer was hauled before a court and found guilty of wrong-doing. Mr Cumming was ordered to value the property taken; the officer was forced to pay the costs.[493]

Auld's tremendous role in ensuring that the rebels were not dealt with mercilessly was not only evident in his interactions with Cumming and the Secretary for Native Affairs. Some rebels asked him to visit them in the bush in order for them to deliver themselves up. For example, a Lujilo resident, Ngobo, requested Auld's presence in preparation for coming out of the hiding place. Auld was accompanied by Nzanzana and Festile to Lujilo, where they reported their presence and objectives at the camp. The officer there expressed his joy that the rebels wished to deliver themselves up and offered to give Auld an escort. However, Auld turned down the offer and went down to the bush with the two men. Though they searched and called for Ngobo, there was no sign of any human being hiding in the vicinity of the bush.

---

490 Auld, 'Reminiscences', in *Blythswood Review*, December 1924, 137.
491 Ibid.
492 Ibid.
493 Ibid.

Hence, they gave up their mission for the day. On returning to the camp, they learnt that two days before an attack had been made on the same bush by the troops; two men were killed and one taken prisoner. They reasoned that Ngobo had been killed.

Ten days later, Cumming received a message from Gomna, one of Sandile's sons, that he come down, so that Gomna, Ngobo and others could deliver themselves up.[494] On arriving in the bush, Cumming and Auld did not wait long before Gomna, Ngobo and some 50 others came out. They were taken to Mgwali, from where they were sent to the magistrate at Greytown. Unfortunately, all "who delivered themselves up, … [including] those taken prisoners by the troops were deported to the Western Province where they were imprisoned or served for a term of years."[495]

The Ninth Frontier War of 1877-1878 had far-reaching results for the abaThembu as well. The War of Ngcayechibi was prompted by Africans' desire to regain their land taken by the Cape Government to the loyal amaMfengu. Thus, this war was an attempt by African kingdoms and chiefdoms to check the tide of white control.[496] The last straw to break the camel's back was a scuffle between the amaGcaleka and amaMfengu at a wedding feast hosted by Ngcayechibi. The Cape Government used this fray as an opportunity to crush uKumkani Sarhili's power by siding with the amaMfengu. The colonial government's interference "in the conflict fuelled resentment amongst chiefs, who chafed under the yoke of magistrates".[497] AmaXhosa and some abaThembu took up arms as a last desperate attempt to restore their autonomy and independence. Interestingly, thousands of Christians sided with the abaThembu and amaXhosa against the colonial army, "as they had not in earlier wars [of dispossession]",[498] which was a harbinger of future ecclesiastical protest movements that were later initiated by Reverend Xoxo Nehemiah Tile in 1884.

Living in the Tambookie location, ooNkosi Gungubele and Mfanta were ready for the war cry from uNkosi Sandile, the late uNkosi Maphasa's old ally. Even though uNkosi Gungubele did not immediately participate in the war, bundles of assegais were found by John Hemming's spies in the hut of uNkosi Mfanta, and this was interpreted as an indication that Mfanta was preparing for the war.[499] In the ensuing battle with Hemming's troops in Gwatyu, uNkosi Gungubele lost between 100 and 150 men; 60 horses were captured; and his Great Place

---

494 Ibid.
495 Ibid., 138.
496 Saunders, "Annexation of Transkei", 185 and 190.
497 Mager, "Gungubele and the Tambookie Location", 1172; R.J. Bouch, "The Colonisation of Queenstown (Eastern Cape) and its Hinterland, 1852-1886" (PhD. Thesis, University of London, 1990), 140-161; Price, *Making Empire*, 353.
498 H. Pretorius and L. Jafta, "A Branch Springs Out: African Initiated Churches", in Elphick and Davenport (eds), *Christianity in South Africa: A Political, Social and Cultural History* (Cape Town: David Philip, 1997), 213.
499 *Blue Book on Native Affairs 1877*, G.17 – '78, John Hemming, Civil Commissioner, to J.X. Merriman, Commissioner of Crown Lands, 11 January 1878, 195; *Queenstown Free Press*, 5 January 1878.

(Komkhulu) was set alight.⁵⁰⁰ On 24 January 1878, ooNkosi Gungubele and Mfanta's troops regrouped and launched an attack on the colonists in the bloody battle of the Gwatyu. They lost 180 men; Msheshwe, Gungubele's cousin, was accused of being a traitor, informing colonists of sensitive information. Hence "he was pierced by more than 30 assegai heads" until he died.⁵⁰¹ The colonial attack on 4 February 1878 by Commandant Griffith of the Frontier Armed and Mounted Police on uNkosi Gungubele's stronghold led to a group of women and children surrendering to the colonial forces. As Mager describes the tragic outcomes of the encounter:

> By the end of February, the Gwatyu was a wasteland and St Peter's lay in smouldering ruins. Gungubele took refuge among the amaNgqika south of the Tambookie location. On 9 April, he and fourteen councillors (among them a man who had been employed as a detective in the colonial service for 17 years) handed themselves over to the Queenstown magistrate. Soon after, Mfanta and Sitokhwe Tyali (who took up arms late in the war) were arrested.⁵⁰²

During this war, the divisive and disruptive role of white magistrates became apparent. It led to a division in the abaThembu attitude and reaction to the war and whites. Their action and participation was not united. For example, Major Elliot soon enlisted the support of the abaThembu against amaXhosa. Scott, the magistrate of Mqanduli, raised the abaThembu force. Having been reinstated in 1876, uKumkani Ngangelizwe fought on the colonial side during the War of Ngcayechibi and the Transkei Rebellion.⁵⁰³

While most abaThembu under uKumkani Ngangelizwe joined the war on the side of the Cape Government, the amaQwathi of Dalasile refused to aid the Cape Government. UNkosi Mathanzima stood aloof. UNkosi Sitokhwe Ndlela of the amaQwathi took sides with amaXhosa. UNkosi Mfanta also rendered valuable military assistance to uKumkani Sarhili. Despite outside assistance, uKumkani Sarhili and his allies were decisively beaten at the Battle of Centani in February 1878.⁵⁰⁴ Following this defeat, uNkosi Dalasile paid a high price for defying the orders of the Chief Magistrate, Major Elliot. He was fined a hundred head of cattle. OoNkosi Sitokhwe Tyhali of the amaVundle, Mfanta and Gungubele were charged with treason and sedition, while their supporters were sentenced to three years' hard labour.⁵⁰⁵ OoNkosi Sitokhwe Tyhali and Mfanta were imprisoned by the Cape Government. Having appealed conviction of treason and death sentence, Chief Gungubele was incarcerated in Robben Island, and separated from Chief Mfanta who was imprisoned in the Breakwater prison. Subsequent to uNkosi Gungubele's imprisonment, the amaTshatshu royal family was

---

500 *Queenstown Free Press*, 26 January 1878.
501 Mager, "Gungubele and the Tambookie Location", 1173. See Yali-Manisi, "Idabi LaseGwatyu", 63.
502 Mager, "Gungubele and the Tambookie Location", 1173.
503 Wagenaar, "History of the Thembu", 246.
504 W.D. Hammond-Tooke, *Command or Consensus: The Development of Transkeian Local Government* (Cape Town: David Philip, 1975), 2.
505 *Queenstown Free Press*, 26 July 1878.

removed to and relocated in Qitsi, Cofimvaba. On being released from Robben Island in 1888 on the occasion of Queen Victoria's Jubilee, uNkosi Gungubele was taken to and settled in Qitsi where he died in 1925.[506]

The colonial appeal for military assistance from the abaThembu only served to widen the gap within the House of Ngubengcuka. Since his reinstatement in 1876 and the subsequent treatment of him by the Cape Government as the highest native official in the country, uKumkani Ngangelizwe had remained loyal to the colonial government. Also important to note is that uNkosi Mathanzima, the then prominent leader in Emigrant abaThembuland, stood aloof from the Ninth Frontier War, and his attitude was detrimental to abaThembu cohesion. His non-participation was another factor illustrating the negative effects of the colonial government's interfering in the abaThembu internal affairs.

Furthermore, the Ninth Frontier War "enabled the colony to seize [ama]Gcalekaland, and [ama] Bomvanaland as well."[507] Sarhili's land was divided into Gatyana (Willowvale) and Dutywa districts before being incorporated in Dutywa and amaMfenguland to become Transkei under the chief magistracy of Captain Blyth. Being one of the bloodiest frontier conflicts, the Ninth Frontier War, however, considerably influenced the pace of whites' extension of control over the abaThembu kingdom. The Cape administration that was imposed on abaThembuland, amaGcalekaland and amaBomvanaland had no legal validity, and therefore required that formal annexation be effected forthwith.

Thus, the period 1877 to 1881 could best be termed the troubled years "for relationships between the colonial power and Africans in the Eastern Cape generally, and the trials afflicting Glen Grey were part of that experience".[508] It was the main period of crisis in the Transkei.[509] It was characterised by a sense of discontent amongst the abaThembu king, chiefs and commoners owing to the fact that the Cape Government had begun to tighten the screws in its control of the abaThembu and other abeNguni communities. After the war, the Cape Prime Minister, J. Gordon Sprigg (1878-1881) enacted what Redding terms the "ill-named Peace Preservation Act"[510] in 1878 in order to step up the rendering impotent of the southern abeNguni communities' military potential.[511] This disarmament legislation was designed to deprive Africans of their weapons of warfare.[512] It provided for the full introduction of colonial law in all its aspects into the African territories.[513] The Act was greeted with resentment and opposition by Africans. Kawa regards the Disarmament Act as follows:

> Instead of healing the illness, the amaBandla ka Nibe (whites) have introduced discriminatory colour laws, (a) they don't want a black person to

---

506 Imvo Zabantsundu, 9 May 1889; 24 March 1914.
507 Saunders, "Annexation of Transkei", 187.
508 Bouch, "Glen Grey before Cecil Rhodes", 6.
509 J. Benyon, *Proconsul and Paramountcy in South Africa*, 146.
510 Redding, "Sorcery and Sovereignty", 256.
511 Mvenene, "Reverend Auld", 33.
512 Macquarrie, *Sir Walter Stanford, vol. i*, 103.
513 Saunders, *Annexation*, 66.

have a voice in higher government matters, that is to say the vote – Franchise (b) a black person does not have the right to enter the Defence Force – the army (c) a black person's education is selective. They want him to have a thin education, bare bones which will not help him to make a man. His education is of such a low standard, that it is fit only for a mouse (d) He is excluded from the work of the Big House. The small salaries given to black people are only just enough to stop the breath from leaving the body, just enough to enable them to become servants, to work on the mines, to shear the sheep, hew the wood, carry the water ... Whites pretend to heal one's wounds, but they scratch them instead. Whereas with blacks, it is: good for good, friendship for friendship, each hand must wash the other.[514]

AbaThembu regarded this Act and magisterial rule with disapproval and loathing. More upsetting to the Emigrant abaThembu was that in addition to surrendering their guns, they were instructed to pay hut tax in 1879. Before 1879, the colonial government had "borne expenses of maintaining establishments without deriving any direct revenue from the [abaThembu], except a trifling amount from the few European traders and farmers in Tembuland Proper".[515] In addition, rumours were afloat that in addition to hut tax, house duty was to be levied on the abaThembu. In this connection, Redding asserts that "the issue of taxation was central to the 1880 revolt and the peace that followed".[516] Redding traces taxation to 1876 wherein adult African men and some women were compelled to pay yearly taxes of ten shillings on each dwelling hut. Surprisingly, these taxes (hut tax and house duty) were not intended for the benefit of Africans, but made provision for the financial development of the Cape Colony. They were "both a symbol and a constituent element of state control".[517]

OoNkosi Mathanzima, Gecelo, Sitokhwe Ndlela and Ndarhala resented this and presented a petition to the Cape Parliament opposing the Act. In spite of that, however, the Cape Parliament continued with the implementation of the Act. Thus, the Peace Preservation Act and abaThembu fear of annexation precipitated a rising, which came to be known as the Transkeian Rebellion,[518] but for it to succeed it needed unity amongst abaThembu chiefs and king.[519] Nevertheless, dissensions amongst the African kingdoms were still apparent, and were accompanied by collaboration with the Cape Government.

Owing to the implementation of the Act, there was a rising – the Transkeian Rebellion. The rebellion originated from abeSuthuland in 1880, when ooNkosi Mhlontlo and Mditshwa "had come out in sympathy with the Basotho during the Gun War, and Mhlontlo's warriors

---

514 Kawa, *Ibali LamaMfengu*, 70-71.
515 *Blue Book on Native Affairs*, 1885, 34.
516 Redding, "Sorcery and Sovereignty", 250.
517 Ibid.
518 Redding refers to the rebellion as the amaMpondomise Rebellion or Hope's War. See Redding, "Sorcery and Sovereignty", 249.
519 Bongani Hector Ncokazi, Interview, Mpheko Village, Mthatha, 10 September 1994; Mlahleni Xundu, Interview, 16 April 1996; Headman Ntsikelelo Sotyatho, Interview, 28 June 1995; Sigqibo Pikashe, Interview, Nkondlo Village, Ngcobo, 16 July 1995.

had murdered the Qumbu [resident] magistrate, Hamilton Hope [and two of his white clerks] near Sulenkama [on 23 October 1880]".[520] Thus, having started in abeSuthuland, the rebellion soon spread to Qumbu and Tsolo[521] before reaching abaThembuland (Ngcobo, Mthatha, Xhalanga and Cofimvaba) in October 1880. The former Transkei ooNkosi Mhlontlo of the Qumbu amaMpondomise and Mditshwa of the Tsolo amaMpondomise decided to put their differences in the background, and face the common challenge. Schism within the abaThembu became more evident as Thomas Phoswayo and Mbekeni (loyal abaThembu headmen) and Ncanywa Zibi (amaMfengu headman at Cwecweni) alerted magistrate Stanford of an imminent rising brewed by uNkosi Dalasile. News spread to Major Boyes, a magistrate at Mjanyana. Under these circumstances there could be no abaThembu concerted reaction against the extension of white rule. Consequently, when the Transkeian Rebellion of 1880-1881 erupted, amaMfengu, amaBhaca and Ngangelizwe's abaThembu took sides with the colonial government; amaGcaleka-Xhosa, amaMpondo and Mathanzima's grouping stood aloof; amaMpondomise and the Griqua were at the forefront of the rebellion. Also, ooNkosi Dalasile of amaQwathi of Ngcobo and Sitokhwe Ndlela of the amaQwathi in Emigrant abaThembuland joined forces against the colonial government. UNkosi Gecelo's subjects also rebelled against the colonial government.[522] In abaThembuland Proper, uNkosi Joyi's son, Gobinamba, and uNkosi Jumba's son, Mdukiswa, resolved to take arms against the Colony. That uKumkani Ngangelizwe fought on the side of the government while Mathanzima stood aloof, was a cause for alarm amongst most abaThembu as that marked the escalation of a division of reaction to whites. UNkosi Mathanzima's non-commital attitude suggested a split in the House of Mthikrakra. Further, Mathanzima's non-participation was good news for the colonial government. The clear implication is that abaThembu polity was not united in their struggles against the imposition of white domination and Cape colonial rule. This lack of unity presented the colonial government with a golden opportunity to strengthen with ease their control over the politically and socially divided abaThembu polity.

UNkosi Dalasile's participation in the rebellion emanated from fear that the enforcement of disarmament in Emigrant abaThembuland would soon be extended to himself and Ngangelizwe.[523] The Emigrant abaThembu participation in the rebellion was due to both their discontent with magisterial rule and the absorption of their land by amaMfengu and other landless or displaced people, like the Khoekhoe, encouraged to settle in their land by whites.[524] These displaced people or refugees would, on being given land, set their own boundaries and claim rights over the land. It was generally the practice of the Cape Government to encourage

---

520 W.D. Hammond-Tooke, "The Transkeian Council System, 1895-1955: An Appraisal", *Journal of African History*, 9, 3 (1968), 457.
521 Mvenene, "Reverend Auld", 33.
522 UNkosi Jonginyaniso Mthikrakra, Interview, 5 February 2013; uNkosi Dalagubha Joyi, Interview, 6 March 2010; uNkosi Sindile Zwelodumo Mthikrakra, Interview, 9 June 2018; *Blue Book on Native Affairs*, 1885, 36.
523 J.W. Macquarrie (ed.), *Reminiscences of Sir Walter Stanford, vol. ii, 1885-1929* (Cape Town: Van Riebeeck Society, 1962), 10; *Walter Stanford Papers*, D.8, 6 November 1883.
524 *Blue Book on Native Affairs*, G.8 – '83, 15.

emigration of non-abaThembu people into Emigrant abaThembuland. This notorious practice led to the abaThembu seeking "to get rid of the officials and Fingoes who were oppressing us".[525] The practice was carried out so that these non-abaThembu people "would form a power in the event of a rising of the Tambookies".[526]

In spite of disunity within Africans kingdoms and chiefdoms, the Transkeian Rebellion proved to be the most formidable attempt by Africans to resist white intrusion and to cast off white control and magisterial rule.[527] Though initially the abaThembu did not resist white control during the Ninth Frontier War, they had by 1880 borne the brunt of white rule. Being the Africans' expression of their objection to the government divisional policy, the rebellion, like the war of 1877-1878, was an attempt to check the tide of white control. Both delayed the move towards the annexation of African kingdoms and chiefdoms. The rebellion warned the Cape Government of the potential danger inherent in ruling east of the Nciba River. Even though the rebellion was quelled early in 1881, the Cape Government could sense that African kingdoms and chiefdoms could not tolerate assault on their political power. When uNkosi Dalasile surrendered, there was considerable agitation in abaThembuland, brewed and fostered by Reverend Nehemiah Xoxo Tile.[528]

At the end of the rebellion by March 1881, confidence in white authority was shattered as many lives were lost on both sides. The rebellion also resulted in loss of land and cattle for the rebels,[529] as "white magistrates deposed rebellious chiefs and replaced them with loyalists".[530] The districts of Indwe and Elliot were confiscated. In consequence of such confiscation and the selling to whites of rebel territory by the colonial government, Africans were "much more closely packed".[531] That "land sequestered from the rebels fell into white hands",[532] was a heavy economic, political and social blow for the former. Significantly, the rebellion also led to the further weakness of uKumkani Ngangelizwe's power, while uNkosi Mathanzima was gradually gaining in prominence. OoNkosi Siqungathi, Mbambonduna and Falo suffered severely; uNkosi Gecelo was deposed; Sitokhwe Ndlela and Gecelo were expelled by the colonial government from their lands around Indwe and Elliot, and their lands were distributed amongst white settlers. Gecelo was thenceforth sent to Robben Island, as uNkosi Dalasile's part of territory, Maxongo's Hoek, was ceded to white farmers. The so-called loyal Africans gained some land in Emigrant abaThembuland under individual land tenure and without due regard to, and observance of, these loyal Africans' tribal relationship.[533] This arrangement and resettlement scheme was intended to foster conflict between the abaThembu and these loyal

---

525 Ibid.
526 Ibid.
527 Brownlee, *Native Territories*, 53.
528 Macquarrie, *Sir Walter Stanford*, vol. ii, 10.
529 Maylam, *History of African People*, 101; Redding, "Sorcery and Sovereignty", 251.
530 Redding, "Sorcery and Sovereignty", 251.
531 *Blue Book on Native Affairs*, G.8 – '83, 13.
532 Saunders, *Dictionary of South Africa*, 174.
533 Brownlee, *Native Territories*, 37.

Africans. The severity with which rebel chiefs were treated could be gauged from Sprigg's assertion that "nothing would give him [Sprigg] greater pleasure than to hear that that man [Mhlontlo] was hanged ... so that he might receive the reward of his misdeeds".[534] It was reported that some abaThembu rebel chiefs fled to abeSuthuland.[535]

It was yet another heavy blow to abaThembu that their land was further divided. For example, out of former districts of Southeyville (Lubisi) and Xhalanga, the Cape Government created a separate magisterial district, Cala, to be under the magistracy of C. Levey. Some rebel chiefs were stationed there. Also, part of Southeyville, formerly under ooNkosi Mathanzima and Ndarhala, was turned into part of St Mark's as a separate district under the diplomat R.W. Stanford. In terms of these arrangements, therefore, Emigrant abaThembuland consisted of three separate magisterial districts, viz. St Mark's and Cala occupied by Africans, and Xhalanga inhabited by whites.

The foregoing survey indicates that whites had sought by all possible means to disrupt martial ties between the amaGcaleka-Xhosa and abaThembu kingdoms. The Cape Government's tradition of playing one kingdom against the other had given rise to conflict and envy between uKumkani Sarhili and uKumkani Ngangelizwe. Manipulating potential envy amongst the southern abeNguni chiefdoms and kingdoms, the colonial government so devastatingly attacked chiefly power, control and authority that by the 1870s and 1880s chiefly and kingship power had alarmingly declined.[536] Furthermore, Hodgson states that by the 1880s, after one hundred years of war, the Xhosa-speaking people, from the Zuurveld in the Eastern Cape to amaMpondoland, had been incorporated under British sovereignty, suffering dispossession of their ancestral land, destruction of their polities, and displacement and domination by alien rulers. Every aspect of their daily lives, their customs, and their beliefs had come under sustained attack from missionaries.[537] The missionaries' actions were in support of the colonial government's aims of subjugating traditional African chiefdoms and kingdoms.[538]

The crumbling of the inner threads that had held the abaThembu cohesively, and the consequent disunity of the abaThembu-Gcaleka kingdoms, led to the shifting of these kingdoms' collectivism to singularly and disjointedly face their enemies. The resultant weakness of the abaThembu gave rise to collaboration. UKumkani Ngangelizwe had been utterly despised by the Cape Government, the magistrates, headmen, abaThembu chiefs and subchiefs and most of the alien clans. However, even though the abaThembu were disunited at the time of their incorporation, they could confidently boast that they had lost minimal land to the colonists.

---

534 *House of Assembly Debates*, 27 July 1894, 373.
535 *Blue Book on Native Affairs*, G.8 – '83, 159.
536 Mvenene, "Reverend Auld", 33.
537 Hodgson, "A Battle for Sacred Power", 78.
538 Mvenene, "African People of Gcalekaland", 59.

6

TILE AND THE FORMATION OF THE AFRICAN SEPARATIST CHURCH MOVEMENT IN ABATHEMBULAND, 1881-1894

In spite of the abaThembu armed uprisings generally "led by chiefs at the head of the military forces of their precolonial units",[539] whites continued to forcefully extend and impose their rule on the abaThembu kingdom. Whites had done everything possible to "crush the chiefs, to convert and 'civilise' the African population"[540] so as to incorporate them into the colonial system of economy and politics. In consequence of these colonial government strategic counteractions, by the 1880s all attempts by the traditional leaders to halt the extension of effective colonial rule had failed.[541]

Not only did the colonial government drive a wedge within the House of Ngubengcuka, but it also took it upon itself to depose some abaThembu traditional leaders without the consent of the abaThembu. This and other defiant actions of the Cape Government on the southern abeNguni kingdoms and chiefdoms were typical examples of the colonial attack on kingship and chieftainship. These actions incurred the anger of commoners who had witnessed their traditional leaders being undermined by whites. As the traditional leaders vainly resisted colonial control and division of their land, it is not surprising that the church leaders came to the forefront of African resistance to the extension of colonial rule and its fatal consequences.

In this chapter, an attempt is made to examine Nehemiah Xoxo Tile's endeavours to resist the extension of white control and the division of abaThembuland. An examination of Tile's attempts to unite abaThembuland will stand the reader in good stead to perceive the fatal effects of colonial assault on kingship, and the rift that occurred as a consequence of colonial activities. An analysis of how Tile

---
539 Beinart and Bundy, "State Intervention and Rural Resistance", 273.
540 Ibid.
541 Mvenene, "Reverend Auld", 35.

tried to unite the church and the Thembu under one king and one magistrate will enable the reader to understand the nature of the division that had plagued the political, social and religious lives of the abaThembu.

An umThembu himself, Tile had become familiar with the abaThembu experiences and their conflicting interests with the Cape Government. He had witnessed the abaThembu king and chiefs vainly resisting the extension of white control. He had also witnessed how the abaThembu had tried to reverse the tide of white rule during the War of Ngcayechibi and the Transkeian Rebellion. Having been exposed to a great wealth of experiences within and outside the church, Tile witnessed how the colonial authorities extended their contemptuous treatment of Africans to the Wesleyan Methodist Church.[542] He was disturbed by the division of Christians and fully-fledged evangelists on the basis of their skin colour. African ministers were not accorded by Church authorities the same treatment as white ministers. With all his missionary education and acquisition of English, Tile could not remain silent on the provocative and derisive actions of whites. He became more antagonistic to whites' maltreatment of Africans in and outside the Church. As such, the Church had become a terrain of resistance to white control and a platform from which to articulate abaThembu aspirations.[543] Even though Africans had realised that they should express their sentiments of disgust through the Church, it was unfortunate that African Christians were numerically few. What was more, the 1870s saw the emergence of a deep-seated cleavage amongst the Africans.

As the division was taking shape within the House of Ngubengcuka, African Christians were also discriminated against by white Church officials. They were not judged according to their ability but rather the colour of their skin determined their fate within the Church. In this way, the Church had become a political instrument to assault commoners. Yet the division between African Christians and non-Christians remained intact. It was encouraged by the missionaries of the various societies.[544] Davenport maintains:

> Methodists, like almost all whites, assumed that white culture was radically superior to black, most missionaries considering that African converts should abandon undesirable cultural practices. Methodists set up different circuits for black and for white churches but without sufficient integration at the clerical level.[545]

Thus, the missionaries did not only work towards eroding chiefly power so that their religion could thrive well, but they also planted seeds of enmity amongst African Christians and non-Christians.[546] Furthermore, those in Church felt the brunt of racial discrimination.

---

542 Bongani Hector Ncokazi, Interiew, 10 September 1994; Professor Wandile Kuse, Interview, 8 September 1994; Sigqibo Pikashe, Interview, 16 July 1995.
543 UNkosi Dalagubha Joyi, Interview, 16 April 1996 and 6 March 2010.
544 Mda Mda, Interview, Xhugxwala Village, Mthatha, 22 May 2014; James Kati, Interview, Luhewini Village, Ngcobo, 30 July 1997.
545 R. Davenport, "Settlement, Conquest, and Theological Controversy: The Churches of Nineteenth-Century European Immigrants", in Elphick and Davenport (eds), *Christianity in South Africa* (Cape Town: David Philip, 1997), 65.
546 Zakade Bhuka, Interview, 14 July 1995 and 10 August 2006.

Tile and the formation of the African Separatist Church movement in AbaThembuland, 1881-1894

In their great sustained assault on abaThembu kings and chiefs and abaThembu culture, customs and their way of life, the missionaries could not go unchallenged. It was under these circumstances and in spite of these forces, factors and influences that emerged a man who could best be termed the father of the African indigenous Church movement in South Africa, Xoxo Tile.

An outspoken Christian, Tile viewed the affairs of the Church in the light of how whites treated Africans outside the Church and perceived some continuities that needed immediate attention. In this way, therefore, the Church had become politically charged and so had "a wide significance than has been hitherto acknowledged".[547] It had, as a result of Tile's political outlook on life, become a channel of expressing abaThembu protest against all forms of extension of white control and its divisive tendencies. Tile did all he could to blockade the divisional politics of the Wesleyan Methodist Church, which had begun to ordain African ministers in 1871.[548] Not only did Tile concentrate on the Methodist Church of which he was an evangelist, but he also extended his area of operation to the Great Place (Komkhulu) and sought to use the abaThembu king, Ngangelizwe, for the benefit of the entire abaThembuland. In this sense, one can talk of Tile as a man who sought to unite the Church and abaThembu. However, Yekela claims that Reverend Tile "symbolised the colonialist's traditional ally, the Christian church".[549]

Tile had exerted much and decisive influence on uKumkani Ngangelizwe. He had him consenting to the establishment in 1874 of a chapel at Cwecweni in the Ngcobo district. His involvement in abaThembu politics as early as 1874, "had as its visible benefit spiritual gratification for the colonial government rather than genuine political gain for the non-christianised Ngangelizwe".[550]

When serving as an evangelist at Cwecweni, Tile distinguished himself as a capable, active and dynamic Christian. Hence, he was sent to Healdtown College near Fort Beaufort by the Wesleyan Church to take the theological course. It was at eNxukhwebe (Healdtown) that Tile established a significant association with such later prominent Church figures as Richard Tainton Kawa, whose favourite *ingoma* (song) was *Umhlaba weAfrika uyalila*,[551] and James Mata Dwane. Kawa (1854-1924) criticised

> [t]he major manifestations of black oppression in the Eastern Cape,... such as taxes, land tenure, the franchise, the temptations of liquor and the degradation of chiefship ... he emphasised the over-riding importance of unity, citing both the prophet Ntsikana and the English slogan, 'Unity is strength'.[552]

---

547 Saunders, "Tile and the Thembu Church: Politics and Independency on the Cape Eastern Frontier in the Late Nineteenth Century", *Journal of African History*, 11, 4 (1970), 554.
548 Davenport, "Settlement, Conquest, and Theological Controversy", 65.
549 Yekela, "Unity and Division", 43.
550 Ibid.
551 Mqhayi, *Ityala Lamawele*, 66.
552 Nhanha and Peires, "Introduction", i.

Their influence on Tile during his three-year theological training at Healdtown bloomed when Tile served as a minister on trial at Morley (south-east of Mqanduli) in 1879, Qokolweni in 1882 and Xhorha in 1883. Their influence had far-reaching effects and wide implications for the abaThembu.[553]

While serving as a probationer-minister at Xhorha in 1883, Tile's political activities brought him into conflict with his superior and superintendent of the Clarkebury educational institution, Reverend Theophilus Chubb. The conflict resulted from the Wesleyan Church's discriminatory practices, which were anathema to Tile. In April 1883, the first Conference of the Wesleyan Methodist Church of South Africa was held. Tile and other African probationer-ministers were denied a say in the discussion of such important affairs as the funding of the Church and matters pertaining to the ordination of African probationer-ministers. More exasperating was that Tile, in spite of his long, successful probationer service, was refused ordination, like African probationer-ministers before him. It was his colour that disadvantaged and barricaded him from being promoted to senior Church positions. These Church malpractices incurred the wrath not only of Tile but also of other African ministers who had been equally disadvantaged.[554]

Being debarred from participating in the deliberations around the distribution of Church funds and disheartened by the Church's denial to have him ordained as a fully-fledged minister, Tile remained uKumkani Ngangelizwe's close adviser. He soon became more entangled and active in Cape politics. His political activities, particularly his involvement in abaThembu politics, were cause for conflict with the Church. Though not eager to antagonise the Church, nevertheless, Tile was determined to oppose the white political and social attack on the abaThembu.[555] This was sure to infuriate Church authorities. Hence, Tile was summoned to the disciplinary hearing by Chubb. At the disciplinary proceedings, a series of allegations were laid against Tile. These allegations were, inter alia, that he had incited the abaThembu and their king, Ngangelizwe, against the magistrates; had addressed public meetings on a "Sabbath"; had not apprised his superior, Chubb, of his political activities and had donated an ox at the circumsion ceremony of Prince Aliva, uKumkani Ngangelizwe's heir.[556]

On a wider plane, these allegations against Tile were an indication of whites' sustained efforts to maintain and consolidate their position of superiority in all spheres of life. They illustrate the extent to which whites went out of their way to keep Africans to a level of subservience.

---

553   Ibid., vi-vii.
554   Saunders, "Tile and the Thembu Church", 555; P. Hinchcliff, *The Church in South Africa* (London: S.P.C.K., 1968), 90; Omer-Cooper, *History of Southern Africa* (Johannesburg: David Philip, 1994), 161.
555   UKumkani Buyelekhaya Zwelibanzi Dalindyebo, Interview, Bumbane Great Place, Mthatha, 15 November 2010; uNkosi Royal Zululiyazongoma Mnqanqeni, Interview, Clarkebury Village, Ngcobo, 25 January 1996 and 4 October 2014.
556   J. Pampallis, *Foundations of the New South Africa* (Cape Town: Maskew Miller Longman, 1991), 56; Saunders, "Tile and the Thembu Church", 556.

They prove how whites sought to maintain the status quo where magistrates had supreme power over the traditional leaders. According to tradition it was entirely in order that Tile generously donated an ox for the circumcision ceremony of Prince Aliva. It was – and still is – traditionally and customarily justifiable that on the occasion of a traditional leader having a ceremony of whatever kind, his subjects would assist him by donating what would please the king or chief. Thus, charging Tile for the generosity he showed to the abaThembu king was out of place with regard to abaThembu tradition. It clearly showed that the colonial authorities had extended their terrain of attack on kingship, chieftainship, traditional religion and practices, and on customs in the Church. It was an intense measure to erode King Ngangelizwe of prominent *amaphakathi* (councillors), and more importantly, to alienate the abaThembu king and his advisers. It was an attempt to weaken the abaThembu more than ever before.[557] It would not be far-fetched to point out that the charges against Tile were unfounded. No wonder then that Tile, without bothering to refute these charges, left the Wesleyan Church. The secession of Tile from the Wesleyan Church in 1883 was important, as it marked the turning point in the history of the Wesleyan Church with all its discriminatory practices. It ushered in a new era in abaThembu Church politics where the articulation of African independence from white control was expressed in both political and religious terms.[558] This should be seen in the context of abaThembu hopelessness in their military power, the influx of whites into Emigrant abaThembuland in 1882 and 1883 and Tile's resentment of the white-led Church.

Having seceded from the Wesleyan Methodist Church, Tile soon championed the interests of the abaThembu. At a meeting held at the Great Place in August 1883, Tile's unwavering opposition to magisterial rule culminated in Ngangelizwe and his three sons signing a petition to the Cape Government. The petition insisted that there should be one magistrate for the entire abaThembuland and that all subordinate magistrates should be removed. However, this petition was not heeded by the Cape Government. Subsequently, uKumkani Ngangelizwe and his family, chiefs and subchiefs signed and sent another petition to the Cape Government insisting that subordinate magistrates be removed. At the centre of these petitions for one magistrate was Tile. More motivating to Tile was that Ngangelizwe had realised the existence of separatist tendencies enshrined in chiefs and subchiefs having their own magistrates.[559] It had dawned upon him that one magistrate would unify chiefs and subchiefs under one king.

The abaThembu petition coincided with the Cape Government's desire to reduce expenditure in the administration of the Transkeian territories. It sought to abolish four magistracies in abaThembuland as a way of cutting down on expenditure to the east of the Nciba River.

---

557 Ntshumayelo Sotyatho, Interview, Clarkebury Village, Ngcobo, 26 June 1995 and 31 July 1997; uKumkani Buyelekhaya Zwelibanzi Dalindyebo, Interview, 29 April 1994; Saunders, "Tile and the Thembu Church", 557-558.
558 Pampallis, *Foundations*, 56; Saunders, "Tile and the Thembu Church", 557.
559 Mncedi Phondolwendlovu Nyoka, Interview, 29 April 1994; Saunders, "Tile and the Thembu Church", 557-558.

When this decision to reduce magistracies was relayed by the Secretary for Native Affairs to Walter Stanford, the latter entertained fears that this might be interpreted as submission to abaThembu petitions. This decision had the effect of promoting Tile's insistence on making demands on the Cape Government. However, the coming into power of Thomas Upington as Prime Minister of the Cape (1884-1886) in May 1884 marked a slight change in the policy of retrocession. There was a massive desire to extend colonial control to the east of the Nciba River. In 1885, Prime Minister Upington incorporated Transkei Proper into the Cape Colony.[560] His bill in the 1886 session of parliament that "the Transkei should be represented by two members: one elected by whites, possessing the ordinary qualifications, and by Africans holding land worth £500 in individual tenure, the other chosen indirectly by a Native Elective Council, itself elected by all male Africans who paid the hut tax"[561] was met with considerable opposition and was dropped. Though this move surely frustrated Tile's dreams of a united abaThembuland under one king, it did not completely deter his agitation for the end of colonial rule.[562]

Tile went on to apply pressure on the Upington prime ministry that there should be a cessation of the hut tax. This gave rise to the fear that Tile might influence people at Mqanduli against the payment of the hut tax. While Tile's demand for the end of the hut tax was an attempt to thwart magisterial control in abaThembuland, Arthur Stanford, magistrate at Mthatha, and other white officials viewed this with disapproval. To them it was no less than a challenge to the fabric of colonial administration. Tile proceeded to send statements to the press supporting uKumkani Ngangelizwe's petition for one magistrate and one king.

September 1884 saw Jacobus de Wet, the new Secretary for Native Affairs, addressing an abaThembu meeting in Mthatha. Tile stood up as spokesperson for the abaThembu and requested the removal of all magistrates except one Chief Magistrate to act as a Resident Agent representing the Cape Government.[563] Tile further proposed "the restoration of the judicial power of the chiefs with the right of appeal only to the Chief Magistrate."[564] More disturbing to De Wet was Tile's utterance that even the Chief Magistrate had also "in the end to go from the scene".[565]

Even though Tile sought a united abaThembuland free from white rule, he nevertheless did not reject altogether white aid, help from the Cape Government and missionaries' occupation of abaThembuland.[566] There was still an apparent division of attitude within the abaThembu. For instance, after a warning by De Wet to King Ngangelizwe, *amaphakathi* (councillors) as Cuthalele, Mnyaka, Nkqayi and an educated Silas Phantshwa stood up and showed their

---

560 Hammond-Tooke, "The Transkeian Council System, 1895-1955", 459.
561 Ibid.
562 Ukumkanikazi No-Moscow Dalindyebo, Interview, Bumbane Great Place, Mthatha, 28 June 1994 and 10 September 2004; uNkosi Zwelidumile Joyi, Interview, 18 April 1996 and 5 July 2005.
563 Macquarrie, *Stanford, vol. ii*, 10.
564 *Cape Mercury*, 16 March 1893.
565 Ibid.
566 *Cape Argus*, 23 June 1884; *Walter Stanford Papers*, D.8, 15 September 1884.

aversion to Tile's demands.⁵⁶⁷ More divisive was the fact that uNkosi Mgudlwa had chosen not to attend the abaThembu meeting, entertaining fears that Tile would stir up abaThembu emotions. Futhermore, uKumkani Ngangelizwe, feeling the pressure exerted on him by chiefs and councillors who had repudiated Tile's demands, "attended at the Chief Magistrates, in Umtata, on the 17th November, and formally repudiated all that had been said in favour of their separating from the Colonial Government".⁵⁶⁸

On the basis of the divisive attitude within abaThembu, white officials claimed that Tile did not express the wishes of all abaThembu. Nevertheless, it was clear that "beyond the Kei, the Thembu were a significant group, but only one among many."⁵⁶⁹ De Wet soon expressed his anger at Tile's utterances by deriding King Ngangelizwe "as an intrigue against loyal Tembus, acting in, undoubtedly upon the instigation of Nehemiah Tile".⁵⁷⁰ He further suggested that Tile be expelled from his country of birth, or be arrested "for the purpose of removing him from the Territory".⁵⁷¹ In another context, De Wet threatened King Ngangelizwe by insisting that "submission to law and order is the primary condition to happiness".⁵⁷² He expressed his disappointment that King Ngangelizwe "allowed that man Tile to speak for yourself at the meeting of Tembus with me at Umtata".⁵⁷³ He reiterated that even though Tile claimed that the abaThembu sought independence from the Cape Government, the people did not see eye to eye with him.

In spite of Tile's attempts to frustrate colonial rule, the Cape Government could still use its strategies to keep the greater part of the abaThembu in their net. In its strategy of divide-and-rule, the Cape Government had forced into its orbit the abaThembu king's chief councillors who, in turn, could influence their king into aligning himself with the colonial government. Not only did the colonial authorities seek with determination to alienate Tile from the abaThembu king, chiefs and commoners, but they also compelled Ngangelizwe to submit to colonial rule by being submissive to the existence of many magistrates in his territorial domain. They set out to convince Ngangelizwe that the abaThembu did not want independence. De Wet had attacked Tile as no more than a commoner who wanted to mislead the abaThembu.⁵⁷⁴ He thenceforth advised Ngangelizwe to have nothing to do with Tile, lest the latter did harm to the abaThembu.⁵⁷⁵

Even though De Wet had recommended that Tile be arrested, or expelled from aba-Thembuland, J. Rose-Innes, the Under-Secretary for Native Affairs, advised against these measures noting that Tile "has been quiet of late [and that] it would not be judicious to take

---

567 Macquarrie, *Stanford, vol. ii*, 10.
568 *Cape Mercury*, 16 March 1893.
569 Saunders, "Tile and the Thembu Church", 559.
570 De Wet to CMT, 30 September 1884, CMT 1/8.
571 Ibid.
572 De Wet to Ngangelizwe, 28 November 1884, enclosed in USNA to CMT, 25 April 1885, CMT 1/9.
573 Ibid.
574 *Walter Stanford Papers*, D.8, 15 September 1884.
575 De Wet to Ngangelizwe, 28 November 1884, enclosed in USNA to CMT, 25 April 1885, CMT 1/9.

action against him so long as he remains so".[576] He further sounded a warning that, "while Tile has not rendered himself liable to any punishment in consequence of what he has done, his conduct should be carefully watched."[577] One can note that the colonial authorities had divergent opinions regarding the treatment to be meted out to Tile. They did not have a clear-cut pattern of dealing with progressive figures in the Transkeian territories.

Notwithstanding Tile's support of the abaThembu king, tragedy struck abaThembuland in December 1884, when uKumkani Ngangelizwe, after a long period of severe suffering at the hands of the colonial authorities, died.[578] He was survived by his son, Aliva, who had been born in 1865 (see Umnombo 8). Prince Aliva came to power in 1885, and on accession to the throne, he took the name Dalindyebo. And he was to be thenceforth saluted, A! Dalindyebo!

Like his father, uKumkani Dalindyebo was also a Christian. He not only faced political contempt as a king whose power, control and authority were tottering, but he was also subjected to discrimination by the Church. And in terms of southern abeNguni tradition, the king's dignity permeates all facets of life, and the commoner (or *umntu omnyama*) has to pay respect to the king or chief (or *umntwana wegazi*). More devastating to kingship power was that it was a common practice for missionaries to regard abaThembu religion, social life, culture and beliefs "with revulsion and loathing".[579] More derisive and appalling was that missionaries looked down upon the abaThembu way of life to such a degree that they used adjectives of disgust and contempt when dealing with the abaThembu.[580] They thus had adopted a view that "was often indistinguishable from that of the Colony".[581]

Following the death of uKumkani Ngangelizwe in December 1884, Tile was arrested on the recommendations of Blakeway, the magistrate at Mqanduli. Tile was charged for "inciting certain chiefs to resist lawful authority, in advising them to refuse to pay Hut Tax to [Blakeway], but to take it to the Chief Magistrate".[582] In spite of Tile's concerted effort at ending hut tax, by 1894 there was no outstanding hut tax in the District of Xhalanga.[583] In the District of St Mark's, however, outstanding revenue was reported as £924 for hut tax in 1893.[584] In the district of Ngcobo, the hut tax arrears stood at £1,420.[585] However, in the district of Mthatha there were no arrears on hut tax.[586] Nevertheless, the Attorney-General ruled that Tile's arrest

---

576 USNA to CMT, 4 December 1884, CMT 1/8.
577 Ibid., 3 September 1883, CMT 1/7.
578 Wagenaar, "History of the Thembu", 246.
579 Mostert, *Frontiers*, 595.
580 Ibid.
581 Ibid., 832.
582 USNA to Blakeway, 30 January 1885, CMT 1/9.
583 *Blue Book on Native Affairs*, 1887-1894, Charles J. Levey, Resident Magistrate Xhalanga District, Cala, 3 January 1894, 64.
584 *Blue Book on Native Affairs*, 1887-1894, H.H. Bunn, Resident Magistrate St Mark's District, 31 December 1893, 65.
585 Ibid., A.H. Stanford, Resident Magistrate Ngcobo District, 3 January 1894, 66.
586 Ibid., C.J. Sweeney, Resident Magistrate Mthatha District, 1 January 1894, 67.

and detention were illegal, and so Tile was released. Nevertheless, the Attorney-General recommended that Tile should be reprimanded in the presence of the king, chiefs, headmen and commoners as a way of demotivating him.

Umnombo (Genealogy) 8: The House of Dalindyebo

Dalindyebo	iNdlu yaseKunene	iQadi of (iNdlu eNkulu)
Jongilizwe	Dabulamanzi	Jongintaba
Jonguhlanga	Fulinzima	Justice
Zwelibanzi		

Subsequent to his expulsion from the Wesleyan Methodist Church for participating in political affairs, Tile founded the abaThembu Independent Church in 1884. As Tile had a close connection with the Great Place, the abaThembu Church grew from strength to strength. His Church became more Africanist in outlook. While the Wesleyan Church was associated with extension of white control, the abaThembu Church espoused allegiance to the abaThembu king. It viewed politics and religion as closely interwoven. It projected an independent African image. It was an expression of African "opposition to European control [and] a positive desire to adopt the message of the Church to the heritage of the Tembu tribe".[587] And as it drew members from various African national groups, the abaThembu Church was, therefore, a unifying element. The abaThembu Church was supported by uKumkani Ngangelizwe and his son, Prince Aliva. Ngangelizwe was held in high regard by abaThembu Church leaders, as though he was its pope. Stressing its natural outlook, Lea regards the formation of the abaThembu Church as heralding the coming into being of the African separatist Church movement in South Africa.[588]

As pointed out elsewhere in this chapter, the year 1885 saw Prince Aliva assume power as the king of the abaThembu. He was since called Dalindyebo. UKumkani Dalindyebo had attended school at Clarkebury Seminary and St James Mission School in Mthatha. Like his father before him, Dalindyebo fell in favour with Tile. Tile's role as chief adviser to the king became more pronounced. However, the colonial government's intrusion in Tile–Dalindyebo relations resulted in Tile's influence gradually diminishing until the end of 1890. The Cape Government worked earnestly to break cordial relations between Tile and the Great Place.[589] Hence, by the end of 1885 Tile and the king were no longer allies against the imposition of white rule. In spite of all these changing relations between Tile and the Great Place, owing to the Cape Government's threats to Dalindyebo that his opposition to magisterial control

---

587 Macquarrie, *Stanford, vol. ii*, 10.
588 A. Lea, *The Native Separatist Church Movement in South Africa* (Cape Town: Juta, 1927), 23.
589 Hinchliff, *Church in South Africa*, 91.

"must inevitably end in the destruction of the chief's power",[590] abaThembuland was annexed to the Cape Colony in 1885. A process of annexation, which had been delayed by the Ninth Frontier War and the Transkeian Rebellion was now half-way through with the annexation of abaThembuland, amaGcalekaland and amaBomvanaland to the Cape Colony.[591]

It was in terms of Act No. 3 of 1885 that abaThembuland, amaGcalekaland and amaBomvanaland were annexed in 1885. However, chiefs of the amaGcaleka and uKumkani Sarhili "fumed at their military defeat and political demotion even as they outwardly acknowledged the overlordship of the Cape".[592] It should be noted that besides the annexation of abaThembuland, the process of annexation of African kingdoms was completed in 1894 with the annexation of amaMpondoland. As an attempt by the colonial government to diminish kingship and chiefly control, the annexationist policy could be understood in the context of J.C. Warner who had held that, "until the power of the chiefs [and kings] was completely broken, Christianity and [Western] civilization would make small advance among the Bantu."[593] Clearly, the motive behind embarking on annexing African kingdoms was that annexation "will bring the tribes ... under the direct control and administration of the Colonial Government".[594] In this connection, Yekela points out that "the late nineteenth-century annexations of the Transkeian Territories dealt chieftainship a further blow, though the annexations were, in a sense, a testimony to the failure of Grey's mid-century politics because resistance to colonial intrusion continued".[595] It is, therefore, not surprising that when Dalindyebo sought to oppose colonial rule, he was told that he should not deviate from his father's amicable course, "and not so soon after his [Ngangelizwe] death".[596]

On being annexed, abaThembuland was not treated as a united territory under one king. It continued to be treated as abaThembuland Proper (made up of Mthatha, Mjanyana, Ngcobo and Mqanduli) and Emigrant abaThembuland (comprising Xhalanga and iSidutyini or St Mark's). Since then, the magistrates were to have "jurisdiction in all civil cases".[597] The Governor was vested with power to allot land, which was to be divided into districts or wards. Each district was to be under a government-appointed headman who was responsible not to the chief or king but to the Chief Magistrate. It was the headman who recommended to the Chief Magistrate who should be allotted land. Those allotted land were thenceforth to pay annual hut tax to the magistrate.[598] These strategies were one of a series of colonial assaults on traditionalism and chiefly control.

---

590 *Cape Mercury*, 16 March 1893.
591 Mvenene, "Reverend Auld", 34.
592 Redding, "Sorcery and Sovereignty", 254.
593 Macquarrie, *Stanford, vol. ii*, 126.
594 USNA to CMT, 31 January 1885, CMT 1/9.
595 Yekela, "Unity and Division", 13.
596 USNA to CMT, 29 April 1885, CMT 1/9.
597 *Government Gazette*, No. 6642, 1 September 1885: Proclamation 140, 8 January 1895, 510-511.
598 *Government Gazette*, No. 5950, 16 September 1879: Proclamation 110, 8 January 1877.

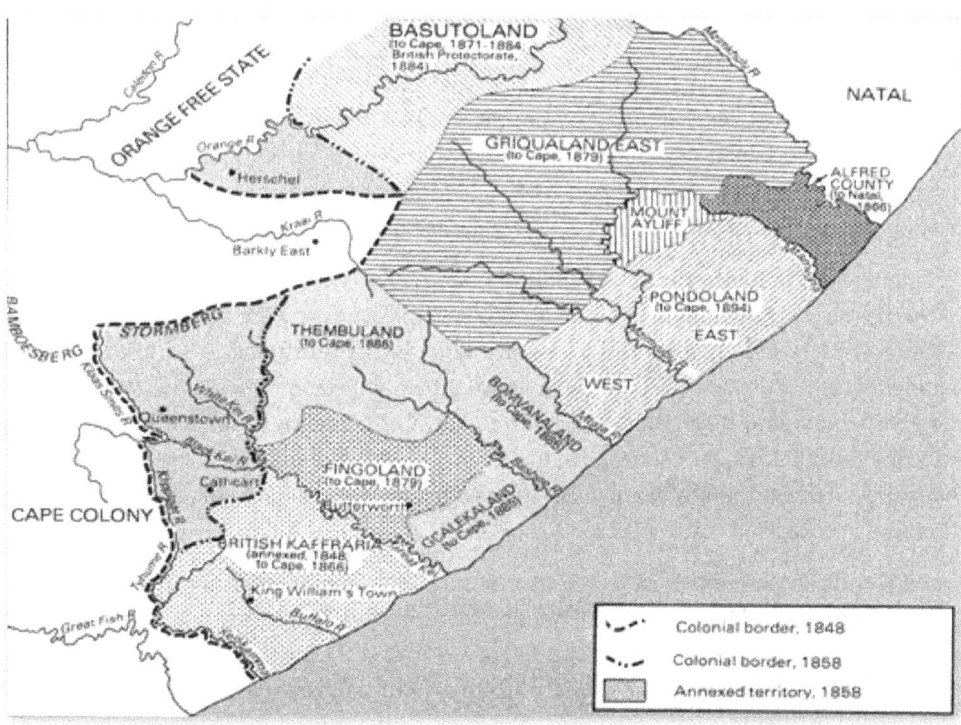

MAP 8: British annexations on the Eastern frontier, 1848-1894[599]

Magistrates were known for maladministering the annexed territories. They were responsible for administrative duties, including drawing up the hut tax registers, hearing court cases, assigning land for use by African families and enforcing the laws.[600] It was common practice that a magistrate could administer "justice according to the best of his judgement".[601] As a matter of fact, "Chief Magistrates were really political agents".[602] Being the representative of the colonial government, a resident magistrate, it was claimed, was looked upon as the chief by Africans.[603] In addition to being detectives, settling disputes and assisting in collecting hut tax in their locations, headmen were generally "to keep the authorities informed of all matters connected with the administration of the people in their charge".[604]

Redding argues, and rightly so, that the hut tax was a tax on wives, and points out that

> each wife had her own household hut ... had her own plot of arable land, and women were primarily responsible for producing the staple crops of maize,

---

599 J. Benyon, "The British Colonies", in T. Cameron and S.B. Spies (eds), *A New Illustrated History of South Africa* (Johannesburg: Southern Book Publishers, 1986), 171.
600 Redding, "Sorcery and Sovereignty", 255.
601 *Legislative Council Debates*, 15 April 1886, 21.
602 *Legislative Council Debates*, 30 April 1886, 86.
603 *Blue Book on Native Affairs*, G.27 – '74, 58.
604 Ibid., 59; USNA to CMT, 4 March 1885, CMT 1/9.

sorghum and cultivated vegetables ... the more wives a man had, the more income the wives could produce.[605]

In the circumstances, one can deduce from the duties of magistrates and headmen that the power of the kings and chiefs was completely shattered by 1885. More prominence was given to commoners as could be perceived in Stanford's practice of keeping on using chiefs, headmen and *amaphakathi* (councillors) as assessors both in civil and criminal cases.

Like the withdrawal from the abaThembu Church of uKumkani Ngangelizwe and his return to the Wesleyan Church, uKumkani Dalindyebo's displeasure at Tile's political activities was a slap in the face of Nehemiah Tile. It was as a result of the pressure exerted by the colonial authorities on uKumkani Dalindyebo following the annexation of abaThembuland that the abaThembu king dissociated himself from Tile. Consequently, from 1885 to 1890 Tile's activities lessened. However, towards the end of 1890 Tile became more dynamic and influential amongst the abaThembu. He stepped up his political and religious agitations by impressing on the king that it was time to unite.[606]

Consequently, in November 1890, the abaThembu king sought ways and means whereby abaThembuland could be united. And here Tile played a significant role. Tile proposed, amongst other things, "that the Thembu Church should now be recognised as the Church of the kingdom".[607] Giving the abaThembu Church an Africanist image, Tile proposed that no white ministers should conduct services. And soon a rift between the Wesleyan Church and abaThembu Church widened further as many members from the Wesleyan Church began drifting to the abaThembu Church. There was also a widened gulf between Tile and some abaThembu chiefs who clung to the Wesleyan Church. For example, uNkosi Mathanzima along with John Thengo Jabavu (1859-1921) unsuccessfully attempted to steer uKumkani Dalindyebo back to the Methodist Church.[608]

This attitude of uNkosi Mathanzima and Jabavu illustrated a conflict situation between Western religion and African religion, which gave rise not only to the division within the House of Ngubengcuka but also to antagonism within the abaThembu. In this sense, the Western religious beliefs and practices, attached to Christianity, were to a large degree incompatible with traditional religion, and as a consequence were responsible for a split within the abaThembu.

In 1891, Tile died having proclaimed Kula, Gqamani and Mkhize his successors. Nevertheless, these three men did not have the ability to organise the abaThembu Church. Though dead, Tile's influence could make its presence felt far and wide. African Wesleyan ministers in the Transvaal expressed their aversion to, and contempt for, the white missionaries who treated

---

605 Redding, "Sorcery and Sovereignty", 255.
606 Ntshumayelo Sotyatho, Interview, 31 July 1997; Nomishini Mthikrakra, Interview, Mqhekezweni Village, Mthatha, 8 July 1994; uNkosi Royal Zululiyazongoma Mnqanqeni, Interview, 25 January 1996 and 4 October 2014.
607 Saunders, "Tile and the Thembu Church", 562.
608 *Cape Mercury*, 16 March 1893.

them with disdain on account of the colour of their skin. This disaffection with white mission superiors culminated in African missionaries marching out of a mission conference in 1892 under the leadership of Mangena Mokone (1851-1936).[609]

Tile's death resulted in uKumkani Dalindyebo feeling desolate in so far as having a chief adviser whose ideas measured up with those of Tile. As a consequence, he was pressurised into ultimately cutting off ties with the abaThembu Church in 1895. He switched over to the Wesleyan Church and until his death in 1920, uKumkani Dalindyebo remained a Wesleyan in spite of Tile's attempts to conscientise him into the importance of uniting the abaThembu around their Church.[610]

Despite setbacks to Tile's activities, his founding of the abaThembu Church had marked a new era of a widespread movement. Due to Tile having led the first breakaway, in 1883, from the Methodist mission church,[611] large numbers of independent Churches, founded by Africans, sprang up after his death. They all rejected white control in all its forms. These Churches prepared the ground for African leadership and the rise of African political consciousness. Having drawn members from various African national groups, the abaThembu Church then joined the Ethiopian Church (iBandla lase Tiyopiya) in 1895. The latter Church had been founded in 1892 by Reverend Mangena Mokone, who had seceded from the Wesleyan Church in Pretoria, and whose expression of disgust with racial discrimination as was practised in the Wesleyan Methodist Church fell on deaf ears.[612] Mokone's Church then affiliated with the African Methodist Episcopal Church (AME) in 1896.

The year 1898 saw Reverend Pambani Mzimba, having been influenced by the formation of an Ethiopian Church in the Transvaal, playing a leading part in the secession from the Free Church of Scotland towards the formation of the Presbyterian Church of Africa in Lovedale.[613] In the same vein, Reverend James Mata Dwane was at the centre of a breakaway from the Anglican Church and formed his own Order of Ethiopia in 1900.[614] P.J. Mzimba had gone through financial disputes and problems with the Church, and had made a great contribution to the emergence of black nationalism.[615] In 1906, Burnet Gabha, the great-grandson of the Xhosa Christian prophet, Ntsikana,[616] had "foreshadowed and inspired the formation of AICs [African Initiated Churches]",[617] and had broken away from the Free Church of Scotland

---

609 Parsons, *New History*, 209.
610 Mncedi Phondolwendlovu Nyoka, Interview, 29 April 1994 and 7 September 1994; Ntshumayelo Sotyatho, Interview, 26 June 1995 and 31 July 1997.
611 Hodgson, "A Battle for Sacred Power", 87.
612 Pretorius and Jafta, "African Initiated Churches", 214.
613 L. Mzimba, "The African Church", in J.D. Taylor (ed.), *Christianity and the Natives of South Africa* (Lovedale: Lovedale Press, 1928), 89.
614 S. Dwane, *Issues in the South African Theological Debate* (Johannesburg: Skotaville, 1989), 88.
615 Nhanha and Peires, "Introduction", vii.
616 Ntsikana (d.1822) was popularly known for his *ingoma*: *ulo Tixo mkulu/ uloNgub'enkulu*, which was recorded in 1844 by Ludwig Dohne, a German missionary working among the amaXhosa. See Jacob Ludwig Dohne, *Das Kafferland und sein Bewohner* (Berlin, 1844), 69-70.
617 Pretorius and Jafta, "African Initiated Churches", 213.

and founded the Ntsikana Memorial Church at Pirie in 1911.[618] In 1907, the amaMfengu in Ngqushwa displayed a growing wave of nationalistic tendencies by instituting an annual amaMfengu Emancipation Day, celebrations being held on 14 May every year at Mqwashini. Under the milkwood tree they made a three-fold oath, which their forefathers had taken in 1835. As with one voice, their forefathers, having been settled by Governor D'Urban in Ngqushwa (Peddie), Kamastone and Oxkraal (both being amaMfengu reserves near Komani) promised to be faithful to God, to be loyal to the British King and to do all in their power to support their missionaries and educate their children, as confirmation of their allegiance to the colonial government.[619] In 1910, the amaXhosa had initiated a yearly celebration in which they honoured Ntsikana by forming the Saint Ntsikana Memorial Association.[620] The celebrations were known as *uManyano Lobuzalwana Bohlanga Lwama Xhosa* (the Union of the Brotherhood of the amaXhosa Nation).

The historical significance of Nehemiah Xoxo Tile lies in the fact that he left an indelible mark amongst African ministers. He was one of the African dynamic spiritual leaders who presented a formidable threat to the mainline Churches controlled by European missionary societies.[621] He proved that the Church could be adjusted to the realities of life. Since his secession from the Wesleyan Church in 1883, the Wesleyan Church began to witness African protest movements and the beginning of African separatist Churches, which all asserted religious independence. Africans had then realised that change was necessary.[622] He set the pace for people's aspiration for unity against racial discrimination. As father of African protest politico-religious movements espousing African religious autonomy, Tile stressed that religion could not be divorced from politics and the social life of the people.

As Saunders aptly maintains:

> Tile was not only the dominant figure in the early history of the church; he also at the same time led a significant movement of political protest. Together, the religious and political activities with which he was connected constitute probably the most interesting of all the varied responses of Africans east of the Kei to the process of the extension of white rule in that area.[623]

While Wesleyans linked the Church to uKumkanikazi Victoria, Tile saw the Church in relation to the expectations, aspirations and demands of the abaThembu kings and chiefs. He viewed the abaThembu Church and the abaThembu king as the centre on which African political, racial and national consciousness hinged.

---

618 B.W. Ntsikana, *Ityalike ye Sikhumbuzo Sika Ntsikana* (Port Elizabeth, 1945), 5.
619 E.H. Hurcombe, "The Story of our Missionary Society", *Forward*, December 1925, 7003.
620 Hodgson, "A Battle for Sacred Power", 86.
621 R.B. Beck, "Monarchs and Missionaries among the Tswana and Sotho", in Elphick and Davenport (eds), *Christianity in South Africa* (Cape Town: David Philip, 1997), 119.
622 Saunders, "Tile and the Thembu Church", 566; Parsons, *New History*, 208.
623 Saunders, "Tile and the Thembu Church", 554.

On a political plane, Tile's immeasurable impact was also conceivable. He served as a link between uKumkani Dalindyebo and the chief magistrate. As a king's spokesperson, he once "complained on his [king's] behalf about how the boundaries of the [kingdom] had been drawn".[624] Tile's influence bore fruit at a meeting held in November 1890, wherein "ways in which the [aba]Thembu could again urge their demand for a united [aba]Thembuland"[625] were the subject of discussion. Quite correctly, Tile can be described as a "fervent [aba]Thembu nationalist",[626] indicating the political role he played in abaThembuland, in addition to being a religious reformer. Thus, Tile can best be regarded as the root and forerunner of African protest politics in South Africa. Indeed, he was the father of the African indigenous Church movement in South Africa.

---

624 Yekela, "Unity and Division", 44.
625 Ibid., 45.
626 Ibid.

7

COLONIAL ASSAULT ON THE HOUSE OF NGUBENGCUKA, 1894-1920

This chapter examines abaThembu divisive politics from the enactment by the Cape Prime Minister, Cecil John Rhodes (who succeeded Gordon Sprigg in 1890), of the Glen Grey Act of 1894 to the Union of the 'white' South African Government's enactment of the Native Land Act of 1913. It ends with the death of uKumkani Dalindyebo in 1920. To what extent the Glen Grey Act emasculated chiefly power, control and authority is discussed within the context of the abaThembu kingdom. It is also shown how and why the Native Land Act (No. 27 of 1913) reinforced the Glen Grey Act and diminished the status of traditional leaders in their political domains. An attempt is made to highlight the colonial and union governments' assault on the abaThembu kingdom. The spotlight is on abaThembu reaction to white policy and legislation affecting Africans, and how and why these legislations diminished chiefly power and paved the way for the political division of abaThembuland in 1958. It is worth noting that the appointment by the South African Government of Chief Kaiser Mathanzima, A! Daliwonga! as the paramount chief of Emigrant abaThembuland in 1966 is traceable to these legislations.

As was alluded to in the previous chapter, the colonial government's policy of incorporating into the Cape African chiefdoms and kingdoms had divisive effects on the abaThembu. For example, in 1884 Cala had been divided between Xhalanga and isiDutyini (St Mark's). In 1885, abaThembuland, amaGcalekaland and amaBomvanaland were annexed by the Cape Colony in terms of Proclamation No. 140 of 1885.[627] The annexation of abaThembuland coincided with uKumkani Dalindyebo's accession to kingship which, according to Yekela, "implied the demise of that kingdom's genuine political independence".[628] Indeed, the colonial govern-

---

627 *Government Gazette*, No. 6642, 1 September 1885: Proclamation by Sir Hercules George Robert Robinson.
628 Yekela, "Unity and Division", 42.

ment's meddling in the affairs of the abaThembu polity weakened uKumkani Dalindyebo's kingship, status, influence and prestige.[629]

Furthermore, the annexed abaThembu territories were not treated as one united kingdom, but as abaThembuland Proper and Emigrant abaThembuland. Constituting abaThembuland Proper were the Districts of Mthatha, Ngcobo and Mqanduli. Emigrant abaThembuland comprised Xhalanga (Cala) and isiDutyini (St Mark's). By 1894 amaMpondoland was annexed by the Cape Colony in terms of Act No. 5 of 1894.[630] Thus, the 1870s, 1880s and 1890s characterised the great age of the scramble and conquest in Southern Africa. Between 1879 and 1894 all the Transkeian territories, viz. amaGriqualand East, abaThembuland, amaGcalekaland and amaMpondoland were incorporated into the Cape Colony. The annexation of amaMpondoland brought the whole of the Transkei under white domination. The extension of white control, with its divisive tendencies on African culture, religion and kingdom, meant the introduction into the Transkeian territories of magisterial rule. Magisterial rule clashed with the traditional system of justice. After the annexation of Transkeian territories, white magistrates ruled through government-appointed headmen, most of whom were, in some instances, regarded as chiefs by their subjects.

However, one amongst abaThembu chief Mathanzima and his headmen in isiDutyini (St Mark's) "evinced a strong desire to work in harmony with the government".[631] Resident magistrate, H.H. Bunn, noted that: "the government has a strong supporter in the Emigrant Tembu chief Matanzima, he is an exceedingly shrewd and capable man, more popular by far with the people of the territory than his late brother Gangelizwe was ... Matanzima's memorandum of 27th June last agreeing to contribute £3,000 towards a bridge over the Tsomo river can be regarded as a potential indication that he is desirous of living and working actively in the interests of the government and of his people."[632] UNkosi Mathanzima also offered the colonial government a reserve of 5,000 morgen of land for the removal and erection of a new chief magistracy from "the mission lands at St Mark's ... to a central position".[633]

With the increase in the tempo of the scramble for Southern Africa, independent African authority south of the Limpopo River was gradually eliminated. Kings and chiefs were relegated to the level of government-paid servants. Their influence amongst their subjects was lessened; white magistrates gained an upper hand and dominated kings and chiefs.[634] When all the independent southern abeNguni kingdoms and chiefdoms were annexed in 1894, the Cape Government did not open Transkei to large-scale white settlement as the Cape

---

629 Ibid.
630 *Government Gazette*, No. 7645, 28 September 1894: Proclamation No. 331 of 1894 by W.G. Cameron.
631 *Blue Book on Native Affairs*, 1887-1894, H.H. Bunn, Resident Magistrate St Mark's District, 31 December 1893; Charles J. Levey, Resident Magistrate Xhalanga District, Cala, 3 January 1894, 65.
632 Ibid.
633 Ibid.
634 W.D. Hammond-Tooke, "Chieftainship in Transkeian Political Development", *Journal of Modern African Studies*, 2, 4 (1964), 516.

authorities entertained fears of further armed African resistance. As a matter of fact, the Cape Government stepped up its policy of abrogating chiefly power in view of its awareness that for it "to rule east of the Nciba River might involve endless trouble."[635] And it soon stepped up its policy of diminishing chiefly power and control through magisterial rule.

Following incorporation into the Cape Colony, the former Transkei was transformed into a labour pool from which white farmers and mine owners could procure labour. The former Transkei was also used as a place to dump undesirable Africans from British Kaffraria (Ciskei since 1864). The fact that the former Transkei, unlike the former Ciskei, was preponderantly inhabited by Africans who had for so long lived on their land, facilitated the Cape authorities' move to use Transkei as a labour reserve for whites. Africans were thus turned into wage earners within a money-based economy. Their drifting to farms and mines was likely, as it later did, to strain the ties that had held Africans coherently. Their social link with their families and traditional leaders was in some cases curtailed. This was accompanied by detribalisation and contempt for culture.

All attempts by Africans to counteract the Cape Government's endeavours to administratively, geographically and politically divide abaThembuland by using magistrates had aborted owing to whites' persistence with exerting influence on uKumkani Ngangelizwe. Nevertheless, the death of Reverend Xoxo Tile in 1891 did not completely dampen the spirit of Ethiopianism. As will be seen, during the second decade of the twentieth century, Africans could evince an urge for unity in spite of whites' divisive policies. This urge meant that though he was dead, Tile's ideas and dreams of a united Africa lived on.

The incorporation into the Cape Colony of African kingdoms and chiefdoms made it inevitable that the colonial whites would take it upon themselves to direct African administrative policies. It necessitated that a common policy be adopted towards Africans so that Africans could never be politically equal to whites. Thus, administrative and political readjustments were necessary if whites were to remain supreme.[636] Moreover, it was whites' fear of being outvoted by the numerically superior Africans that prompted the colonial government to step up the magisterial rule in the former Transkei. In line with this fear, Rhodes expressed his desire to introduce a bill that would cater for the administration of affairs first at Cacadu (Glen Grey) and then at other proclaimed districts. The bill Rhodes envisaged was also to look into the distribution of land at Cacadu (Glen Grey). More importantly, the bill dealt with questions of primogeniture, land tenure, councils, labour tax and African customs. The result was the passing of the Glen Grey Act (Act No. 25 of 1894), which became law in August 1894.

The origins of Glen Grey are traceable to 1853 when Governor Sir Cathcart (1794-1854) created, west of the Indwe River, a location of 250,000 morgen for occupation by the western abaThembu who numbered approximately 15,000 to 16,000.[637] The creation of Glen Grey was part of a colonial settlement, which culminated in the coming into being of Komani, a

---

635 Saunders, "Annexation of Transkei", 190.
636 *Cape of Good Hope House of Assembly Debates*, 10 July 1894, 25 and 283.
637 Bouch, "Glen Grey before Cecil Rhodes", 3.

new colonial district. Indeed, Glen Grey was part of Komani. At its inception, writes Bouch, "Glen Grey contained four principal chieftainships",[638] under the nominal paramountcy of uKumkanikazi Nonesi and the control of abaThembu agent, Joseph Warner, an ex-missionary "who exercised a broad but unspecific and undefined authority on behalf of the government in Cape Town".[639] No sooner was Glen Grey created than Warner proposed in March 1856 that chiefs who remained on good terms with the Cape Government be paid stipends by the colonial government, as one of the methods of weakening chiefly authority. As Bouch observes, a stipendiary system recently introduced in British Kaffraria in 1855 was intended by Warner "to be a substitute for chiefly income derived from fines [isizi], as in British Kaffraria … [and] would encourage or buy goodwill".[640] Warner proceeded to unilaterally rank chiefs thus: "Manel, a first-class chief under Warner's ranking, was really only a minor sub-chief under Nonese. Petrus Mahonga, erstwhile headman of the White Kei mission station, became a second-class chief under Warner's superintendence, although he had no claim to chiefly standing."[641]

To all intents and purposes the Glen Grey Act was an expression of Rhodes' ideas of separate political institutions and local administration, which heralded racial exclusion and the politics of ethnic separatism in South Africa. Its point of departure was that "…the natives must be treated differently to Europeans".[642] It was based on four premises, which were: to give Africans interest in the land, allow the superior minds amongst them to attend to their local wants, remove the canteens and give Africans a stimulus to labour.[643] The Glen Grey Act was aimed at emphasising racial differences in order to safeguard whites' political position of supremacy. It made provision for the imposition of labour tax to all Africans; it dealt with land and franchise issues. Bouch states that the Glen Grey Act "was intended to meet several purposes: to put in place a land-tenure system based on small plots (4 morgen), inheritable only on the basis of primogeniture, so that the bulk of the male population would take employment in the Colony, spurred on by a labour tax in cash; an extension of previous efforts to limit the extension of African franchise rights by denying Africans possession of land on the terms laid down in the franchise law; and the institution of limited self-government based on local councils."[644] While introducing individual land tenure based on surveyed allotments, it also made provision for the establishment of councils, which were to discuss Africans' land issues and matters of common concern.

Critically looking at how Rhodes justified the Glen Grey Bill, one can note that the Glen Grey Act was a wholly racist and segregationist measure. Bouch identifies the Act as a key precursor of twentieth-century segregation, and an unprecedented device to force Africans

---

638 Ibid.
639 Ibid.
640 Ibid., 4.
641 Ibid.
642 *Cape of Good Hope House of Assembly Debates*, 9 August 1894, 464.
643 *Cape of Good Hope House of Assembly Debates*, 26 July 1894, 363.
644 Bouch, "Glen Grey before Cecil Rhodes", 1-2.

to migrate into labour on the gold mines.[645] Moreover, it was meant for areas mainly inhabited by aboriginal natives, particularly the district of Cacadu (Glen Grey) to the west of the Indwe River.[646] And for that reason it was segregationist. It is, therefore, not far-fetched to say that it was "a further step towards the recognition of racial difference".[647]

What prompted Rhodes to advocate the Glen Grey Act was that he reasoned that Africans were multiplying at such a rate that sooner or later they would not be able to support themselves in view of the scarcity of land. However, the district of Glen Grey, Rhodes' area of experimentation, had a population of about 40,000, while the Cape Colony had 600,000 people. In both areas, Africans were in the majority. In line with his view that Africans were rapidly increasing in numbers, Rhodes sought to give the abaThembu some land, which no whites might enter, except white officials and traders. His overriding aim was to equip the abaThembu to govern, manage, tax and educate themselves. He sought to teach them the concept of labour, to train them to build their own roads and bridges and to grow their own food and forests. Rhodes also sought to teach the concept of the dignity of labour amongst Africans and as a result of the misconception, he felt that they were not accustomed to labouring. Further, Rhodes wrongfully alleged that Africans' minds were no longer occupied since the cessation of the wars of dispossession and resistance. He further alleged that, having nothing to do on account of laziness, Africans enjoyed themselves in the canteens, and therefore should be made to seek and depend on rendering labour to whites.

Thus, the Glen Grey Act was based wholly on Rhodes' misconceptions of Africans' mode of labour. Though Rhodes did not support whites' general feeling that Africans "were a distinct source of trouble and loss to the country",[648] he nevertheless firmly believed that Africans ought to be used and made a great source of assistance and wealth to whites. To render such assistance, Africans were to be a source of labour and thus were, according to Rhodes, used to good purpose. By providing labour to whites away from their place of abode, Africans gradually lost touch with their culture, beliefs, religion and traditional practices.

Continuing his misconception of Africans, Rhodes viewed them as indolent. He further reiterated that the Cape Government should "remove these poor children out of their state of sloth and laziness".[649] Thus, Rhodes' concept of labour was in direct contrast to the African concept of labour. Undoubtedly, the Glen Grey Act was based on misconceptions. Africans could live without working for whites. Their staple food was maize, meat and milk. They herded their cattle. They were not generally poor. Rhodes' insistence that Africans seek work elsewhere was to erode their unity as they would most likely shift their economic unit and no longer pay collective allegiance to their traditional leaders. Families were consequently set apart as men had to leave their families behind when moving to white farms and industries to supply labour.

---

645 Ibid., 2.
646 *Government Gazette*, No. 6637, 31 August 1894, 1682.
647 Saunders, *Annexation of Transkeian Territories*, 141.
648 *Cape House of Assembly Debates*, 26 July 1894, 362.
649 Ibid., 363.

Clearly, the Glen Grey Act had as its main concerns taxation, land tenure, the franchise and local administration. It was in an attempt to induce non-working men to go and seek work on white farms and industries that Rhodes moved that a labour tax be levied on all African men. Rhodes hoped that the imposition of labour tax would serve as a gentle stimulant to them.[650] The labour tax was in addition to the already existing hut tax. The labour tax of 10 shillings and the hut tax were meant to relieve the Cape Government of the economic burden of administering the Transkeian territories. Such expenses, as were incurred in building schools, roads and other infrastructure, were catered for through local taxation of all African men. As it was compulsory for all African men to pay labour tax, it was in turn a must that non-working men devised ways and means whereby they could procure money and pay tax. It was, therefore, inevitable that men should go and seek work in order to be in a splendid position to meet the labour tax demands. The labour tax was thus a measure to promote amongst Africans the importance of providing labour to whites.

In terms of the Glen Grey Act, individual land tenure replaced communal land ownership. Africans were entitled in accordance with the Glen Grey Act to have title deeds and plots. The Location Boards were in charge of these plots. White farms were turned into locations, each of which had a Location Board. The Location Boards were constituted by three men nominated by the Cape Government. Each location consisted of 2,700 morgen of pastoral ground and 300 morgen of agricultural ground.[651] A title deed for each head of each family was inalienable for three to four years. This inalienation was intended to prevent any possible transfer of land to any family. This had the effect of forcing those without land out to seek labour and fend for themselves on white farms and industries.

By making provision for, and implementing the principle of, individual property and land rights, the Glen Grey Act negated the traditional system of communal land ownership. Thus, it undermined the power and authority of the traditional leaders whose duty was, amongst others, to allocate lands to individual family members. By limiting land to one family and by making provision that those granted title should pay an annual quitrent of 15 shillings, the Glen Grey Act sought to fix Africans on the land and to force the increasing population to go out and work. By recognising the law of primogeniture, which ruled that allotments were to descend to the eldest son, the Glen Grey Act did not only deny land rights to younger sons who would consequently flock to the labour market, but it also limited African producers. By forbidding African and white mixed settlements, Rhodes laid the foundations for segregation. Rhodes had reiterated that no whites could live "in the midst of savages just emerging from barbarism".[652]

It has become clear that recognition of the law of primogeniture meant that the heir would inherit his father's land, while his younger brothers would have to seek employment or move to unsurveyed districts. This cut off the link within the sons of a family as the younger sons

---

650 Ibid., 365.
651 Ibid., 363.
652 *Cape House of Assembly Debates*, 26 July 1894, 367-368.

had nothing to gain on their father's limited small land. While in industrial cities or in mine-compounds, they would not always be keen to return home, and would gradually lose respect for the traditional leaders and rural life circumstances.

Furthermore, all unalienated land at Glen Grey was divided into locations. Unsurveyed land was treated as commonage. The former Transkei was divided into twenty-seven districts. Each district consisted of thirty locations, and was in turn subdivided into four electoral wards or areas. That the authority, power and control of traditional leaders were diminished while magisterial rule gained in prominence became evident.[653] In control of each district was a white magistrate appointed by the Governor-General. Senior chiefs' position and authority dwindled as a result. White magistrates heading locations wielded much power and authority in their respective locations. For example, the white magistrate was both judicial officer and administrator in one. He was also a tax collector and dispenser of justice. Above district magistrates was a chief magistrate. White magistrates had veto power over the kings' and chiefs' deliberations and resolutions. Kings and chiefs were relegated to the role of arbitrators, in which case they had to apply the customary law. Even there they had no final word. Generally, white magistrates appointed loyal Africans to head districts. These loyal Africans who became headmen were paid officials of the Cape Government who were responsible to white magistrates.[654] Thus, the power of traditional leaders was severely curtailed. Indeed, the Cape Government had succeeded in wielding decisive influence over the abaThembu and other southern abeNguni kingdoms and chiefdoms.

The Glen Grey Act also dealt with the franchise issues as affecting Africans. Even though the abaThembu held land under individual land tenure, clause 26 of the Glen Grey Act ruled that individual land tenure on the Glen Grey model would count as communal land ownership for franchise purposes. In this way, the Glen Grey title did not count as the franchise qualification. That the Glen Grey title did not qualify Africans for the vote was responsible for the exceedingly low percentage (between 15 and 16 between 1892 and 1910) of African voters in the Cape Colony. Thus, this measure of excluding land held under Glen Grey was the whites' attempt to protect themselves from being outvoted by Africans whom Rhodes described as "children, and as the Government protected their land"[655] could under no circumstances claim a vote on it.

Furthermore, there was a re-adjustment of African franchise qualifications. Such readjustment was prompted by the increase of potential African voters following the incorporation of Africans into the Cape Colony. Before the annexation of the Transkeian territories (between 1879 and 1894), the property franchise qualification for all males irrespective of colour was to the value of twenty-five pounds; it was then raised to seventy-five pounds. Alternatively, it was required of all males to earn fifty pounds per annum. In addition, a prospective voter was also to pass a literacy test (test of civilisation) whereby he was expected to be able to sign his

---

653 Maylam, *History of African People*, 102.
654 Bouch, "Glen Grey before Cecil Rhodes", 10.
655 *Cape House of Assembly Debates*, 26 July 1894, 365.

name and write his address and occupation. This re-adjustment was meant to disenfranchise as many Africans as possible. It was intended to exclude Africans from the vote. While individual land tenure diminished chiefly power and control over land distribution, it was a heavy blow to Africans that the Cape non-racial franchise was "circumscribed by high property qualifications".[656]

The Glen Grey Act also made provision for local government. Rhodes argued that Africans should direct their own local affairs. He justified local politics and the council system as intended "to keep the minds of the natives occupied ... to think of their roads and their bridges".[657] He further insisted that, "Having proposed that they should form councils, so that it should be a farce, let them tax themselves, and give them funds to spend in the matter of building bridges."[658] Rhodes justified African involvement in local affairs and district councils by stating that some chiefs had expressed the complaint that "they had nothing to do but grow mealies and think of mischief; they did not understand concepts of parliamentary rights and racial equality ... they did care about matters of local interest".[659] However, it was later revealed in newspapers that Rhodes' assertion was not a true reflection of the abaThembu aspirations. Africans did not clamour for councils.[660]

In the spirit of the Glen Grey Act, the Cape Government introduced the council system in 1895. It was in all probability "an extension of the system of magisterial rule",[661] as will be clear from the way its representatives were nominated and elected. Under the council system, each district was divided into four wards or electoral areas. The white magistrate called all registered taxpayers for each of the four electoral wards to a central place, usually a store. Landowners and taxpayers of each electoral area elected one member, while the native commissioner nominated two members to form a local district council of six members. A local native commissioner chaired a local district council. Each district council nominated at its November meeting two from amongst its members, with the Governor-General appointed a third member, to represent the district council on the General Council. Under Proclamation 352 of 1894, provision was made for the establishment of councils in Gcuwa (Butterworth), Dutywa, Ngqamakhwe and Tsomo.[662] And this was carried out in 1895. In terms of Proclamation 319 of 1899, the council system was extended to the District of Centane (Kentani).[663] Before a Select Committee of the Cape Assembly, whose mandate was to assess the working and administration of the Glen Grey system, Enoch Mamba, a labour agent of Dutywa and chairperson of the Transkei Vigilante Association, complained:

---

656 Worden, *Modern South Africa*, 29 and 31.
657 *Cape House of Assembly Debates*, 26 July 1894, 366.
658 Ibid.
659 Ibid., 367.
660 *Cape Times*, 28 February 1895; *Imvo*, 29 January 1895.
661 L. Hailey, *An African Survey* (Oxford: Oxford University Press, 1957), 353.
662 Hammond-Tooke, "The Transkeian Council System, 1895-1955", 461.
663 Ibid., 462.

> The councils in the Transkei ... are appointed by the headmen, and not by the people. Owing to the wording of the Proclamation, the ratepayers are not referred to at all, so that when the District Councils hold a meeting, the people know nothing about the proceedings ... and what is more, in that Council they ask for certain laws to be made for the Transkei about which the people know nothing. The Government take it that they represent the people, whereas they only represent the headman. Then again, the real efficient men are outside the Council; there are men outside the Council who are far superior to the men on the Council. I know for a fact that if the appointment of Councillors was in the hands of the ratepayers, a better feeling would exist in favour of the Glen Grey Act. In districts like Qumbu, say, for the first two years, although people may be allowed to elect members of Boards and Councillors, they may appoint Headmen as members first and the people would change the position themselves after.[664]

Mamba's criticism fell on deaf ears as the Select Committee defended the system as being beneficial to Africans and proceeded to extend it to seven districts in abaThembuland and East amaGriqualand.

The General Council was a platform for discussing Africans' land issues and matters of common concern. It consisted of two members from each district council and white magistrates who had no voting rights. Its chairperson was the chief magistrate. This system was first applied in the district of Cacadu (Glen Grey). White magistrates controlled and checked any criticism by Africans against the council system and rather ensured that discussions were around matters of a local nature. All attempts were made not to have mixed white and African councils, and with this view in mind the northwestern portion of Glen Grey was excluded from the district council of Glen Grey and was transferred to the district council of Wodehouse.[665] Though Africans were taxed to finance the activities and administration of councils, white farmers were free from taxation, as they had their own system of government.

Considering the nature and mode of elections and nominations of council members, it can be maintained that these councils were a means to curb African electoral power. They were unrepresentative of Africans and provided an appearance or illusion of local self-government. Chaired, and its discussions directed by white magistrates, councils had no authority to change white laws. Furthermore, they acted in an advisory capacity, that is advising white officials on what Africans needed, and indeed they focused on local issues and less on political affairs. Used by whites as strategies to effectively exclude Africans, particularly the Glen Grey abaThembu, from the Cape's non-racial franchise, the council system was a forerunner to the system of the Transkei Territories General Council (TTGC) of 1903, the United Transkeian Territories General Council (UTTGC) of 1931[666] and the Bantu Authorities Act of 1951. The UTTGC, as a culmination of a federation of the various district councils, formed

---

664 Report of Minutes of Evidence Taken before the Select Committee on the Glen Grey Act, 1903, 155.
665 *Cape House of Assembly Debates*, 30 July 1894, 379.
666 Yekela, "Unity and Division", 14.

the *Bhunga*.⁶⁶⁷ Encouraging elected but non-traditional leaders to participate in local affairs, the Bhunga played a major role in sidelining the chiefs. To be exact, not only did the council system breathe the spirit of segregation, as is clear from its propagation of separate district councils, but it "was only a vehicle for the propagation and the execution by the [Cape] Government of its own aims and decisions".⁶⁶⁸

With the introduction of the council system came the split of all annexed Transkeian territories into twenty-seven districts and the formation of three chief magistracies, viz. Transkei Proper, abaThembuland and East amaGriqualand (with amaMpondoland). These chief magistracies had separate capitals. Butterworth became the capital of Transkei Proper, Mthatha of abaThembuland and Kokstad of East amaGriqualand.⁶⁶⁹ Furthermore, the Cape Government then divided Mqanduli into abaThembu, amaBomvana and amaHegebe chiefdoms, each of which was subdivided into locations. Each chiefdom was to consist of approximately thirty locations. In these chiefdoms, headmen assumed administrative and key positions as they were relied upon by whites during elections for councils.⁶⁷⁰ The fruits of their loyalty to the Cape Government became apparent when they were given chairmanship in meetings relating to canvassing and elections.⁶⁷¹

Cases from the headmen's court were directed to the resident magistrate who had more judicial power than chiefs and headmen. It was not uncommon that chiefs' courts were bypassed. Thus, the council system went contrary to the traditional system of administration. The fact that locations were subdivided and each placed under government-appointed paid officials – the headmen – meant that district councils curtailed the traditional system of justice. It is therefore no wonder that people began to look down upon kingship and chiefly authority.

That kings and chiefs were also to be members of district councils if they won elections or were nominated, necessitated that they had to pander to the wishes of the people. As a result of the introduction of the council system, kings' and chiefs' fate depended on their ability to satisfy the people. Yet, although they were the traditional trustees of the people, they could not issue instructions or make final decisions in their areas of jurisdiction, as these might be vetoed by white magistrates. Under these conditions chiefs and kings largely relayed to their people instructions issued by white magistrates. Hence, they appeared as agents of the colonial administration, or as Hammond-Tooke puts it, "as Government stooges".⁶⁷² White magistrates set out to control and check any criticism levelled against the council system. The Glen Grey Act and its provisions was not only a forerunner for segregation, but it was

---

667 The word *Bhunga* comes from the isiXhosa word meaning to discuss in secrecy, and is used for 'council'.
668 Brownlee, *Reminiscences*, 138.
669 Hammond-Tooke, "The Transkeian Council System, 1895-1955", 457.
670 *Queenstown Free Press*, 22 December 1893.
671 *Queenstown Free Press*, 9 August 1898; *Cape Times*, 9 February 1904.
672 Hammond-Tooke, "Chieftainship", 518.

also a slap in the face of traditional leaders as it promoted non-traditional leadership in all its facades. It usurped the power, control, influence and authority of traditional leaders.

In 1902, all judicial power in Transkeian territories was vested in the chief magistrates for Transkeian territories. All other chief magistrates came under one chief magistrate whose seat was in Mthatha. An assistant chief magistrate in each district was to "assist the chief magistrate in the execution of his duties".[673]

The year 1903 saw the chief magistrates of Transkei Proper, abaThembuland, East amaGriqualand and amaMpondoland incorporated and becoming known as the Transkeian Territories General Council (TTGC) under the chief magistrate in Mthatha. Each of the twenty-seven districts was divided into thirty wards or locations. Hammond-Tooke asserts:

> Each [location was] under a government-appointed headman, directly responsible to the magistrate for the welfare and good governance of his people: the chiefs were allowed to remain as titular heads of their tribes, but [with] severely curtailed powers. They received stipends in lieu of tribute, their powers of making war and exercising criminal jurisdiction were removed and, although they still tried civil cases involving customary law (provided such custom was not 'repugnant to natural justice'), appeals from their courts were tried de novo in the magistrates' courts. Tribesmen were free to by-pass both chief's and headman's courts if they so wished.[674]

The TTGC had limited powers and restricted responsibility as it focused purely on local and practical affairs like education, customary law, cattle-dipping to combat diseases, limitation of stock, fencing, agriculture, irrigation, water conservation, road building and markets.[675] It did not have any power to deal with matters pertaining to wider political issues affecting Africans. No wonder, therefore, that it was regarded as a strategy to implement political segregation. Its influence on the South African Government was minimal. The Bhunga, as the UTTGC was popularly known, met annually in Mthatha under the chairmanship of the chief magistrate of the Transkeian Territories.[676] The Bhunga was constituted of twenty-six magistrates and three members of each district council appointed by members of each district council. Kings of abaThembuland, Eastern amaMpondoland and Western amaMpondoland served as ex officio members.

However, most provisions of the Glen Grey Act were greeted with African opposition and could therefore not be translated into effective policy. For example, individual land tenure, non-divisibility of land held under Glen Grey title and the principle of primogeniture fell away in 1903. Labour tax was dropped in 1905. Land tenure provisions were largely confined to the Glen Grey district. Be that as it may, the Glen Grey Act laid a foundation for the introduction of local and self-government in the former Transkei.

---

673 *Government Gazette*, No. 8456, 11 July 1902: Proclamation 112, 3 July 1902, 65.
674 Hammond-Tooke, "The Transkeian Council System, 1895-1955", 457.
675 Carter, Karis and Stultz, *South Africa's Transkei*, 92.
676 Hammond-Tooke, "The Transkeian Council System, 1895-1955", 463.

The Glen Grey Act and its provisions aside, the South African War broke out in 1899. The war was fought by both whites and Africans. It was fought to determine which white authority held real power in South Africa. And, writes Worden, it "marked the completion of the process of conquest begun in the 1870s."[677] Both Boers and Britons agreed that Africans should not participate in the war and that Africans should be unarmed for fear that they would thenceforth shake off white control. In a bid to maintain their prestige in the face of Africans who constituted about eighty percent of the inhabitants of South Africa, whites were united in prohibiting Africans from joining any warring party.

However, when the war started both Boers and Britons seemed not to stand by their word of not arming Africans. Nor did they bother about keeping Africans out of the war. Therefore, Africans, including the abaThembu, participated in the South African War (1899-1902), hoping that they would be given equal political rights with whites. But that was not to be. Africans were promised by Britons the postwar extension of the non-racial franchise to the former Boer republics, the regaining of access to land and liberation of Africans from Boer slavery. Putting Boers in a poor light, Britons promised Africans that the war was necessary as it marked "an end to the oppressive treatment"[678] of Africans by Boers, which had been disgraceful, brutal and unworthy of a civilised power. In this way, Africans' hopes were increasingly raised, though they were later to be dashed.

As a result of pre-war promises, the abaThembu participated in the war both as combatants and messengers, scouts, wagon drivers, convoy guards, dispatch riders, watchmen in blockhouses, firewood collectors and trench diggers. They were also stretcher bearers, labourers, servants and attendants for horses. Recruited by uKumkani Dalindyebo, ooNkosi Mgudlwa and Mvuzo Mathanzima, abaThembu levies were mobilised and stationed on the borders of the former Transkei. The amaMfengu and abaThembu levies, along with the Cape Mounted Rifle detachments, repulsed the Boer commandos from ravaging Transkei. UKumkani Dalindyebo's, the Chief of Native Intelligence, and other abaThembu chiefs' active involvement in the war could be seen in the context of abaThembu collaboration with whites.[679]

In December 1899, four hundred amaMfengu and abaThembu forces were mobilised; the abaThembuland field force comprising one hundred and eighty whites and one thousand one hundred levies under the command of Major Elliot were stationed at Ngcobo; five hundred men were stationed between Cala and Indwe and they all advanced dauntlessly towards the Wodehouse and Barkly East. These forces were determined to defend the former Transkei against imminent Boer attacks. However, Africans were divided in their assistance of whites.

---

677 Worden, *Modern South Africa*, 25.
678 P. Warwick, *Black People and the South African War, 1899-1902* (London: Cambridge University Press, 1983), 111.
679 Pampallis, *Foundations*, 44; S.B. Spies, "British Supremacy and South African Unification", in B.J. Liebenberg and S.B. Spies (eds), *South Africa in the 20th Century* (Pretoria: Academica, 1993), 10-11.

Colonial assault on the House of Ngubengcuka, 1894-1920

MAP 9: The South African War, 1899-1902[680]

For example, approximately 100,000 aided Britons on the borders of Transkei, while in the Transvaal about 10,000 Africans rendered service to the Boers.[681] Many levies were drawn from Gatyana (Willowvale), Gcuwa (Butterworth), Ngcobo and Xhalanga. Africans had a divided attitude and reaction in giving assistance to whites. This could be viewed as one of a series of factors leading to the social, administrative and political division of abaThembuland. It could be seen in the context of divisions before and after the war. The war was not only destructive of life and property, but it also led to antagonism between Boers and Britons. How devastating the war was to all South Africans is clear from the fact that approximately 22,000 Britons died during the war, while 26,000 Boer women and children and 14,000 Africans died in the concentration camps.[682] Thus, the South African War caused "equal suffering to whites and blacks".[683]

The war itself had wider repercussions for twentieth-century South Africans and momentous consequences for the abaThembu as well. For Africans, the war was destructive; for whites, it was curative. As the British conquered the Transvaal and the Orange Free State, the way was paved for the unification of 'white' South Africa. The war did not promote unity amongst

---
680 T. Pakenham, "The Anglo-Boer War, 1899-1902", in T. Cameron and S.B. Spies (eds), *A New Illustrated History of South Africa* (Johannesburg: Southern Book Publishers, 1986), 212.
681 Pampallis, *Foundations*, 46.
682 Warwick, *South African War*, 60-61.
683 Worden, *Modern South Africa*, 30.

Africans, and rather "led to divisions within communities and families".[684] In spite of their involvement and loss of lives during the war, however, the abaThembu were disillusioned. All their hopes, encouraged by British rhetoric before and during the war, were dashed.[685] The Peace of Vereeniging brought in its train traumatic consequences for Africans. Both Boers and Britons put their differences in the background and united in hindering Africans from gaining equal political rights with whites. Whites feared that should they grant equal political rights to Africans, they would be outvoted by the numerically superior Africans. In line with whites' fear of the 'black peril', article 8 of the *Peace of Vereeniging* denied Africans the vote, much to the chagrin of the abaThembu who had hoped, and rightly so, that after the South African War their political conditions would be improved.

As Switzer puts it, "Black war victims received little if any compensation, and those who had rendered support to the British during the conflict were not supported in the postwar dispensation."[686] Adding their voice, Beinart and Bundy put it thus: "dismayed by this betrayal, black South Africans were disappointed in other ways by the British."[687]

Thus, Africans were politically sidelined in the envisaged new South Africa. Their clamour that they should be given a vote before the union of 'white' South Africa came into being fell on deaf ears. What became clear was that before and after the union of 'white' South Africa, Africans were viewed by both Boers and Britons, particularly Louis Botha, as a major threat to South African politics and so ought to be kept in check lest they outvoted whites. While Botha saw Africans as 'black peril', Milner, the British High Commissioner, viewed them as a problem to whites' political survival, and so the 'native question' became South Africa's major and burning issue. Then the question of political and land rights for Africans received wide attention.

The attitude of Boers to Africans can be seen within the context of J.C. Smuts, the Colonial Secretary of the Transvaal, who had in 1906 expressed to J.X. Merriman, the leader of the Afrikaner Bond, which later became the South African Party, and the British Government, his disbelief in granting political rights to Africans. This expression illustrated that Africans were to be disenfranchised. Smuts reiterated that all matters pertaining to Africans and their franchise be shelved so that these would be solved by a united South Africa. He, however, suggested that the existing franchise conditions be retained.[688] This idea was accepted by Merriman for the sake of compromise. Similarly, the South African Native Affairs Commission (SANAC) backed Smuts for the sake of implementing a policy of segregation. This was followed by the granting of self-government to the Transvaal and Orange River Colonies in 1907.

---

684 Ibid., 29.
685 Ibid., 29 and 31.
686 Switzer, *Power and Resistance in an African Society*, 164.
687 Beinart and Bundy, *Hidden Struggles in Rural South Africa*, 47.
688 D.W. Kruger, *The Making of a Nation: A History of the Union of South Africa, 1910-1961* (Johannesburg: Macmillan, 1969), 35.

Thus, rather than fulfilling pre-war and wartime promises, Britons resorted to political evasion by claiming that Africans' political position was to be later decided by white majority after the introduction of self-government for the union of 'white' South Africa. As self-government meant white rule and therefore the rejection of African political rights, it was not to be expected that Africans would be enfranchised in the foreseeable future.[689]

On the basis of the contents of article 8 of the Peace of Vereeniging (see Appendix 3), one can argue that Africans were betrayed. Having a decisive role to play in deciding the future of Africans, Botha set out to unite Afrikaans and English speakers against Africans who wanted to be enfranchised. Rather than granting Africans equal political rights with whites, Botha regarded Africans as posing, on account of their large numbers, a major threat and danger ('swart gevaar') to their political dominance in South Africa.[690]

Following in the wake of the Peace of Vereeniging of 1902 and the granting of self-government to the Transvaal and Orange River Colonies in 1907, were attempts by Boers and Britons in 1908 to decide the future of South Africa with a view to uniting the former Boer republics, viz. the Orange Free State and the Transvaal, and the British colonies, viz. the Cape Colony and Natal. Africans were not invited to these discussions though they constituted the majority of South Africans. It was, therefore, surprising that the outcomes of these conventions were perceived as affecting Africans whose ideas had not been sought. What was more of an insult to Africans was the entrenchment of article 137, which pertained to Africans' non-franchise. Worse still, it was also decided at these conventions that only white "men were eligible for membership of parliament".[691]

The Act of Union of 1908 united two British colonies and two Boer republics and made provision for the union of 'white' South Africa of 1910. It also formalised the conquest of African land and entrenched white political power. As a result of this union, the two diverse white population groups could work together in dealing with Africans. And so they did. The Act of Union restricted the franchise to whites, except in the Cape. However, Africans in the Cape were denied seats in the national legislature and thus could vote only for white candidates. In this way, political power resided with whites.

While the South African War brought former colonies and republics under one flag, the union of 'white' South Africa can best be termed as "the artificial creation of a new state"[692] and a compromise by whites, which enshrined the principle of South Africa as the white man's country.[693] All the united territories differed in political and cultural background. Their differences and mutual distrust following the South African War characterised the post-union South Africa.

---

689 Davenport, *South Africa*, 202.
690 Guise, *Freedom*, 11; Pampallis, *Foundations*, 47.
691 Kruger, *Union of South Africa*, 42.
692 Ibid., 3 and 4.
693 H. Pretorius and L. Jafta, "A Branch Springs Out: African Initiated Churches", in Elphick and Davenport, *Christianity in South Africa*, 215.

In spite of the abaThembu participation in the South African War and whites' betrayal of Africans, headmen still supported whites during elections. This support was due to the fact that headmen received white support against traditional leaders. In election meetings, headmen were strategically given chairmanship by whites.[694] Headmen were regarded as the most reliable and cooperative people within African communities by the South African Party candidates. UKumkani Dalindyebo's collaborative tendencies became apparent during these meetings. He had influenced many, if not all, of his followers to collaborate with whites. Collaboration ensured white support against enemies. For example, at a meeting organised by Colonel Stanford in 1907, uKumkani Dalindyebo and his *amaphakathi* (councillors displayed their loyalty to white candidates by insisting that all should vote for Stanford whom, as Dalindyebo claimed, they had known for so many years as the chief magistrate of the Transkei.[695]

It is clear that before and after the union of 'white' South Africa, segregation had become the answer to the 'swart gevaar' (see Appendices 4 and 5). While kingship and chiefly power had been taken away by the Cape Government, chief magistrates had become "supreme chiefs of African tribes".[696] As Africans' political position was put in the background in the Act of Union and its constitution, the union of 'white' South Africa was nothing more than a white unitary state. It was, therefore, the union, not of South Africa, but of white South Africa. The Act of Union's assault on the traditional system of justice was clear from the fact that after 1909 chiefly power shifted to the Governor-General, who assumed supreme position amongst Africans. As Peires correctly concludes about traditional leadership both in South Africa and Africa during the colonial times:

> Chiefs in South Africa, as elsewhere in Africa during the colonial period, have long depended on the government rather than their people for both political recognition and financial support. They cannot be regarded as a 'traditional' ruling class because they have entirely ceased to represent the dominated remnants of the pre-colonial social order, although this fact has been deliberately obscured for ideological purposes.[697]

It was a heavy blow that Africans had been deprived of political rights in South Africa by being excluded from being members of parliament. This was followed by a series of repressive legislations, such as the Native Labour Regulation Act, the Mines and Works Act of 1911 and the Defence Act of 1912. In terms of the Native Labour Regulation Act of 1911, it was an offence for Africans to break a labour contract and participate in a strike. The Act further "stipulated that blacks involved in industrial accidents would receive less compensation than

---

694 *Cape Times*, 30 January 1904; *Cape Mercury*, 23 March 1908.
695 *Imvo*, 5 November 1907; *Cape Mercury*, 23 March 1908.
696 A. Stadler, *The Political Economy of Modern South Africa* (Cape Town: David Philip, 1987), 129.
697 Peires, "The Implosion of Transkei and Ciskei", *African Affairs*, 91 (1992), 384.

whites".[698] The Mines and Works Act of 1911 imposed job reservation by reserving skilled work for whites, thus advocating racial bars on wage and jobs rights. The Defence Act of 1912 debarred Africans from military training.

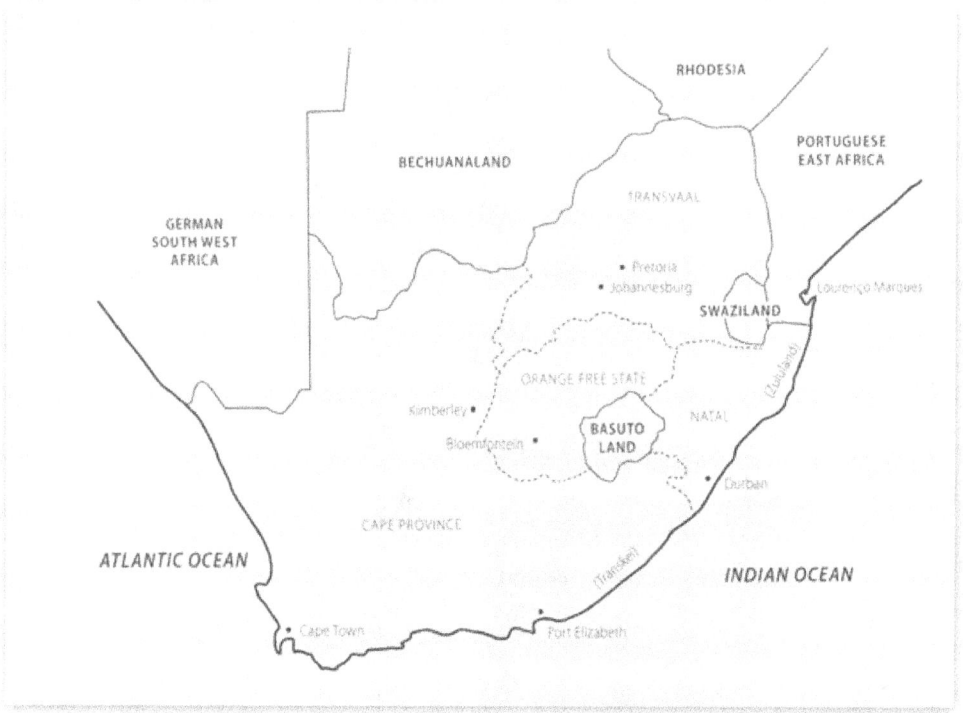

MAP 10: South Africa in 1910, showing the four provinces of South Africa (Transvaal, Orange Free State, Cape Province and Natal). Swaziland and Basutoland were separate British Crown territories.[699]

In response to these repressive acts, Africans came to realise that they should form a country-wide organisation to unite Africans against white domination. Hence, the founding of the South African Native National Congress (SANNC) in Bloemfontein on 8 January 1912. The SANNC (from 1923 to be known as the African National Congress) was an outcome of a meeting of "a number of secular and religious leaders banded together ... [which was] the first national political organisation of Africans",[700] convened by Pixley ka Isaka Seme, a newly-qualified advocate.[701] The SANNC was formed by teachers, clergymen and clerks, businessmen, journalists and builders, all educated in missionary schools in the nineteenth century, as well

---

698 S.B. Spies, "Unity and Disunity, 1910-1924", in T. Cameron and S.B. Spies (eds), *A New Illustrated History of South Africa* (Johannesburg: Southern Book Publishers, 1986), 234.
699 K. Shillington, *History of Southern Africa* (London: Longman, 1987), 137.
700 Pretorius and Jafta, "A Branch Springs Out", 215.
701 H. Holland, *The Struggle: A History of the African National Congress* (New York: George Braziller Inc., 1990), 39.

as chiefs and kings wearing leopard skins that marked their status as traditional leaders.[702] The traditional leaders were robed in traditional chiefly dress (a leopard-skin cloak) as well as in traditional kingly dress (a lion-skin cloak). After the opening speeches, maintains Meli, the gathering sang Reverend Tiyo Soga's hymn, *Lizalis' idinga Lakho, Thixo Nkosi Yenyaniso* (Fulfil thy Promise, God, Thou Lord of Truth[703]), which became the SANNC's *uMhobe weSizwe* (National Anthem) until their adoption of Enoch Sontonga's *uMhobe weSizwe* (National Anthem) and after 1994, the African National Congress (ANC) adopted the new version of *uMhobe weSizwe* (National Anthem) (see Appendices 1 and 2).

The SANNC. opposed racial discrimination and tribalism. It was intended to be "a permanent national organisation to represent African political interests in the new union of [white] South Africa and in the adjacent British protectorates [viz. Basutoland (Lesotho), Bechuanaland (Botswana) and Swaziland]".[704] It transcended race, colour and creed in favour of a united nation of Africans, whites, Indians and coloureds. Linked to the SANNC was the Bantu Women's League formed in 1918, which "included many black women members from the English-speaking churches".[705] The formation of the Bantu Women's League, and its protest against the Pass Laws, signified the important role played by women not only in the Church but also in the society. Rejecting narrow nationalism, the formation of the SANNC in 1912 marked the birth of a wider South African nationalism. As African hopes of political equality with whites were shattered, the SANNC became an organisation for expressing African political aspirations. And in its stance to oppose segregation, the SANNC was to change the course of South African history in many ways.[706] With regard to the formation of the SANNC and its Christian element, Elphick concludes that "Christian leadership provided much of the impetus for the founding, in 1912, of the African National Congress, the most influential black opposition to white rule, and now the dominant political party in South Africa."[707]

As a unitary organisation the SANNC. had traditional leaders as its members. It had an Upper House of kings and chiefs and a Lower House of Executive Commoners. The Upper House of nobles had the role of advising, as per the draft constitution, the elected committee of twelve Executive Commoners.[708] Reverend John Langalibalele Dube, who combined three careers – international Christian leader, educator and African politician[709] – became the first president of the Lower House. Alfred Mangena, Reverend Walter Benson Rubusana, Meshack Pelem

---

702 Ibid., 40.
703 F. Meli, *A History of the ANC: South Africa Belongs to us* (London: James Currey, 1988), 38.
704 Switzer, *Power and Resistance in an African Society*, 175.
705 J.W. de Gruchy, "Grappling with a Colonial Heritage: The English-Speaking Churches under Imperialism and Apartheid", in Elphick and Davenport, *Christianity in South Africa*, 170.
706 Zakade Bhuka, Interview, 14 July 1995; James Kati, Interview, 30 July 1997; Phongomile S. Fadana, Interview, 27 August 1994.
707 R. Elphick, "Introduction: Christianity in South African History", in Elphick and Davenport, *Christianity in South Africa*, 1.
708 Switzer, *Power and Resistance in an African Society*, 176.
709 Elphick, "The Benevolent Empire and the Social Gospel: Missionaries and South African Christians in the Age of Segregation", in Elphick and Davenport, *Christianity in South Africa*, 361.

and Sam Makgatho were elected vice-presidents. Thomas Maphikela was elected as Speaker. Montsioa became the recording secretary. Reverend Mqoboli of the Wesleyan Church was Chaplain-in-Chief while Reverend H.R. Ngcayiya served as his assistant.[710] Pixley ka Isaka Seme was elected as the treasurer, while Solomon Plaatje was a secretary.[711] According to Holland, Plaatje was "an interpreter from Kimberley who, despite a Standard Three education, had translated five Shakespearian plays into Setswana and was the first black to have written a novel in English."[712]

UKumkani Dalindyebo, along with Montsioa of Barolong, Dinizulu of amaZulu, Lewanika of aBarotseland (now part of Zambia), Khama of Botswana, Marelane of amaMpondoland, Moepi of the Kgatla and Letsie II of Lesotho constituted the Upper House. Letsie II became the president of the Upper House as other traditional leaders were honorary presidents of the SANNC. The traditional leaders were part of the organisation, representing "the rural masses who were the majority of the people at the time and the section most affected by land robbery".[713] Having fought against colonialism and land dispossessions, most of them had been deposed, banished and victimised.[714]

The inclusion of traditional leaders gave the SANNC wide recognition and significance. It helped to give it more stature and hearing amongst the masses of South African people. The SANNC's significance lay in its bid to blur the old divisions between and within different nationalities, and in its quest to unite all political organisations against white domination.

Thus, not only the traditional leaders constituted the SANNC, but also the Church had made its appearance felt in the movement. For example, Ethiopians such as Henry Ncayiya, who became the senior chaplain of the movement and president of the Ethiopian Church; Charlotte Maxeke, founder of the movement's Women's Section and an active African Methodist Episcopal Church (AMEC) laywoman; Dr Alfred Bathini Xuma (1893-1962), ANC and AMEC president; and R.W. Msimang, drafter of the ANC constitution, and a leader in his father's Independent Methodist Church, participated in the founding of the SANNC in 1912.[715]

In a bid to counteract and deal with the 'swart gevaar', the union government promulgated the Native Land Act (No. 27 of 1913) in 1913, which was an expression of territorial segregation. The Native Land Act was designed to deprive Africans of the right to own land outside the reserves. African land was already crowded and, as such, whites would settle there only for trading purposes.[716] Similarly, whites were debarred from buying land in the reserves. Africans were restricted to 8% of South Africa's land surface. Yet, of the total South African population

---

710 Meli, *A History of the ANC*, 38.
711 Elphick, "The Benevolent Empire and the Social Gospel", 357.
712 Holland, *The Struggle*, 41.
713 Meli, *A History of the ANC*, 39.
714 Ibid.
715 Pretorius and Jafta, "A Branch Springs Out", 215; W.G. Mills, "Millennial Christianity, British Imperialism, and African Nationalism", in Elphick and Davenport, *Christianity in South Africa*, 344.
716 T. Karis and G.M. Carter (eds), *From Protest to Challenge: A Documentary History of African Politics in South Africa, 1882-1964* (California: Hoover Institution Press, 1972), 131.

of 5,973,394, Africans numbered 4,019,006. Whites numbered 1,276,242, coloureds 525,943 and Indians 152,203. Africans, who outnumbered whites by five to one, were thenceforth evicted from white-owned land to the already overcrowded and poverty-stricken reserves. In this connection, Holland concludes that

> black families were evicted from white farms in their thousands. Loading their belongings on to their heads, they trudged for days and nights in the middle of winter, driving small herds and carrying children from one white farm to the next as they begged for shelter.[717]

It seemed paradoxical that the majority of South Africans who formed 67,3% of the population were given such a small percentage of land. Debarred by the Land Act from buying land in white areas, Africans lived in the reserves.[718] As these reserves could not support them owing to increasing soil erosion and overgrazing, Africans had to move to white areas in search of work. Even here they could only stay for the period that they were providing labour to whites. Thus, the Land Act allowed Africans to stay in white areas only as long as they offered labour, and indeed Africans became tenants and wage-earners, as reserves could not adequately support the increasing population.

Judging from the aims of the Native Land Act, it can be argued that the Act was one of segregation legislations passed by the union of 'white' South Africa. It was one of the union's attempts to entrench white supremacy over Africans. Having had no voice in the planning, formation and administration of the union of 'white' South Africa, Africans found themselves pariahs in their fatherland. The Land Act was one of the whites' strategies, which rendered the economic self-sufficiency of African kingdoms and chiefdoms to nothingness as their limited land was impoverished by overcrowding, soil erosion and overgrazing. Being insufficient, African land could not adequately cater for such a big population. The Native Land Act was the basis for territorial separation and, like other Acts passed by the same government, it was one of the segregation Acts that "completed the subordination of traditional chiefly power to the central government".[719]

The SANNC. strongly rejected the Native Land Act by staging a major protest campaign against the implementation of the Act. It sent a deputation to the Minister for Native Affairs expressing aversion to the Act and its clause prohibiting Africans from purchasing land in white areas, and the granting of rights to white farmers to expel Africans from the land they had for so long been occupying. Failing to receive a positive response, the SANNC sent another deputation to London to protest against the Act. The second deputation consisted of the Congregationalist leader John Langalibalele Dube, the first president of the SANNC and "a cautious Zulu headmaster from Natal and recipient of an honorary University of South Africa doctorate for his efforts towards establishing the first industrial school for blacks",[720] Solomon

---

717 Holland, *The Struggle*, 41.
718 Stadler, *Political Economy*, 129.
719 Ibid.
720 Holland, *The Struggle*, 41.

Thekisho Plaatje, A. Msane, T.M. Maphikela and Dr W.B. Rubusana. Even here, the SANNC did not meet with a positive reaction, and so all attempts to have the Act rescinded were to no avail. Thus, while the Land Act was intended to divide South Africa into African reserves and white areas, the SANNC was to unite all South Africans. In spite of all these attempts, however, South African land was divided. And this contributed to the division of abaThembuland.

The period from 1894 to 1913 was characterised by whites' attempts to step up the policy of divide-and-rule. And to that effect, whites set out to introduce political structures, which reinforced and buttressed segregation. They also used those who saw security and protection in collaborating with whites to promote and consolidate their policy of divide-and-rule. AbaThembu king's, chiefs' and headmen's collaborative tendencies were partly responsible for the success of the whites' policy. Furthermore, a series of segregation Acts were promulgated to deprive Africans of any access to voting rights and land rights in greater South Africa. Be that as it may, the formation of the SANNC in 1912 heralded a period of heightened opposition to the vicious and segregationist policies of the union of 'white' South Africa. The SANNC fought tooth and nail against the Native Land Act of 1913, which deprived Africans of 87% of the land's surface.

The South African War (1899-1902) broke out during the reign of uKumkani Dalindyebo. UKumkani Dalindyebo, the son of uKumkani Ngangelizwe and uKumkanikazi Notasi, had been born in 1865. He came to power after the death of his father in December 1884. Being educated in mission schools, uKumkani Dalindyebo evinced much interest in educational matters and Christianity. He actively participated in the abaThembuland General Council. His abaThembu favourably responded to the British call that the abaThembu should protect the Transkeian borders against Boer invasions during the South African War, which cost over 16,500 African lives. The participation of the abaThembu in the war pointed to the significant historical position of the abaThembu of uKumkani Dalindyebo. It also demonstrated the trust the colonial government had in the abaThembu king.

That uKumkani Dalindyebo had, unlike his father, "peaceful reign"[721] earned him respect. He was respected by prominent Africans, such as Alfred Mangena, the first black South African to practise as a barrister, Reverend Walter Benson Rubusana and Thengo Jabavu. In 1904, uKumkani Dalindyebo distinguished himself by being amongst the kings who attended the coronation of Edward VII. Reverend W.B. Rubusana accompanied the Christian abaThembu king.

Having been acquainted with white liberals, uKumkani Dalindyebo was current on contemporary issues. Consequently, he was in 1911 accompanied to the Universal Race Congress in London by Thengo Jabavu, Reverends W.B. Rubusana, J.S. Moffat, Balmforth and other famous South Africans, such as Sir James Rose-Innes and Oliver Schreiner. This showed uKumkani Dalindyebo's high esteem in the Christian circles and in greater South Africa.

---

721 W.J. de Kock (ed.), *Dictionary of South African Biography, vol. ii* (Johannesburg: Tafelberg-Uitgewers, 1972), 156.

So famous, knowledgeable and respectable was uKumkani Dalindyebo that he was amongst the seven kings to be elected as Honorary Presidents of the SANNC in 1912. The inclusion of kings in the SANNC helped to give it more stature and hearing amongst the masses of the people of South Africa. The importance of King Dalindyebo's active association with the formation of the SANNC on 8 January 1912 lies in that he made a massive contribution in the form of cattle towards catering for the people attending the occasion of the founding of the organisation. Interestingly, his descendant, uKumkani Buyelekhaya Dalindyebo, A! Zwelibanzi! contributed 15 head of cattle on the occasion of ANC celebrations on 8 January 2012.[722]

Significantly, when the SANNC first published its national newspaper, *Abantu-Batho*, in the middle of 1912 with Seme as editor, the amaSwati Queen-Regent, Labotsibeni, had played a major role in financially ensuring its publication in English, isiXhosa, isiZulu, isiSuthu and isiTswana. Pampallis aptly argues that "the participation of the [kings], who still enjoyed considerable prestige among rural people, helped to put the Congress in contact with the masses."[723]

With its primary objectives at its inception of promoting and protecting the "interests of a professional African middle class, such as doctors, teachers, lawyers, businessmen and those of similar status",[724] the SANNC opposed segregation and tribalism in all its forms. With the passage of time, the SANNC cast its net wider and became a mass-based organisation, which transcended race, colour, creed and gender.

While the SANNC initially embarked on a policy of peaceful protests in awakening the 'union' government to recognise black people's rights, its President, J.T. Gumede, vainly attempted to inject some radicalism into the organisation after World War I of 1914 to 1918. His failure to radicalise the SANNC was due to the movement's association with the powerful and influential Communist Party of South Africa (CPSA).

On 24 April 1920, uKumkani Dalindyebo died, just as he was "preparing to attend the 1920 session of the general council".[725] He was survived by his Great Wife, Nohajisi, daughter of uNkosi Makhawula of the amaBhaca, Makhawula, and his son and heir, Prince Sampu, A! Jongilizwe! Prince Silimela, uKumkani Dalindyebo's brother, acted as regent from then to September 1924. Sampu became king of the abaThembu on 1 October 1924. His term of office was shortlived for he died in July 1928, four months before his son and heir, Prince Sabata, was born.[726] He was survived by his Great Wife, uKumkanikazi Novoti, and daughter, Princess Nompucuko, who had been born in 1925. UNkosi Jongintaba, the eldest son but non-heir (*imvelatanci*) of uKumkani Dalindyebo, acted as chief-regent until his death in 1942, whereupon his brother, uNkosi Dabulamanzi, took over as chief-regent until 1954.

---

722 *Daily Dispatch*, 8 January 2012.
723 Pampallis, *Foundations*, 68.
724 L.S. Togui, *The Struggle for Human Rights* (Kenwyn: Juta & Company, 1994), 147.
725 De Kock, *Dictionary*, 156.
726 *Umthunywa*, 19 June 1954, 2.

It is evident that the rule of uKumkani Dalindyebo was not so much convulsed with problems. That of uKumkani Sampu was relatively problem-free, though short-lived. Though uKumkani Sampu died without a symbolical heir, uKumkanikazi Novoti was at the time in the family way and her giving birth to Prince Sabata on 25 November 1928 was obviously and nationally a cause of delight to the abaThembu dynasty. A prince was born.

However, uKumkani Dalindyebo's role in the formation of the SANNC in 1912 helped to put his people, the abaThembu, on the political map of South Africa, and of the liberation struggle in South Africa. His grandson, Prince Sabata, emulated his grandfather.

8

Conclusion

The history of the abaThembu during and after precolonial times was characterised by internal-conflict relations amongst the descendants of the House of Nxeko. These turbid relations fostered secession and fissiparous tendencies that resulted in socio-political and cultural disunity amongst the abaThembu. The division of houses into the iNdlu eNkulu, iNdlu yaseKunene and amaQadi did not serve to unite the abaThembu kingdom and chiefdoms as jealousy and envy set in amongst sons of these houses who jostled for power. Out of these houses, expansion and secession came into being.

The tumultuous atmosphere generated by the Mfecane wars in which the abaThembu had physical encounters with the amaNgwane did not bode well for abaThembu socio-political and cultural cohesion. Equally so, the role of the missionaries, white traders and white governors in dismantling the cohesion of the abaThembu kingdom and chiefdoms was apparent. Owing to these factors, a split within the abaThembu set in, and it rendered them culturally vulnerable, militarily weak and politically impotent.

AbaThembu relations with whites and neighbouring African kingdoms and chiefdoms were not conducive to strengthening the House of Ngubengcuka. They had conflicts with their neighbours over land. Adding combustion to these unhealthy relations was the colonial government's policy of divide-and-rule, which threw the abaThembu into political disarray. At the centre of these gruesome relations was the question of land, as the colonial government was bent on extending colonial control not only to abaThembuland but also to the areas of jurisdiction of other abeNguni kingdoms and chiefdoms. In its bid to achieve its aim, the colonial government worked hand-in-glove with the missionaries who were vehemently opposed to traditionalism, culture and all that was African. The missionaries' actions were in support of the colonial government's aims of subjugating traditional African chiefdoms and kingdoms.[727]

It should be clear from the foregoing account that the abaThembu kings had formed alliances with the colonial government, but they never derived much benefit from their being collaborators. Instead, the colonial government exploited the political and social cleavages within the abaThembu kingdom, on the one hand, and between the abaThembu and amaXhosa, on the other. In cases where the colonial administrators assisted the abaThembu against amaGcaleka, abaThembu prestige and political status suffered indescribably. Rather than strengthening the abaThembu kingdom, abaThembu collaboration and defection jeopardised the stability of their community. At the centre of these associations, there were mistrust and suspicion. The colonial administration was intent on undermining the military potential of the abaThembu. The white farmers viewed the abaThembu as land seekers who threatened their existence. Though the abaThembu collaborated with the colonial government, they were not spared the treatment meted out to non-collaborators as evidenced by the annexation of their land in 1885. When Africans were disarmed in accordance with the legislation of 1879, the abaThembu were also affected. However, they could confidently boast that they had never been driven away from their land. Emigrant abaThembu were forced to vacate the colonial territory after their participation in the war of 1846-1847, and they were settled in the 'Tambookie' Location by Sir George Cathcart in 1852. Their closeness to, and association with, the whites exposed them to education and Christianity, which easily permeated throughout abaThembu communities. Products of abaThembu mission schools were – and are – the centre around which the cause of African nationalism was fostered.

The colonial government drove a wedge into the abaThembu marital relations with the amaGcaleka kingdom, using the Nomkhafulo affair as an opportunity to fuel tensions between these two kingdoms. Such infiltration epitomised the Cape Government's tradition of playing one kingdom against the other, and it led to physical conflict between uKumkani Sarhili and his son-in-law, uKumkani Ngangelizwe. The colonial government was so intent on attacking chiefly and kingship power and authority that it introduced magisterial rule in abaThembuland. Hence, by the 1870s and 1880s, chiefly and kingship power had alarmingly declined.[728] By the 1880s, abaThembuland was annexed into the Cape Colony. The abaThembu had lost their ancestral lands to the Cape Government. The colonial government placed magistrates and government-appointed headmen in the saddle to rule over these lands.[729] Having been subjected to colonial and missionary attacks, the abaThembu gradually succumbed to collaboration.

---

[727] Mvenene, "African People of Gcalekaland", 59.
[728] Mvenene, "Reverend Auld", 33.
[729] Hodgson, "A Battle for Sacred Power", 78.

Tile's role in uniting abaThembuland under one king, one Church and one magistrate was a turning point in the history of protest politics in abaThembuland. He strongly opposed the unequal treatment of African ministers by white ministers in the Wesleyan Church and drew King Ngangelizwe into his orbit. He was the forerunner in putting pressure on the Wesleyan Church and its white missionaries to respect African ministers as their equals, setting the pace for the abaThembu people's aspiration for unity against racial discrimination. Tile viewed the abaThembu Church and the abaThembu king as the centre on which African political, racial and national consciousness hinged.

The years 1894 to 1913 saw the colonial government advocating pieces of legislation, which were intended not only to step up the policy of divide-and-rule but also to reinforce and buttress segregation. These laws were also designed to deprive Africans of any access to voting rights and land rights in South Africa. It was a result of Africans' objection to these laws and determination to oppose them that the SANNC was formed in 1912. On its formation, the SANNC heralded a period of heightened opposition to the Glen Grey Act of 1894, the South Africa Act of 1909 and the coming into being of the union of 'white' South Africa in 1910 as well as the Native Land Act.

The reign of uKumkani Dalindyebo following the death of his father, uKumkani Ngangelizwe, in December 1884, was a peaceful one. Having been a famous and Christian king, his death in 1920 led to the period of regency in abaThembuland.

Appendices

APPENDIX 1

National anthem (uMhobe weSizwe) in its original form

1. Nkosi Sikelel' I Afrika,
   Maluphakam' uphondo lwayo;
   Yiva nemithandazo yethu-
   Usisikelele,
   Usisikelele.

   Chorus:

   Yihla Moya, yihla Moya,
   Yihla Moya Oyingcwele.

2. Sikelela iiNkosi zethu
   Zikhumbule umDali wazo;
   Zimoyike zezimhlonele,
   Azisikelele,
   Azisikele.

3. Sikelel' amadod' eli lizwe,
   ikelela kwanomlisela;
   Ulithwal' ilizwe ngomonde-
   Uwusikelele,
   Uwusikelele.

4. Sikelel' amakhosikazi,
   Nawo onk' amanenekazi,
   Phakamisa wonk' umthinjana-
   Uwusikelele,
   Uwusikelele.

5. Sikelela abafundisi,
   Beemvaba zonke zeli lizwe
   Ubathwese ngomoya wakho,
   Ubasikelele,
   Ubasikelele.

6. Sikelel' ulimo nemfuyo,
   Gxotha zonk' iindlala nezifo,
   Zalisa ilizwe ngempilo-
   Ulisikelele,
   Ulisikelele.

7. Sikelel' amalinga ethu,
   Awomanyano nokuzakha,
   Awemfundo nemvisiswano,
   Uwasikelele,
   Uwasikelele.

8. Nkosi, sikelel' iAfrika,
   Cima bonk' ubugwenxa bayo,
   Nezigqitho, neezono zayo-
   Uyisikelele,
   Uyisikelele.

APPENDIX 2

National anthem, a combined version of 'Nkosi Sikelel' iAfrika', 'The Call of South Africa' and 'Die Stem van Suid-Afrika'

Nkosi sikelel' i Afrika
Maluphakanyisw' uphondo lwayo,
Yizwa imithandazo yethu,
Nkosi sikelela, thina luswapho lwayo.

Morena boloka setjhaba sa heso,
O fedise dintwa le matshwenyeho,
O se boloke,
O se boloke, setjhaba sa heso,
Setjhaba sa South Afrika –
South Afrika.

Uit die blou van onse hemel,
Uit die diepte van ons see,
Oor ons ewige gebergtes,
Waar die kranse antwoord gee.

Sounds the call to come together,
And united we shall stand,
Let us live and strive for freedom,
In South Africa our land.

APPENDIX 3

The Treaty of Vereeniging, 31 May 1902

General Lord Kitchener of Khartoum, Commander-in-Chief, and His Excellency Lord Milner, High Commissioner, on behalf of the British Government and Messrs S.W. Burger, F.W. Reitz, Louis Botha, J.H. de la Rey, L.J. Meyer and J.C. Krogh, acting as the Government of the South African Republic, and Messrs W.J.C. Brebner, C.R. De Wet, J.B.M. Hertzog and C.H. Olivier, acting as the Government of the Orange Free State, On behalf of their respective Burghers, desirous to terminate the present hostilities, agree on the following articles:

1. The Burgher Forces in the field will forthwith lay down their arms, handing over all guns, rifles, and ammunitions of war, in their possession or under their control, and desist from any further resistance to the authority of His Majesty King Edward vii, whom they recognize as their lawful Sovereign.

2. The manner and details of this surrender will be arranged between Lord Kitchener and Commandant-General Botha, Assistant Commandant-General de la Rey, and Chief Commandant de Wet.

3. Burghers in the field outside the limits of the Transvaal and Orange River Colony, and all prisoners of war at present outside South Africa, who are burghers, will, on duly declaring their acceptance of the position of subjects of His Majesty King Edward VII, be gradually brought back to their homes as soon as transport can be provided and their means of subsistence ensured.

4. The burghers so surrendering or so returning will not be deprived of their personal liberty, or their property.

5. No proceedings, civil or criminal, will be taken against any of the burghers so surrendering or so returning for any acts in connection with the prosecution of the war. The benefit of this clause will not extend to certain acts contrary to the usage of war, which have been notified by the Commander-in-Chief to the Boer Generals, and which shall be tried by Court-Martial immediately after the close of hostilities.

6. The Dutch language will be taught in public schools in the Transvaal and the Orange River Colony where the parents of the children desire it, and will be allowed in Courts of Law when necessary for the better and more effectual administration of justice.

7. The possession of rifles will be allowed in the Transvaal and Orange River Colony to persons requiring them for their protection on taking out a licence according to law.

8. Military administration in the Transvaal and Orange River Colony will at the earliest possible date be succeeded by civil government, and, as soon as circumstances permit, representative institutions, leading to self-government, will be introduced.

9. The question of granting the franchise to natives will not be decided until after the introduction of self-government.

10. No special tax will be imposed on landed property in the Transvaal and Orange River Colony to defray the expenses of the war.

11. As soon as conditions permit, a Commission, on which the local inhabitants will be represented, will be appointed in each district of the Transvaal and Orange River Colony, under the presidency of a magistrate or other official, for the purpose of assisting the restoration of the people to their homes and supplying those who, owing to war losses, are unable to provide for themselves, with food, shelter, and the necessary amount of seed, stock, implements, etc., indispensable to the resumption of their normal occupations.

His Majesty's Government will place at the disposal of these Commissions a sum of three million pounds sterling for the above purposes, and will allow all notes, issued under Law No. 1 of 1900 of the Government of the South African Republic, and all receipts given by the officers in the field of the late Republics or under their orders, to be represented to a Judicial Commission, which will be appointed by the Government, and if such notes and receipts are found by this Commission to have been duly issued in return for valuable consideration they will be received by the first-named Commissions as evidence of war losses suffered by the persons to whom they were originally given. In addition to the above-named free grant of three million pounds, His Majesty's Government will be prepared to make advances as loans for the same purposes, free of interest for two years, and afterwards repayable over a period of years with 3 per cent interest. No foreigner or rebel will be entitled to the benefit of this clause.

Signed at Pretoria this thirty-first day of May in the Year of Our Lord One Thousand Nine Hundred and two.

(Signed)

Kitchener of Khartoum, Milner, S.W. Burger, F.W. Reitz, Louis Botha, J.H. de la Rey, L.J. Meyer, J.C. Krogh, C.R. de Wet, J.B.M. Hertzog, W.C.J. Brebner, C.H. Olivier.

APPENDIX 4

The Afrikaner: 'Civilised' Christian or 'brutal' savage?

In response to the scrapping of all apartheid laws in the early 1990s, conservative Afrikaners have threatened to take up arms to preserve separation of the races and retain land, which they consider is rightfully theirs. To support their right to maintain separation and hold onto the land, they have increasingly resorted to claiming that Christianity and the need to uphold Christian values justify their actions. Thus, on the basis of their Christianity, they claim the right to domination, ownership of land, separation of the races and maintenance of segregation. In addition, any resort to violence and terrorism is justified by the desire to carry out the will of God.

The Afrikaners' claim to this country has long been underpinned by their claim to be Christians. Thus, in the name of Christianity, they repelled the hordes of 'heathens' and occupied South Africa in the name of civilisation and Christianity. Their actions since then are justified in the name of preserving 'civilised' and 'Christian norms and values' in South Africa.

However, the Afrikaner's claim to be Christian is vigorously contested. Christ said, "Not everyone who says Lord, Lord will enter the kingdom of heaven, but ye that doeth the will of my Father." Then again He added: "By their fruits ye shall know them." Thus not everyone who claims to be a Christian is necessarily one. Christianity is a 'doing' word. One is a Christian by the way one acts. One's Christ-like life of kindness, helpfulness, patience, love and understanding is the indication that one is a follower of Christ.

What evidence have Afrikaners given, besides saying so, that they are Christians? A study of the historical past gives massive evidence of the 'savage propensities' and 'inhuman brutality' of the Afrikaner. They dealt savagely with slaves in the 17th century. In the 18th and 19th centuries, they exterminated the Bushmen; they acted brutally towards the Hottentots; they cruelly crushed all African opposition and then greedily grabbed all the best land available.

In the 20th century, they herded Africans like cattle into overcrowded reserves; immorally stripped the coloureds of all political rights; treated Indians like vermin; brutalised all non-whites; and enriched themselves beyond their wildest dreams.

Later, they showed increasing tendencies towards barbarism. The newspapers are full of accounts of Afrikaners boiling Africans alive for suspected theft; tying farm labourers to trees with wire and beating them to death; cutting off water to whole communities and then shrugging their shoulders when children start to die. The police, right-wing vigilantes and the CCB went into townships with 'moering tools' and attacked Africans with baseball bats, pick handles and crowbars for no other reason than that they were black.

At the same time, Afrikaners defrauded the government, plundered the treasury, stole millions through Finrand and other scams, raided the pension fund and gave themselves enormous golden handshakes. Of course, we are not even going to go into detail about the millions of hectares of tribal land virtually 'given' to Afrikaner farmers after the African inhabitants had been removed at gunpoint, nor about the houses bought by whites for a pittance from the hapless victims of the Group Areas Act. Afrikaners destroyed whole nations, tribes and communities. They brought misery, humiliation and destitution to millions.

And now this immoral, greedy, unfeeling, brutal 'savage' has the audacity to claim that he is a Christian. To do so, is to besmirch the name of Christ and taint the image of those who are genuinely Christian and who daily display the "fruits of the Spirit".

APPENDIX 5
Abraham Esau, the Calvinia martyr

Abraham Esau was born in Bushmanland around 1855. He was taught by Wesleyan missionaries and spoke English fairly well. At the time of the Anglo-Boer War, Esau was a man of some prominence in Calvinia.

On 19 May 1890, he organised the celebrations on the market square after the Boer siege of Mafikeng had been ended by British troops. Esau, as undisputed leader of the Calvinia coloured community, made a speech and raised the Union Jack. Their open alliance with the British meant that the Calvinia community were branded by the Boers as collaborators.

Thus, various reports that the Boers were about to attack the town caused consternation in Calvinia. Fearful of the consequences, Esau went to the local magistrate to demand that his people, all loyal subjects, be given arms to defend themselves. Although many of the 'non-white' Calvinia community held the franchise, the magistrate declined to provide them with weapons and instead provided Esau with a few swords. Esau formed a militia that drilled and manned outposts with a system of warning signals whereby the town could be alerted.

Even after the immediate danger had passed, the British authorities refused to arm the 'non-white' community of Calvinia. Undaunted, Esau organised a highly effective intelligence network in the Northern Cape, keeping the British apprised of Boer movements. His activities soon brought him to the attention of the Boers, who decided to take vengeance on him.

On 10 January 1901, a group of Boers, headed by Charles Nieuwoudt, galloped into Calvinia. Unarmed, but inspired by Esau, the 'non-whites' of Calvinia put up a resistance with sticks and stones, but were severely lashed and a number were shot. Esau and local officials were imprisoned.

Esau was responsible for every supposed crime or misdeed. He was accused of inciting labourers to commit arson and maiming stock belonging to Boer sympathisers. What realty infuriated the Boers was Esau's 'arrogance' in refusing to name the members of his organisation, refusing to disclose the location of arms caches, and refusing to publicly renounce his allegiance to Britain. Esau was described as "the most poisonous Hottentot in Calvinia".

Esau's supporters defied a curfew and marched through the streets at night, chanting his name and singing hymns. This upset Nieuwoudt who had three people, chosen arbitrarily, publicly flogged. Esau was dragged out of jail, beaten, smeared with dung and offal, and left chained to a pole in the searing heat of midday. The next day, Nieuwoudt sentenced Esau to twenty-five lashes for having spoken against the Boers and for attempting to arm the natives.

Esau was subsequently tied to a tree and the lashes were administered by Nieuwoudt himself. At the seventeenth stroke, he fainted. When Esau was untied and collapsed to the ground, he was kicked. Throughout the next two weeks he was lashed and beaten again and stoned by the men of Nieuwoudt's commando. Inflammation of the kidneys set in, rendering him very ill.

Finally, on 5 February, he was placed in leg irons, tied between two horses and dragged for about a kilometre, constantly lashed when he protested against his treatment. Just out of town, he was shot. His friends found his body the next day. There was a bullet hole in the back of his head and his body was scored and marked by the lashes he had received.

When news of this atrocity reached the outside world, pro-Boer newspapers in the Cape tried to find justification by saying that Esau had been shot in "self-defence". However, the *Cape Times* described the incident as a "horrible crime" perpetrated by "heartless wretches". The report stated that he died at the hands of "inhuman brutes" who should be "arraigned for murder".

(A full report of Esau's death was carried in the *Cape Times*, March 1901, and a more detailed account can be found in the *Readers Digest's Illustrated History of South Africa, the Real Story*, 258-259.)

Reference List

1. PRIMARY SOURCES

A. Manuscript and Archives Collections

Cory Library, Rhodes University

PR 1272, James M. Auld, 'Reminiscences', in *Blythswood Review*, Dec. 1924.

PR 3665, Sihele, E.G., "Ngobani na AbaThembu, Bevelaphi na?"

The Burton Papers, Glimpses of History, MS. 14, 636.

Jagger Library, University of Cape Town

J.C. Molteno Papers, Barkly to Molteno, 2 September 1875.

Walter Stanford Papers, D.4, 3 August 1857; D.8, 6 November 1883; 15 September 1884; D.10, E.J. Warner's Biography Sketch of his Father; E.J. Warner's Manuscript.

South African Library, Cape Town

MSB 428, *Statement of Silayi*, May 1884.

MSC 57, 26(21), *Statement of Elias Xelo*, Councillor of King Ngangelizwe, 31 March 1882.

Western Cape Archives, Cape Town

Cape Colonial Statute, An Act for More Effectually Preventing Kaffirs from Entering the Colony without Passes, No. 23 (1857); An Act for Preventing Colonial Fingoes, and Certain Other Subjects of Her Majesty, from being Mistaken for Kaffirs, and Thereby Harassed and Aggrieved, No. 24 (1857); An Act for Amending the Law Regarding Certificates of Citizenship, No. 17 (1864).

Cape of Good Hope Blue Book on Native Affairs, 1873, G.27 – '74, 10 June 1873: Thomas R.M. Cole, Civil Commissioner, to Secretary for Native Affairs, 30 March 1874; E. Judge, Civil Commissioner, to SNA, 11 May 1874; W.R.D. Fynn, Tambookie Agent, to SNA, 6 May 1874; C. Brownlee, British Resident, to SNA, 8 August and 3 November 1873; SNA to Colonial Secretary, 5 April 1874.

Cape of Good Hope Blue Book on Native Affairs, 1877, G.17 – '78, John Hemming, Civil Commissioner, to J.X. Merriman, Commissioner of Crown Lands, 11 January 1878.

Cape of Good Hope Blue Book on Native Affairs, 1878, G.17 – '78, John Hemming, Civil Commissioner, to the Honourable J.X. Merriman, Commissioner of Crown Lands, & C, 5 December 1877; 11 January 1878.

Cape of Good Hope Blue Book on Native Affairs, 1878, G.17 – '78, John Hemming, Civil Commissioner Queenstown, 18 January 1878.

Cape of Good Hope Blue Book on Native Affairs, 1883, G.8 – '83: John Hemming, Civil Commissioner, to SNA, 30 December 1882; H.G. Elliot, Chief Magistrate Thembuland, to Under-Secretary for Native Affairs, 3 January 1883; A.H. Stanford, Resident Magistrate, to USNA, I January 1883.

Cape of Good Hope Blue Book on Native Affairs, 1885.

Cape of Good Hope Blue Book on Native Affairs, 1887-1894, H.H. Bunn, Resident Magistrate St Mark's District, 31 December 1893; C.J. Sweeney, Resident Magistrate Mthatha, 1 January 1894; Charles J. Levey, Resident Magistrate Xhalanga District, Cala, 3 January 1894; A.H. Stanford, Resident Magistrate Ngcobo, 3 January 1894.

Cape of Good Hope Debates in the House of Assembly, 10 July; 26 July; 27 July; 30 July; and 9 August 1894.

Cape of Good Hope Debates in the Legislative Council, 9 April; 15 April; 30 April; and 21 June 1886.

Cape of Good Hope Government Gazette, No. 1535, 22 May 1835: Report by W.H. Dutton, Military Secretary, on Hintsa, 3 May 1835.

Cape of Good Hope, Papers of Joseph Cox Warner, Tambookie Agent, 1857-1858, J.C. Warner to Richard Southey, Resident Secretary, King William's Town, 24 February 1857; 11 March 1857; 7 April 1857.

Cape of Good Hope Proceedings of and Evidence taken by Commission on Native Affairs 1865, Joseph Cox Warner's Testimony, 11 February 1865.

Cape of Good Hope Proceedings of and Evidence taken by Commission on Native Affairs 1865, Testimony of A.N. Ella, Field Cornet [local judiciary officer] to Commission on Native Affairs.

Cape of Good Hope, Report and Proceedings of the Government Commission on Native Laws and Customs (Cape Town, 1883).

Cape of Good Hope Report of Sir Langham Dale, Superintendent-General of Education, to House of Parliament, 1873, G.11 – '74.

Cape of Good Hope Reports of Select Committee on Native Affairs, 1873, A.12 – '73: Memorandum on Relations with Gangelizwe and Tambookie Allies by Orpen; C.D. Griffith, James Ayliff and J. Murray Grant, Special Commissioners, to Colonial Secretary, 18 May 1872; E.B. Chalmers, Resident Magistrate, to Colonial Secretary, 29 May and 7 October 1872; C. Brownlee to Colonial Secretary, 24 October 1872; E.J. Warner, Tambookie Agent, to SNA, 19 December 1872; James Ayliff to Colonial Secretary, 25 January 1873.

Cape Parliamentary Paper, Correspondence with Reference to the Principles, Conditions and Detailed Arrangements on Which the Fingo Exodus has been Carried Out, A14 (1867), Currie to Colonial Secretary, 28 July 1865.

Cape Parliamentary Paper, Return Showing the Number of Titles of Land Issued to Fingoes and Correspondence Between the Government and the Resident Magistrate of Fort Beaufort on the Refusal of Zazela and His Tribe to take Out New Certificates, A56 (1865).

Chief Magistrate, Thembuland: CMT 1/7, USNA to CMT, No. 2/413, 3 September 1883; CMT 1/8, USNA to CMT, 2/247, 25 January 1884; CMT 1/8, USNA to CMT, No. 2/241, 6 May 1884; CMT 1/8, USNA to CMT, No. 2/227, 30 April 1884; CMT1/8, USNA to CMT, No. 2/746, 4 December 1884; CMT 1/9, USNA to CMT, No. 2/284, 29 April 1885; CMT 1/9, USNA to CMT, No. 518/47, 4 March 1885; De Wet to Ngangelizwe, 28 November 1884 enclosed in USNA to CMT, No. 3/165, 25 April 1885 and No. 2/289, 30 April 1885; USNA to Blakeway, Resident Magistrate, No. 2/57, 30 January 1885 and No. 2/54, 31 January 1885; Report of Minutes of Evidence Taken before the Select Committee on the Glen Grey Act, 1903.

Government Gazette, No. 1536, 29 May 1835: Proclamation, 29 May 1835.

Government Gazette, No. 3627, 21 October 1864: Government Notice, No. 339, 20 October 1864.

Government Gazette, No. 5950, 16 September 1879: Proclamation, 8 January 1877.

Government Gazette, No. 6637, 31 August 1894.

Government Gazette, No. 6642, 8 January 1885: Proclamation, 1 September 1885.

Government Gazette, No. 6642, 1 September 1885: Proclamation by Sir Hercules George Robert Robinson.

Government Gazette, No. 6564, 6 January 1885: Government Notice, 5 January 1885.

Government Gazette, No. 7330, 22 September 1891: Government Notice, No. 773, 18 September 1891.

Government Gazette, No. 7645, 28 September 1894: Proclamation No. 331 of 15 September 1894 by W.G. Cameron.

Government Gazette, No. 7844, 25 August 1896: Proclamation, 21 August 1896.

Government Gazette, No. 8456, 11 July 1902: Proclamation, 3 July 1902.

Government Gazette Extra-ordinary, No. 2911: Governor's Speech to Parliament, 10 March 1858.

Imperial Blue Book 538 of 1836, Evidence of W. Shaw.

B. Newspapers

South African Library, Cape Town

Cape Argus, 23 July 1884.

Cape Mercury, 16 March 1893; 23 March 1908.

Cape Times, 27 July 1894; 28 February 1895; 30 January 1904; 9 February 1904; 22 November 1965.

Daily Dispatch, 8 January 2012; 16 April 2019.

Eastern Province Herald, 8 and 11 July 1865.

Grahamstown Journal, 15 March 1851; 26 June 1865; 24 October 1880.

Imvo, 29 January 1895; 5 November 1907.

Queenstown Free Press, 5 January 1878; 26 January 1878; 26 July 1878; 22 December 1893; 9 August 1898.

Tembuland News, 28 September 1907; 16 November 1907.

Umthunywa, 19 June 1954.

2. ORAL SOURCES

Bhuka, Zakade (former member of Democratic Party of Transkei), Gqobonco Village, Ngcobo, 14 July 1995; 10 August 2006.

Dalindyebo, Buyelekhaya Zwelibanzi (heir to the Late abaThembu King, Sabata Dalindyebo), Bumbane Great Place, Mthatha, 29 April 1994; 7 September 1994;15 November 2010.

Dalindyebo, No-Moscow (the Great Wife of the Late abaThembu King, Sabata Dalindyebo), Bumbane Great Place, Mthatha, 28 June 1994; 10 September 2004.

Fadana, Phongomile S. (Former Member of D.P. of Transkei), Mhlophekazi Village, Ngcobo, 27 August 1994.

Joyi, Dalagubha (Former Member of D.P. of Transkei), Bhaziya Village, Mthatha, 7 May 1994; 7 September 1994; 16 April 1996; 6 March 2010.

Joyi, Zwelidumile (Former Member of the Transkei National Independence Party), Bhaziya Village, Mthatha, 18 April 1996; 5 July 2005.

Kati, James (Former Member of D.P. of Transkei), Luhewini Village, Ngcobo, 30 July 1997.

Kuse, Wandile, University of Transkei, Mthatha, 20 June 1994; 8 September 1994; 20 April 1996.

Mathanzima, Mbuzo Ngangomhlaba, Myezo, Mthatha, 25 July 2018.

Matiwane, Sizakele, Ntlalukana Village, Ngcobo, 24 June 1995; 29 June 1995.

Matshayana, G.G. Thozamile, Clarkebury Village, Ngcobo, 27 June 1995; 29 June 1995; 17 April 1996.

Mda, Mda, Xhugxwala Village, Mthatha, 22 May 2014.

Mnqanqeni, Ngubethafa, Mbhashe Village, Mthatha, 8 September 1994; 12 September 1994.

Mnqanqeni, Royal Zululiyazongoma, Clarkebury Village, Ngcobo, 25 January 1996; 4 October 2014.

Mnyande, Auto (Former Member of D.P. of Transkei), Luhewini Village, Ngcobo District, 30 July 1997.

Mthikrakra, Jonginyaniso, Sithebe Village, Mthatha, 29 April 1994; 5 February 2013.

Mthikrakra, Nomandla, Qulugqu Village, Ngcobo, 26 June 1995.

Mthikrakra, Nomishini, Mqhekezweni Village, Mthatha, 8 July 1994.

Mthikrakra, Sindile Zwelodumo, Qulugqu Village, Ngcobo, 30 December 2012; 9 June 2018.

Ncokazi, Bongani Hector (Former Deputy President of D.P. of Transkei), Mpheko Village, Mthatha, 10 September 1994.

Njozela, Monakali, Clarkebury Village, Ngcobo, 15 April 1996; 17 June 1997.

Nyoka, Mncedi Phondolwendlovu, Tyhalarha Village, Mthatha, 29 April; 7 September 1994.

Peires, Jeff Brian (Emeritus Professor of History), Telephone Interviews, 30 July 2018; 5 September 2018; 15 April 2020.

Pikashe, Sigqibo (Former Member of D.P. of Transkei), Nkondlo Village, Ngcobo, 16 July 1995.

Sithole, Bongani (the Late King Sabata's Praise Singer), Mpandela Village, Mthatha, 14 April 1996; 19 April 1996.

Sotyatho, Ntshumayelo (Former Secretary of amaHala Tribal Authority), Clarkebury Village, Ngcobo, 26 June 1995; 31 July 1997.

Sotyatho, Ntsikelelo (Headman), Clarkebury Village, Ngcobo, 28 June 1995.

Xundu, Mlahleni, Manzana Village, Ngcobo, 16 April 1996; 19 April 1996.

3. SECONDARY SOURCES
A. Books

Ayliff, J. and Whiteside, J., *History of the Abambo* (otherwise known as Fingoes), Butterworth, 1912.

Beinart, W. and Bundy, C., *Hidden Struggles in Rural South Africa: Politics and Popular Movements in the Transkei and Eastern Cape, 1890-1930* (Johannesburg: Ravan Press, 1987).

Bellwood, W.A., *Whither the Transkei?* (Cape Town: Howard Timmins, 1964).

Bennie, W.G. (ed.), *The Stewart Xhosa Readers Std vi* (Lovedale: Lovedale Press, 1970).

Benyon, J., *Proconsul and Paramountcy in South Africa, 1806-1910* (Pietermaritzburg: University of Natal Press, 1980).

Boyce, W.B., *Memoir of the Reverend William Shaw: Late General Superintendent of the Weslyan Mission in South Africa* (London: Wesleyan Conference Officer, 1874).

Brookes, E.H. and Webb, C. de B., *A History of Natal* (Pietermaritzburg: University of Natal Press, 1965).

Broster, J.A., *The Tembu: Their Beadwork, Songs and Dances* (Cape Town: Purnell Press, 1976).

Brownlee, C.P., *Reminiscences of Kaffir Life and History* (Lovedale: Lovedale Press, 1896).

Brownlee, F., *The Transkei Native Territories: Historical Records* (Lovedale: Lovedale Press, 1923).

Brownlee, W.T., *Reminiscences of a Transkeian* (Pietermaritzburg: Shuter and Shooter, 1975).

Bulpin, T.V., *Discovering Southern Africa* (Cape Town: T.V. Bulpin Publishers, 1980).

Bundy, C., *The Rise and Fall of the South African Peasantry* (Cape Town: Macmillan, 1988).

Callaway, G., *A Shepherd of the Veld* (London: Darton and Company, 1911).

Callinicos, L., *A People's History of South Africa, vol.1, 1886-1892: Gold and Workers* (Braamfontein: Ravan Press, 1981).

Cameron, T. and Spies, S.B. (eds), *A New Illustrated History of South Africa* (Johannesburg: Southern Book Publishers, 1986).

Campion, H., *The New Transkei* (Sandton: Valiant Publishers, 1976).

Carter, G.M., Karis, T. and Stultz, N.M., *South Africa's Transkei: The Politics of Domestic Colonialism* (Evanston: North-Western University, 1967).

Cingo, W.D., *Ibali Laba Tembu* (Palmerton: Mission Printing Press, 1927).

Coulter, J., *They Lived in Africa* (Port Elizabeth, 1988).

Crais, C.C., *The Making of the Colonial Order: White Supremacy and Black Resistance in the Eastern Cape, 1770-1865* (Johannesburg: Witwatersrand University Press, 1992).

Davenport, T.R.H., *South Africa: A Modern History* (London: Macmillan, 1991).

De Kock, W.J. (ed.), *Dictionary of South African Biography, vol. ii* (Johannesburg: Tafelberg-Uitgewers, 1972).

Dohne, J.L., *Das Kafferland und sein Bewohner* (Berlin, 1844).

Duminy, A. and Guest, B. (eds), *Natal and Zululand from Earliest Times to 1910: A New History* (Pietermaritzburg: University of Natal Press, 1989).

Du Plessis, J., *A History of Christian Missions in South Africa* (Cape Town: C. Struik, 1965).

Du Pre, R.H., *The Making of Racial Conflict in South Africa* (Johannesburg: Skotaville Publishers, 1992).

Dwane, S., *Issues in the South African Theological Debate* (Johannesburg: Skotaville, 1989).

Elphick, R. and Davenport, R. (eds), *Christianity in South Africa: A Political, Social and Cultural History* (Cape Town: David Philip, 1997).

Elphick, R. and Giliomee, H. (eds), *The Shaping of South African Society, 1652-1840* (Cape Town: Maskew Miller Longman, 1989).

Els, W.C., de Jager, E.J., Coetzee, C.G., Raum, O.F., Oosthuizen, G.C, Duminy, P.A., Brown, D.L., Smith, J.H. and Holdt, C.C., *The Ciskei: A Bantu Homeland* (Fort Hare: Fort Hare University Press, 1970).

Eveleigh, W., *A Short History of South African Methodism* (Cape Town: Methodist Publishing Office, 1914).

Eveleigh, W., *The Settlers and Methodism, 1820-1920* (Cape Town: Methodist Publishing Office, 1920).

Galbraith, J.S., *Reluctant Empire* (Los Angeles: Greenwood, 1963).

Green, S., *The First Hundred Years, 1873-1973: The Story of the Diocese of St. John's in South Africa* (Umtata: Paul Mission Press, 1974).

Groenewald, C. (ed.), *Oral Studies in Southern Africa* (Pretoria: Human Sciences Research Council, 1990).

Guise, D., *Freedom for All* (Natal: Natal Publishing Press, 1993).

Guy, J., *The Heretic: A Study of the Life of John William Colenso, 1814-1883* (Johannesburg: Ravan Press, 1983).

Hailey, L., *An African Survey* (Oxford: Oxford University Press, 1957).

Halisi, C.R.D., *Black Political Thought in the Making of South African Democracy* (U.S.A.: Maskew Miller, 1999).

Hammond-Tooke, W.D., *Command or Consensus: The Development of Transkeian Local Government* (Cape Town: David Philip, 1975).

Hammond-Tooke, W.D., *The Tribes of Umtata District* (Pretoria: Government Printer, 1956).

Henige, D., *Oral Historiography* (London: Longman, 1982).

Hinchliff, P., *The Church in South Africa* (London: S.P.C.K., 1968).

Holland, H., *The Struggle: A History of the African National Congress* (New York: George Braziller Inc., 1990).

Hutton, J.E., *A History of the Moravian Church* (London: Moravian Publication Office, 1909).

Jackson, A.O., *The Ethnic Composition of the Ciskei and Transkei: Ethnological Publications, No. 53* (Pretoria: Government Printer, 1975).

Karis, T. and Carter, G.M. (eds), *From Protest to Challenge: A Documentary History of African Politics in South Africa, 1882-1964* (California: Hoover Institution Press, 1972).

Kawa, R.T., *Ibali LamaMfengu and Kunganjani Kusiyiwa eKapa? 2nd Edition* (Grahamstown: Cory Library, 2011).

Kirby, P. (ed.), *Andrew Smith and Natal* (Cape Town: David Philip, 1955).

Klein, M. (ed.), *Peasants in Africa* (California: Hoover Institution Press, 1980).

Kruger, W.D., *The Making of a Nation: A History of the Union of South Africa, 1910-1961* (Johannesburg: Macmillan, 1969).

Lea, A., *The Native Separatist Church Movement in South Africa* (Cape Town: Juta, 1927).

Legassick, M., *The Struggle for the Eastern Cape, 1800-1854* (Johannesburg: KMM Publishing Co, 2010).

Liebenberg, B.J. and Spies, S.B. (eds), *South Africa in the 20th Century* (Pretoria: Academica, 1993).

Macquarrie, J.W. (ed.), *The Reminiscences of Sir Walter Stanford, vol. i, 1850-1885* (Cape Town: Van Riebeeck Society, 1958).

Macquarrie, J.W. (ed.), *The Reminiscences of Sir Walter Stanford, vol. ii, 1885-1929* (Cape Town: Van Riebeeck Society, 1962).

Majeke, N., *The Role of the Missionaries in Conquest* (Cumberwood: A.P.D.U.S.A., 1952).

Maylam, P., *A History of the African People of South Africa: From the Early Iron Age to the 1970s* (Cape Town: David Philip, 1986).

Mears, W.G., *Mission to Clarkebury* (Cape Town: Longmans, 1973).

Meli, F., *A History of the ANC: South Africa Belongs to us* (London: James Currey, 1988).

Millin, S.G., *The People of South Africa* (London: Constable and Company Ltd, 1953).

Milton, J., *The Edges of War: A History of Frontier Wars, 1702-1878* (Johannesburg: Juta, 1983).

Molema, S.M., *The Bantu: Past and Present* (Cape Town: Longmans, 1920).

Mostert, N., *Frontiers: The Epic of South Africa's Creation and the Tragedy of the Xhosa People* (London: Jonathan, 1992).

Mqhayi, S.E.K., *Inzuzo* (Johannesburg: Witwatersrand University Press, 1943).

Mqhayi, S.E.K., *Ityala Lama Wele* (Lovedale: Lovedale Press, 1914).

Mtuze, P.T. and Kaschula, R.H. (eds), *Izibongo Zomthonyama* (Cape Town: Oxford University Press, 1993).

Nattrass, G., *A Short History of South Africa* (Johannesburg and Cape Town: Jonathan Ball, 2018).

Nicholls, B., Charton, N. and Knowling, M., *The Diary of Robert John Mullins 1883-1913* (Grahamstown, Rhodes University Department of History, 1998).

Ntsikana, B.W., *Ityalike ye Sikhumbuzo Sika Ntsikana* (Port Elizabeth, 1945).

Odora-Hoppers, C. and Richards, H., *Rethinking Thinking: Modernity's 'other' and the Transformation of the University* (Pretoria: Unisa Press, 2011).

Omer-Cooper, J.D., *History of Southern Africa* (Johannesburg: David Philip, 1994).

Omer-Cooper, J.D., *The Zulu Aftermath: A Nineteenth-Century Revolution in Bantu Africa* (London: Longman, 1966).

Pampallis, J., *Foundations of the New South Africa* (Cape Town: Maskew Miller Longman, 1991).

Parsons, N., *A New History of Southern Africa* (London: Macmillan, 1982).

Peires, J.B., *The Dead Will Arise: Nongqawuse and the Great Xhosa Cattle-Killing Movement of 1856-7* (Johannesburg: Ravan Press, 1989).

Peires, J.B., *The House of Phalo: A History of the Xhosa People in the Days of their Independence* (Johannesburg: Ravan Press, 1981).

Price, R., *Making Empire: Colonial Encounters and the Creation of Imperial Rule in Nineteenth-Century Africa* (Cambridge: Cambridge University Press, 2008).

Saunders, C.C. (ed.), *An Illustrated Dictionary of South African History* (Sandton: Vois Books, 1994).

Saunders, C.C., *Historical Dictionary of South Africa: The Real Story* (London: Reader's Digest Association, 1994).

Saunders, C.C., *The Annexation of the Transkeian Territories, Archives Year Book 1976* (Pretoria: Government Printer, 1978).

Saunders, C. and Derricourt, R. (eds), *Beyond the Cape Frontier: Studies in the History of the Transkei and Ciskei* (London: Longman, 1974).

Shaw, W., *The Story of my Mission in South Eastern Africa* (London, 1860).

Shillington, K., *History of Africa* (London: Macmillan, 1995).

Shillington, K., *History of Southern Africa* (London: Longman, 1987).

Soga, J.H., *The South-Eastern Bantu* (Johannesburg: Witwatersrand University Press, 1930).

Somana, A., *A Preliminary Study of the History of the Thembus of Western Thembuland* (Johannesburg: Nikel Kruse Publishers, 2010).

Stadler, A., *The Political Economy of Modern South Africa* (Cape Town: David Philip, 1987).

Switzer, L., *Power and Resistance in an African Society: The Ciskei Xhosa and the Making of South Africa* (Pietermaritzburg: University of Natal Press, 1993).

Taylor, J.D. (ed.), *Christianity and the Natives of South Africa* (Lovedale: Lovedale Press, 1928).

Templin, J.A., *Ideology on a Frontier* (London: Greenwood, 1984).

Terreblanche, S., *A History of Inequality in South Africa, 1652-2002* (Pietermaritzburg: Macmillan, 2003).

Theal, G.M., *History of South Africa, 1834-1854* (London: Aberdeen University Press, 1893).

Theal, G.M., *History of South Africa since 1795, vol. v* (London, 1908).

Thompson, L. (ed.), *African Societies in Southern Africa* (London: Heinemann, 1978).

Togui, L.S., *The Struggle for Human Rights* (Kenwyn: Juta & Company, 1994).

Van Aswegen, H.J., *History of South Africa to 1854* (Pretoria: Academica, 1990).

Vansina, J., *Oral Tradition: A Study in Methodology* (London: Routledge and Kegan Paul, 1965).

Warwick, P., *Black People and the South African War, 1899-1902* (London: Cambridge University Press, 1983).

Westermann, D., *Africa and Christianity* (London: A.M.S. Press, 1935).

Williams, D., *When Races Meet* (Johannesburg: Longmans, 1967).

Wilson, M. and Thompson, L. (eds), *The Oxford History of South Africa, vol. i* (Oxford: Oxford University Press, 1969).

Wilson, M. and Thompson, L. (eds), *The Oxford History of South Africa, vol. ii* (Oxford: Oxford University Press, 1971).

Worden, N., *The Making of Modern South Africa: Conquest, Segregation and Apartheid* (Oxford: Blackwell Publishers, 1994).

Yali-Manisi, D.L.P., *Izibongo Zeenkosi ZamaXhosa* (Lovedale: Lovedale Press, 1952).

Yali-Manisi, D.L.P., *Yaphum' Ingqina* (Grahamstown: Institute of Social and Economic Research, Rhodes University, 1980).

B. Dissertations

Bouch, R.J., "The Colonisation of Queenstown (Eastern Cape) and its Hinterland, 1852-1886" (PhD. Thesis, University of London, 1990).

Lewis, J., "An Economic History of the Ciskei, 1848-1900" (PhD. Thesis, University of Cape Town, 1984).

Master, V.M., "Colonial Control in Thembuland and Resistance to it, 1872-1885" (M.A. Dissertation, University of Cape Town, 1966).

Mvenene, J., "The Implementation of Indigenous Knowledge Systems in the Teaching and Learning of South African History: A Case Study of Four Mthatha High Schools" (D.Ed. Thesis, Walter Sisulu University, 2018).

Ndima, M., "A History of the Qwathi People from Earliest Times to 1910" (M.A. Dissertation, Rhodes University, 1988).

Seton, B.E., "Wesleyan Missions and the Sixth Frontier War" (PhD. Thesis, University of Cape Town,1962).

Tisani, N.C., "Continuity and Change in Xhosa Historiography during the Nineteenth Century: An Exploration through Textual Analysis" (PhD. Thesis, Rhodes University, 2000).

Voss, M., "Urbanising the North-Eastern Frontier: The Frontier Intelligentsia and the Making of Colonial Queenstown, c.1859-1877" (M.A. Dissertation, University of Cape Town, 2012).

Wagenaar, E.J.C., "A History of the Thembu and their Relationship with the Cape, 1850-1900" (PhD. Thesis, Rhodes University, 1988).

Webster, A.C., "Land Expropriation and Labour Extraction under Cape Colonial Rule: The War of 1835 and the 'Emancipation' of the Fingo" (M.A. Dissertation, Rhodes University, 1991).

Williams, D., "The Missionaries on the Eastern Frontier of the Cape Colony, 1799-1853" (PhD. Thesis, Witwatersrand University, 1959).

Yekela, D.S., "Unity and Division: Aspects of the History of AbaThembu Chieftainship c.1920 to c.1980" (PhD. Thesis, University of Cape Town, 2011).

C. Articles and Papers

Beck, R.B., "Bibles and Beads: Missionaries as Traders in Southern Africa in the Early Nineteenth Century", *Journal of African History*, 30 (1989).

Bouch, R., "Glen Grey before Cecil Rhodes: How a Crisis of Local Colonial Authority Led to the Glen Grey Act of 1894", *Canadian Journal of African Studies*, 27, 1 (1993).

Cobbing, J., "Jettisoning the Mfecane with Perestroika", Unpublished Seminar Paper, University of Cape Town, April 1989.

Cobbing, J., "The Case against the Mfecane", Unpublished Seminar Paper, University of Witwatersrand, 1984.

Cobbing, J., "The Mfecane as Alibi: Thoughts on Dithakong and Mbolompo", *Journal of African History*, 1, 2 (1988).

Comaroff, J. and Comaroff, J., "Through the Looking Glass: Colonial Encounters of the First Kind", *Journal of Historical Sociology*, 1, 1 (March 1988).

Cope, R.L., "Christian Missions and Independent African Chiefdoms in South Africa in the 19th Century", *Theoria*, 2 (May 1979).

De Wet, T., Teugels, J.L. and Van Deventer, P., "Historic Bells in Moravian Missions in South Africa's Western Cape", *Historia*, 59, 2 (November 2014).

Eldredge, E.A., "Sources of Conflict in Southern Africa, c.1800-30: The Mfecane Reconsidered", *Journal of African History*, 33 (1992).

Etherington, N., "Mission Station Melting Pots as a Factor in the Rise of South African Black Nationalism", *Africa*, 47, 1 (1977).

Hamilton, C.A., "An Appetite for the Past: The Recreation of Shaka and the Crisis in Popular Historical Consciousness", *South African Historical Journal*, 22 (1990).

Hammond-Tooke, W.D., "Chieftainship in Transkeian Political Development", *Journal of Modern African Studies*, 2, 4 (1964).

Hammond-Tooke, W.D., "Segmentation and Fission in Cape Nguni Political Units", *Africa*, 35, 3 (April 1965).

Hammond-Tooke, W.D., "The Transkeian Council System, 1895-1955: An Appraisal", *Journal of African History*, 9, 3 (1968).

Hodgson, J., "Mission and Empire: A Case Study of Convergent Ideologies in 19th Century Southern Africa", *Journal of Theology for Southern Africa*, 38 (March 1983).

Hurcombe, E.H., "The Story of our Missionary Society", *Forward* (December 1925).

Hutchinson, B., "Some Social Consequences of Nineteenth-Century Missionary Activity among the South African Bantu", *Africa*, 37, 2 (April 1957).

Keller, B.B., "Millenarianism and Resistance: The Xhosa Cattle-Killing", *Journal of Asian and African Studies*, 13, 1-2 (1978).

Kuse, W., "The Thembu Right Hand House: An Institutional Problem", *Bureau for African Research and Documentation*, University of Transkei, 1991.

Lambourne, B., "Methods of Mission: The Ordering of Space and Time, Land and Labour on Methodist Mission Stations in Caffraria, 1823-1835", African Studies Seminar Paper, University of the Witwatersrand, African Studies Institute, 24 August 1992.

Lewis, J., "Materialism and Idealism in the Historiography of the Xhosa Cattle-Killing Movement 18567", *South African Historical Journal*, 25 (1991).

Lye, W.F., "The Difaqane: The Mfecane in the Southern Sotho Area, 182224", *Journal of African History*, 8, 1 (1967).

Mager, A.K., "Gungubele and the Tambookie Location, 1853-1877: End of a Colonial Experiment", *Journal of Southern African Studies*, 40, 6 (2014).

Mignolo, W., "Delinking: The Rhetoric of Modernity, the Logic of Coloniality, and the Grammar of Decoloniality", *Cultural Studies*, 21, 2 (2011).

Mvenene, J., "A Social and Economic History of the African People of Gcalekaland, 1830-1913", *Historia*, 59, 1 (May 2014).

Mvenene, J., "Embedding Chiefs' Bulls and Iminombo in Decolonising South African History in the Further Education and Training Phase", *Indilinga, African Journal of Indigenous Knowledge Systems*, 18, 1 (2019).

Mvenene, J., "Reverend James Macdonald Auld and the Disintegration of Traditional Leadership in Xhosaland", *African Historical Review*, 48, 2 (2016).

Peires, J.B., "Matiwane's Road to Mbholompo: A Reprieve for the Mfecane?", *The Mfecane Aftermath: Towards a New Paradigm*, University of Witwatersrand (September 1991).

Peires, J.B., "The Central Beliefs of the Xhosa Cattle-Killing", *Journal of African History*, 28, 1 (1987).

Peires, J.B., "The Implosion of Transkei and Ciskei", *African Affairs*, 91 (1992).

Redding, S. "Sorcery and Sovereignty: Taxation, Witchcraft and Political Symbols in the 1880 Transkeian Rebellion", *Journal of Southern African Studies*, 22, 2 (June 1996).

Saunders, C.C., "Tile and the Thembu Church: Politics and Independency on the Cape Eastern Frontier in the Late Nineteenth Century", *Journal of African History*, 11, 4 (1970).

Schapera, I., "Christianity and the Tswana", *Journal of the Royal Anthropological Institute*, 58, 1 (January–February 1958).

Stapleton, T.J., "Oral Evidence in a Pseudo-Ethnicity: The Fingo Debate", *History in Africa*, 22 (1995).

Stapleton, T.J., "The Expansion of a Pseudo-Ethnicity in the Eastern Cape: Reconsidering the Fingo 'Exodus' of 1865", *International Journal of African Historical Studies*, 29, 2 (1996).

Stapleton, T.J., "The Memory of Maqoma: An Assessment of Jingqi Oral Tradition in Ciskei and Transkei", *History in Africa*, 20 (1993).

Watson, R.L., "Missionary Influence at Thaba Nchu, 1833-1854: A Reassessment", *International Journal of African Historical Studies*, 10, 3 (1977).

Webb, C. de B., "The Mfecane", in *Perspectives on the Southern African Past*, University of Cape Town, 1979.

Wright, J., "Political Mythology and the Making of Natal's Mfecane", *Canadian Journal of African Studies*, 23, 2 (1989).

Wright, J., "Popularizing the Precolonial Past: Politics and Problems", *Perspectives in Education*, 10, 2 (1988).

Zarwan, J., "The Xhosa Cattle-Killings, 1856 57", *Cahiers d' Etudes Africaines*, 16, 63-64 (1976).

www.ingramcontent.com/pod-product-compliance
Lightning Source LLC
Chambersburg PA
CBHW080224170426
43192CB00015B/2746